WORMWOOD
GENTLEMAN CORPSE

CALAMARI
RISING

BEN TEMPLESMITH + IDW PUBLISHING

IDW PUBLISHING
SAN DIEGO, CA

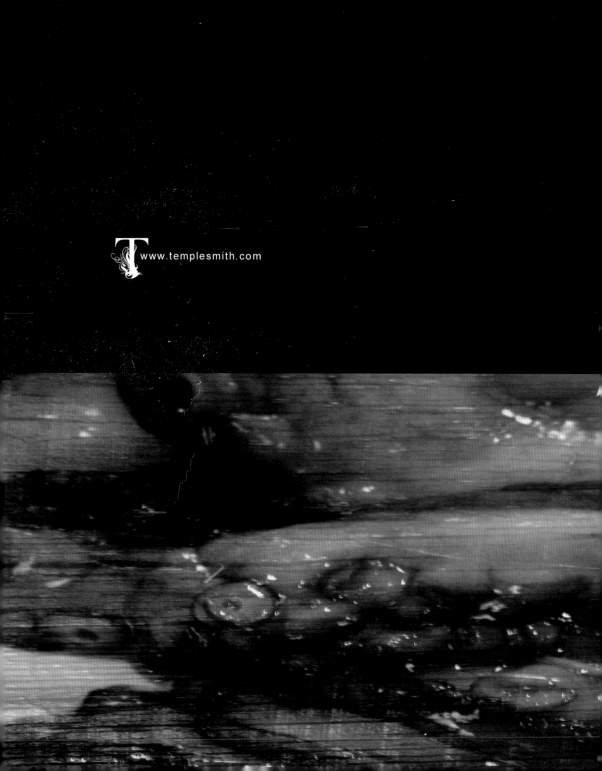

www.templesmith.com

WORMWOOD
GENTLEMAN CORPSE | CALAMARI RISING

created, written & drawn by
Ben Templesmith (for Singularity7 Pty Ltd)

redneck assistance & lifestyle advice by
Greg White

letters by
Chris Mowry, Robbie Robbins, and Neil Uyetake

foreword by
Rob Schrab

edits, charisma and general good looks
Chris Ryall & Denton J. Tipton

collection edtis by
Justin Eisinger

Templesmith logo by Babe Elliot Baker | spiritform.com

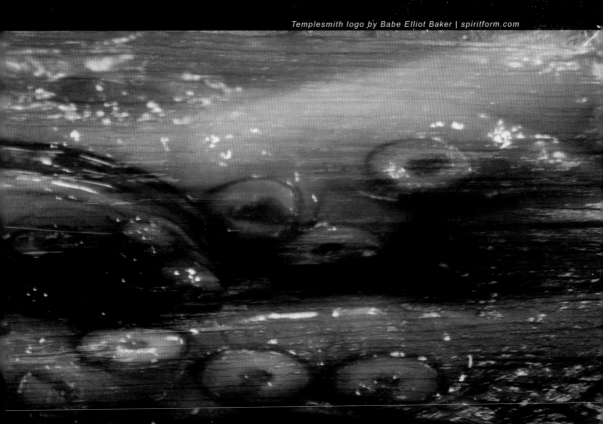

IDW founded by Ted Adams, Alex Garner, Kris Oprisko, and Robbie Robbins | International Rights Representative, Christine Meyer: christine@gfloystudio.com

ISBN: 978-1-60010-183-0 15 14 13 12 2 3 4 5

IDW®

Ted Adams, CEO & Publisher
Greg Goldstein, President & COO
Robbie Robbins, EVP/Sr. Graphic Artist
Chris Ryall, Chief Creative Officer/Editor-in-Chief
Matthew Ruzicka, CPA, Chief Financial Officer
Alan Payne, VP of Sales

Become our fan on Facebook **facebook.com/idwpublishing**
Follow us on Twitter **@idwpublishing**
Check us out on YouTube **youtube.com/idwpublishing**
www.IDWPUBLISHING.com

Originally published as WORMWOOD: GENTLEMAN CORPSE: CALAMARI RISING Issues #1 to 4.

Life is a funny old bugger. Many thanks to all the people
who've supported Wormwood to make it as far as it has
by buying the books.

Thanks also to Ted, Robbie & Chris, and
everyone else at IDW Publishing for
the opportunites and support.

And how could I forget, big cheers to Warren Ellis, Jim Mahfood,
Jeff Shagawat, Jeanne Duperret, David Guelou, Thierry Mornet, Rob Schrab,
Erica Farjo, David Slade, Jeff Henderson, Lorelei Bunjes, Arni Gunnarsson,
Greg White, Ben Wooller & all the usual suspects
who remind me why I do comics and keep it so fun.

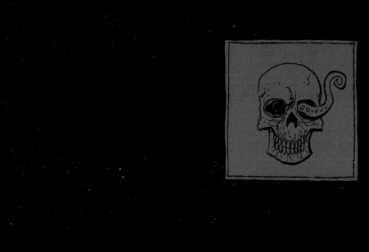

Templesmith.

Roughly translated: builder of churches, "*temple-smith.*"

Holy shit I love monsters. I love monsters and guns. I'm 38 years old and I'm supposed to like white wine and *Frasier*. Fortunately, something's wrong with me because I freaking love 7UP and *Wormworm: Gentlemen Corpse.*

Ben Templesmith's art is electric. Seriously, hold this book up to your face. Feel that? It actually generates **heat** it's so badass.

Tentacles, demons, bombs, bars and neon cobras crackle off each page. Good lord, I eat this stuff up! Ben's dimension is populated with fresh visions of perdition that wow me up the ying-yang (take **that**, Frasier). Wormy is the best, how can you compete with a pub-crawling, chain smoking dead guy fighting octopuses from hell? For real, this book was made for me—and you too, my friend. Lucky us.

The Templesmith has forged yet another church with *Wormwood: Gentleman Corpse* and I am pleased as shite to be apart of its congregation.

Amen.

Rob Schrab

Rob Schrab is a comedian, comic book creator, actor, writer, and is active in both television and film production. He grew up in Mayville, Wisconsin. Schrab is currently producing the final chapter to his comic book, Scud: The Disposable Assassin, *as well as directing the second season of* The Sarah Silverman Program.

Chapter 1

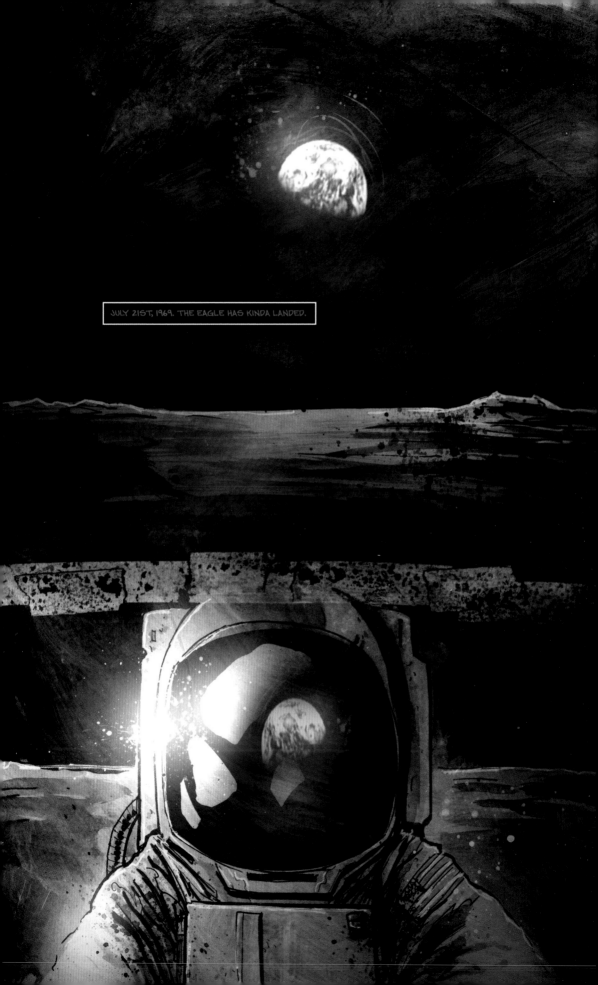

JULY 21ST, 1969. THE EAGLE HAS KINDA LANDED.

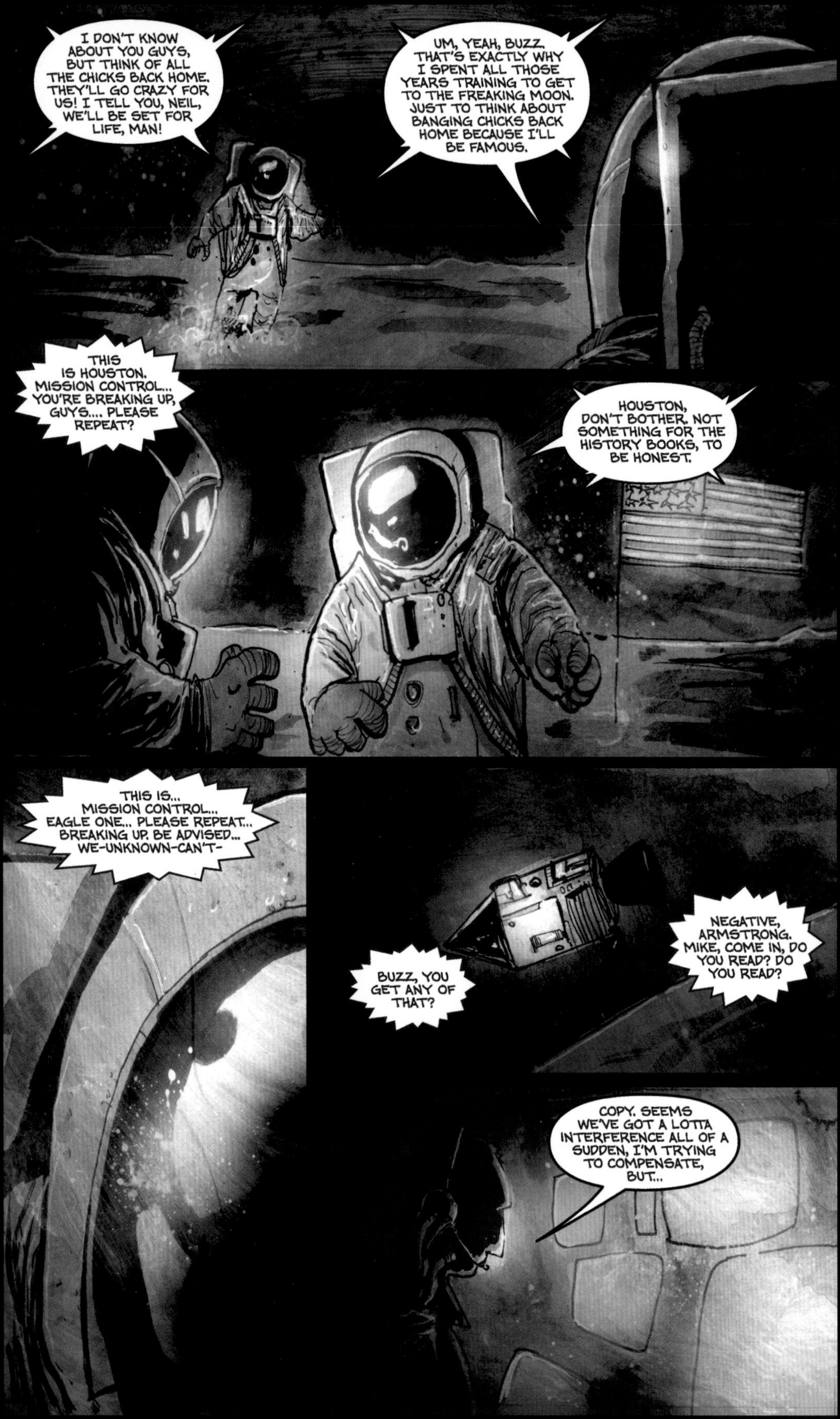
I DON'T KNOW ABOUT YOU GUYS, BUT THINK OF ALL THE CHICKS BACK HOME. THEY'LL GO CRAZY FOR US! I TELL YOU, NEIL, WE'LL BE SET FOR LIFE, MAN!
UM, YEAH, BUZZ. THAT'S EXACTLY WHY I SPENT ALL THOSE YEARS TRAINING TO GET TO THE FREAKING MOON. JUST TO THINK ABOUT BANGING CHICKS BACK HOME BECAUSE I'LL BE FAMOUS.
THIS IS HOUSTON. MISSION CONTROL... YOU'RE BREAKING UP, GUYS.... PLEASE REPEAT?
HOUSTON, DON'T BOTHER. NOT SOMETHING FOR THE HISTORY BOOKS, TO BE HONEST.
THIS IS... MISSION CONTROL... EAGLE ONE... PLEASE REPEAT... BREAKING UP. BE ADVISED... WE-UNKNOWN-CAN'T-
BUZZ, YOU GET ANY OF THAT?
NEGATIVE, ARMSTRONG. MIKE, COME IN, DO YOU READ? DO YOU READ?
COPY. SEEMS WE'VE GOT A LOTTA INTERFERENCE ALL OF A SUDDEN, I'M TRYING TO COMPENSATE, BUT...

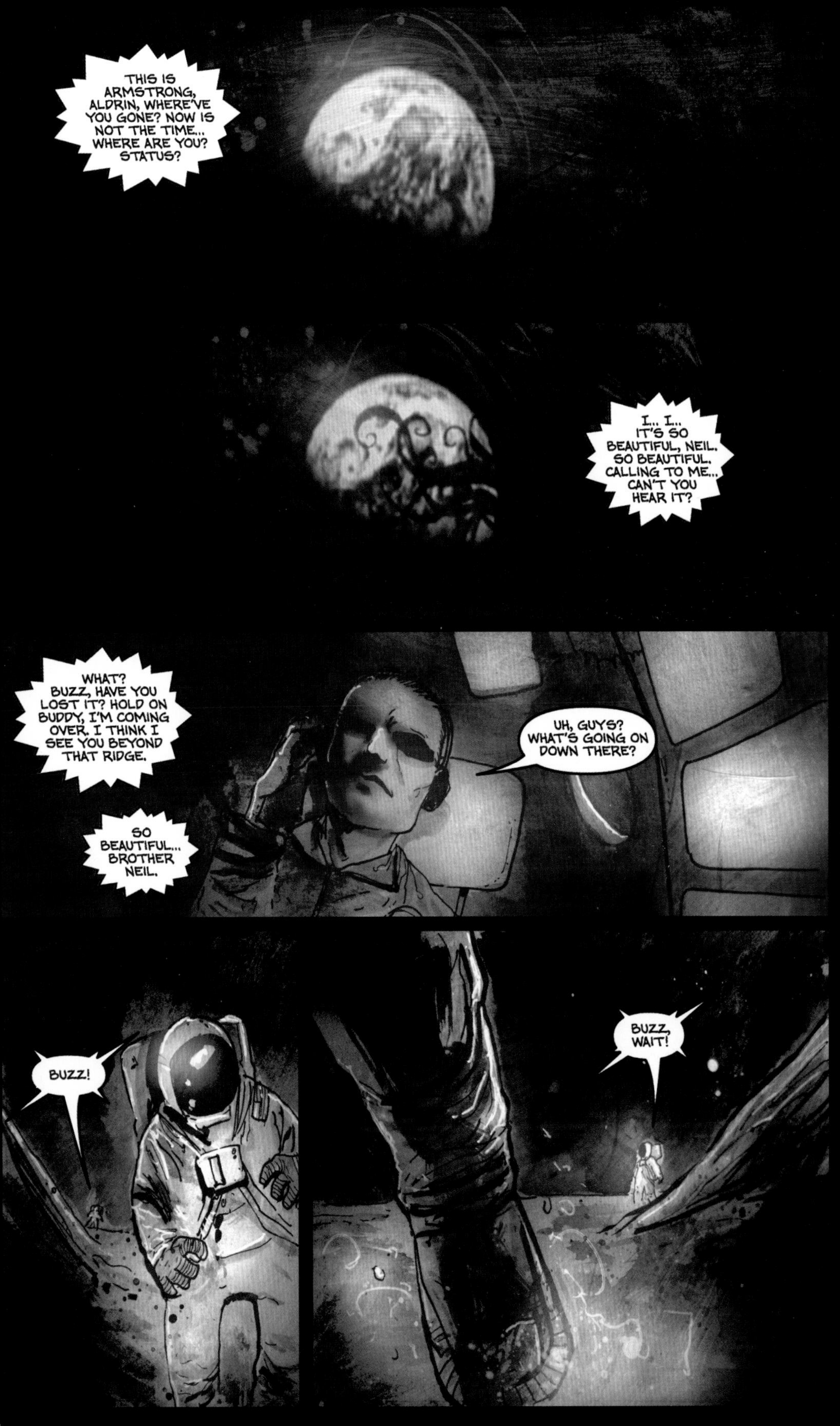

THIS IS ARMSTRONG, ALDRIN, WHERE'VE YOU GONE? NOW IS NOT THE TIME... WHERE ARE YOU? STATUS?
I... I... IT'S SO BEAUTIFUL, NEIL. SO BEAUTIFUL. CALLING TO ME... CAN'T YOU HEAR IT?
WHAT? BUZZ, HAVE YOU LOST IT? HOLD ON BUDDY, I'M COMING OVER. I THINK I SEE YOU BEYOND THAT RIDGE.
UH, GUYS? WHAT'S GOING ON DOWN THERE?
SO BEAUTIFUL... BROTHER NEIL.
BUZZ!
BUZZ, WAIT!

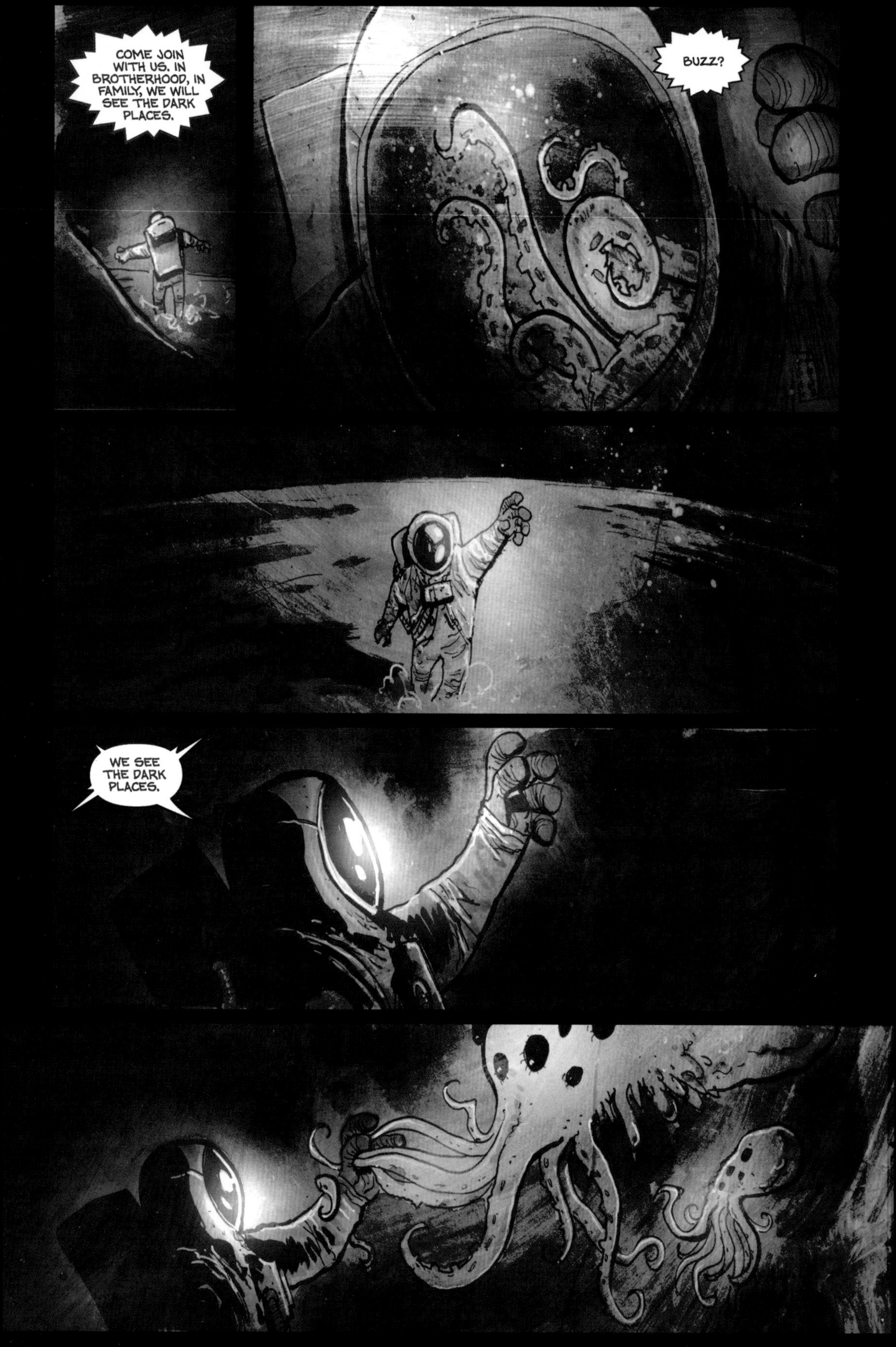
COME JOIN WITH US. IN BROTHERHOOD, IN FAMILY, WE WILL SEE THE DARK PLACES.
BUZZ?
WE SEE THE DARK PLACES.

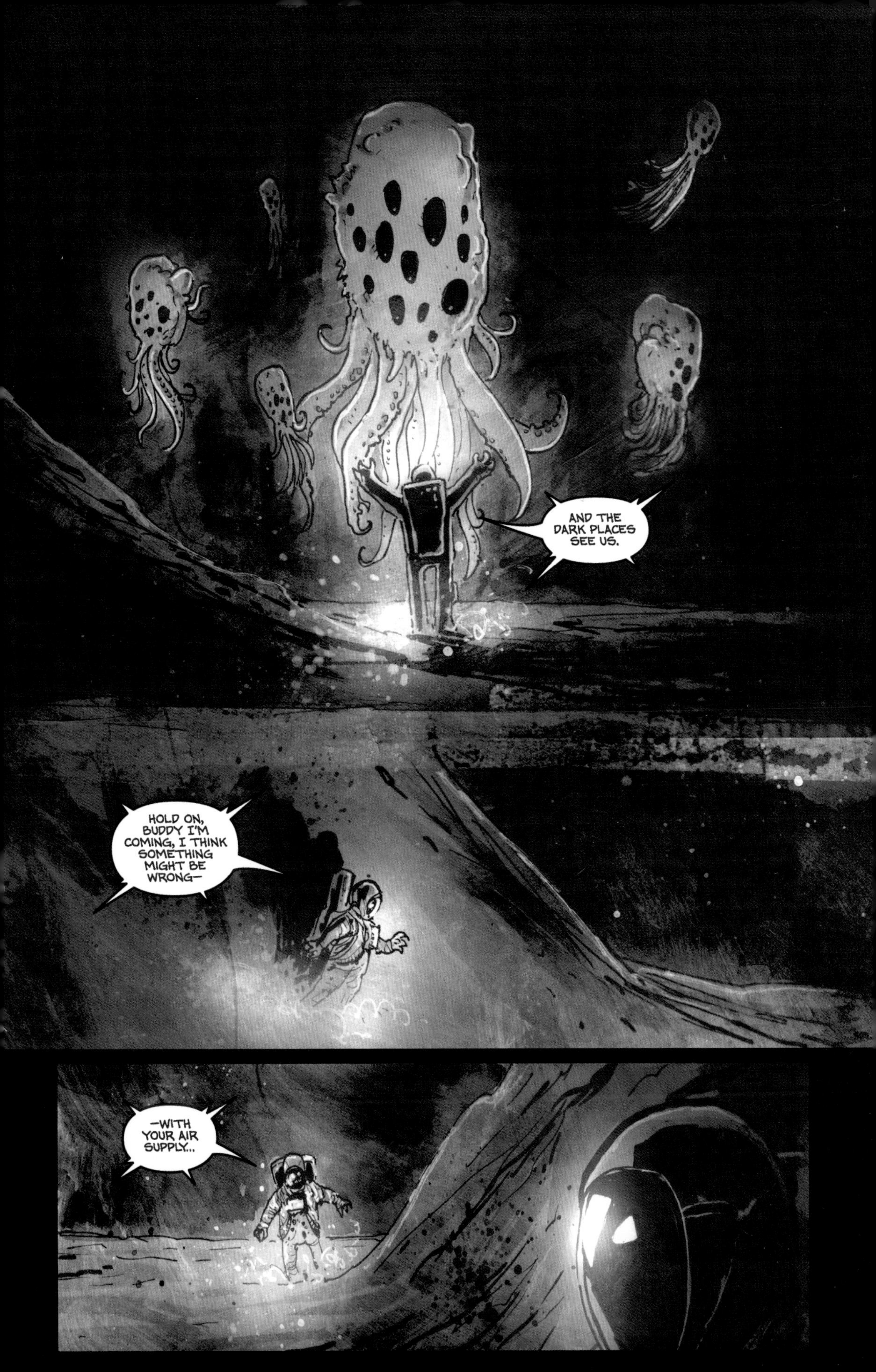
AND THE DARK PLACES SEE US.
HOLD ON, BUDDY I'M COMING, I THINK SOMETHING MIGHT BE WRONG—
—WITH YOUR AIR SUPPLY...

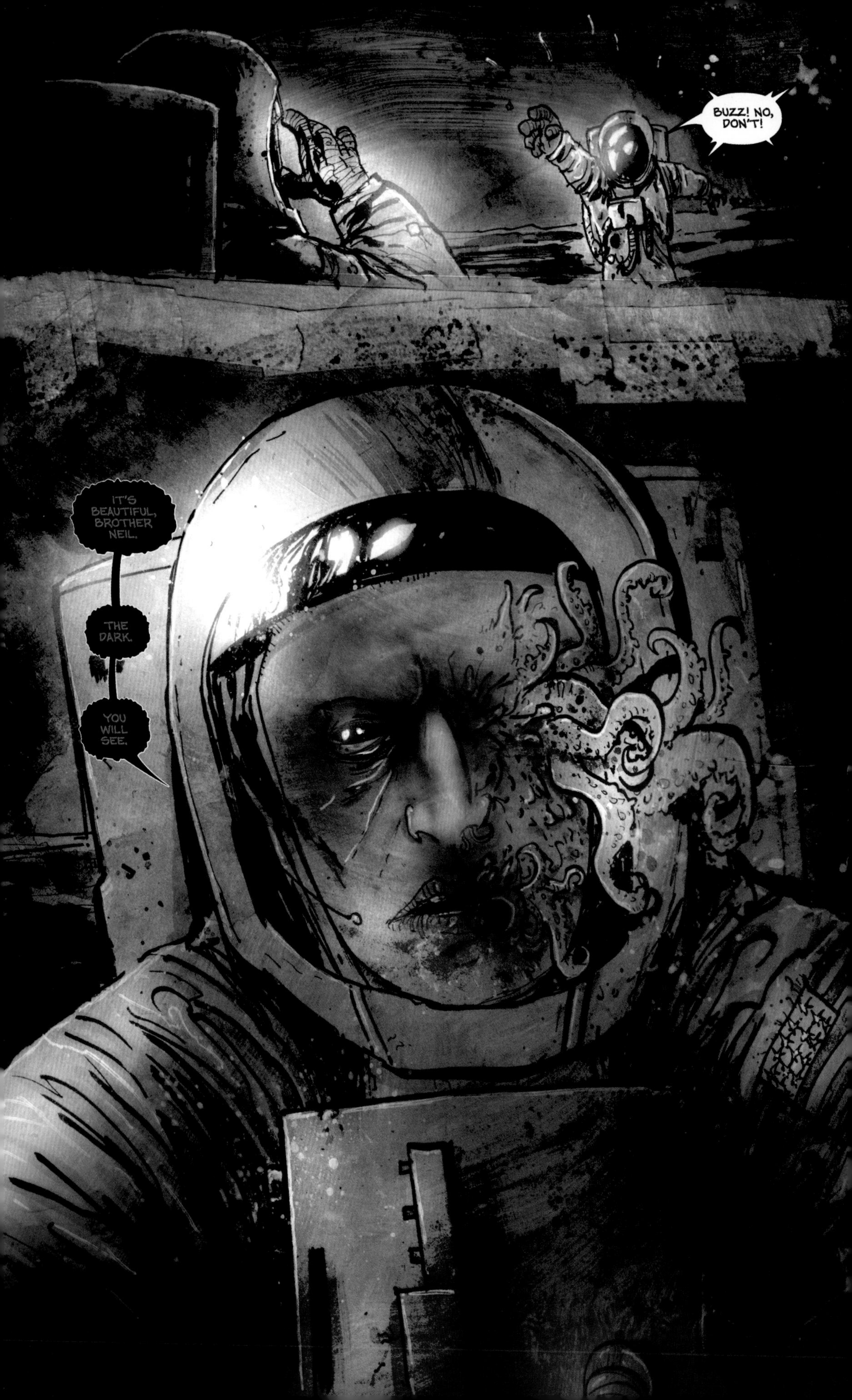
BUZZ! NO, DON'T!
IT'S BEAUTIFUL, BROTHER NEIL.
THE DARK.
YOU WILL SEE.

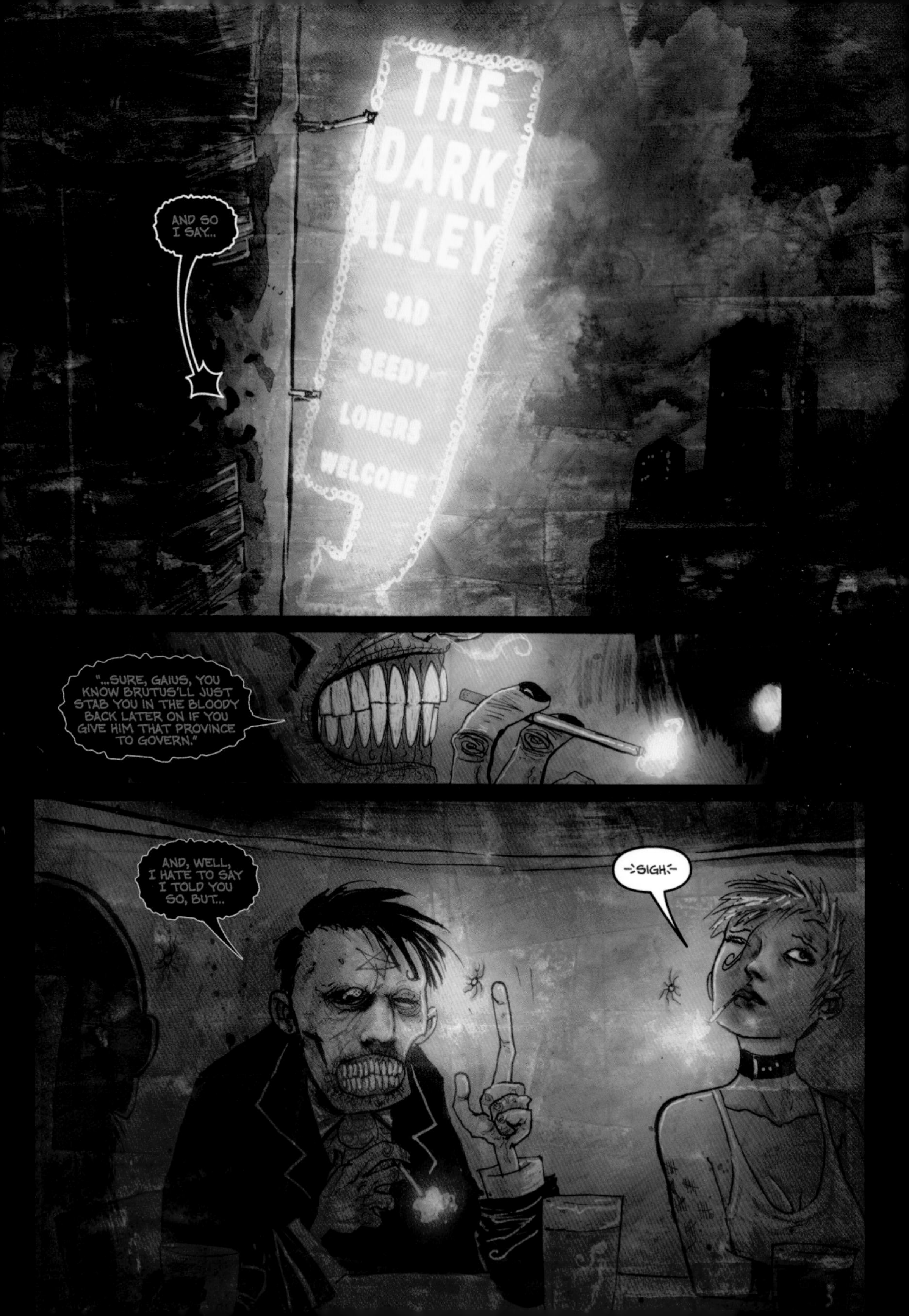
THE DARK ALLEY
SAD
SEEDY
LONERS
WELCOME
AND SO I SAY...
"...SURE, GAIUS, YOU KNOW BRUTUS'LL JUST STAB YOU IN THE BLOODY BACK LATER ON IF YOU GIVE HIM THAT PROVINCE TO GOVERN."
AND, WELL, I HATE TO SAY I TOLD YOU SO, BUT...
SIGH

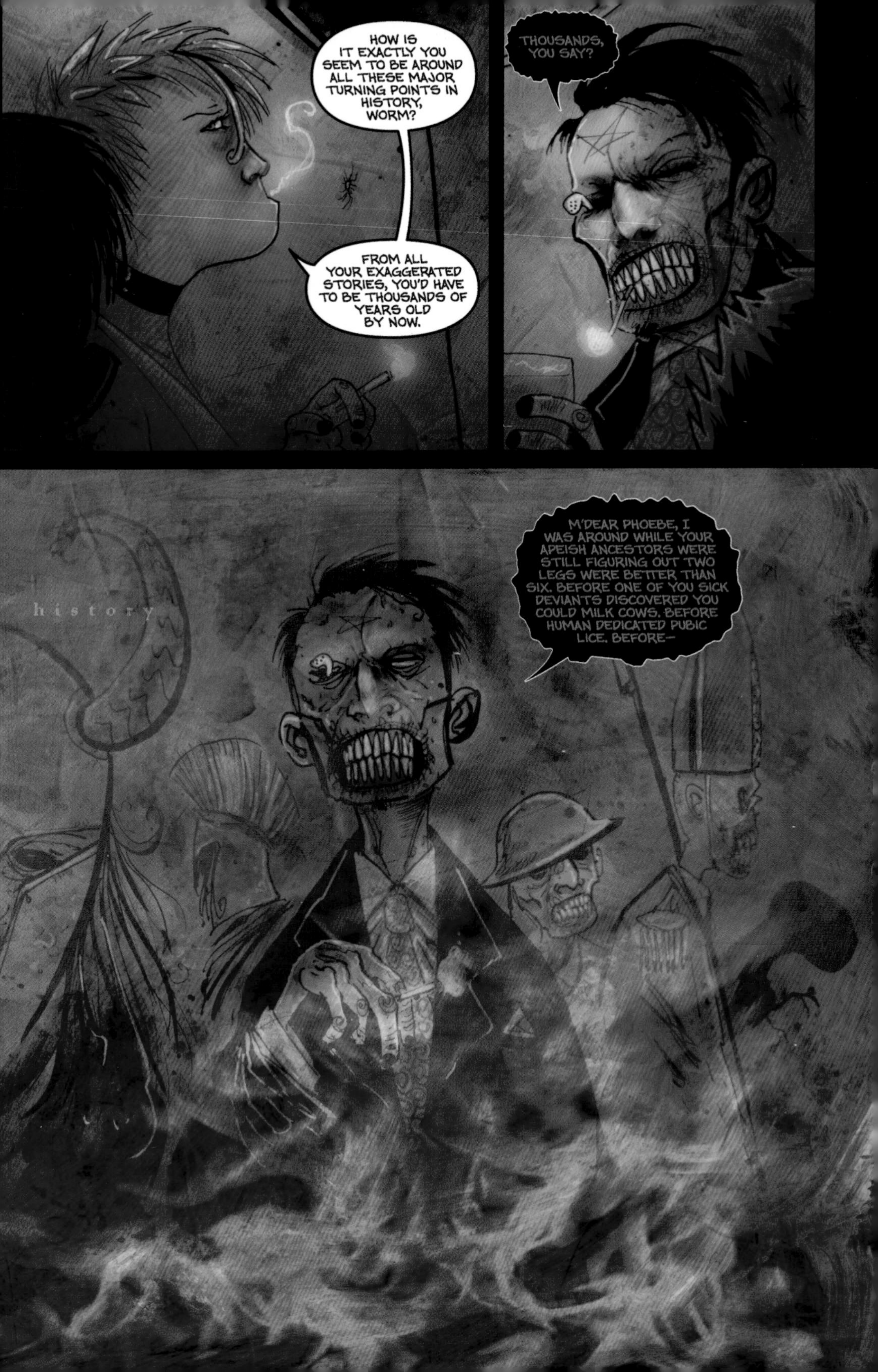
HOW IS IT EXACTLY YOU SEEM TO BE AROUND ALL THESE MAJOR TURNING POINTS IN HISTORY, WORM?
FROM ALL YOUR EXAGGERATED STORIES, YOU'D HAVE TO BE THOUSANDS OF YEARS OLD BY NOW.
THOUSANDS, YOU SAY?
history
M'DEAR PHOEBE, I WAS AROUND WHILE YOUR APEISH ANCESTORS WERE STILL FIGURING OUT TWO LEGS WERE BETTER THAN SIX. BEFORE ONE OF YOU SICK DEVIANTS DISCOVERED YOU COULD MILK COWS. BEFORE HUMAN DEDICATED PUBIC LICE. BEFORE—

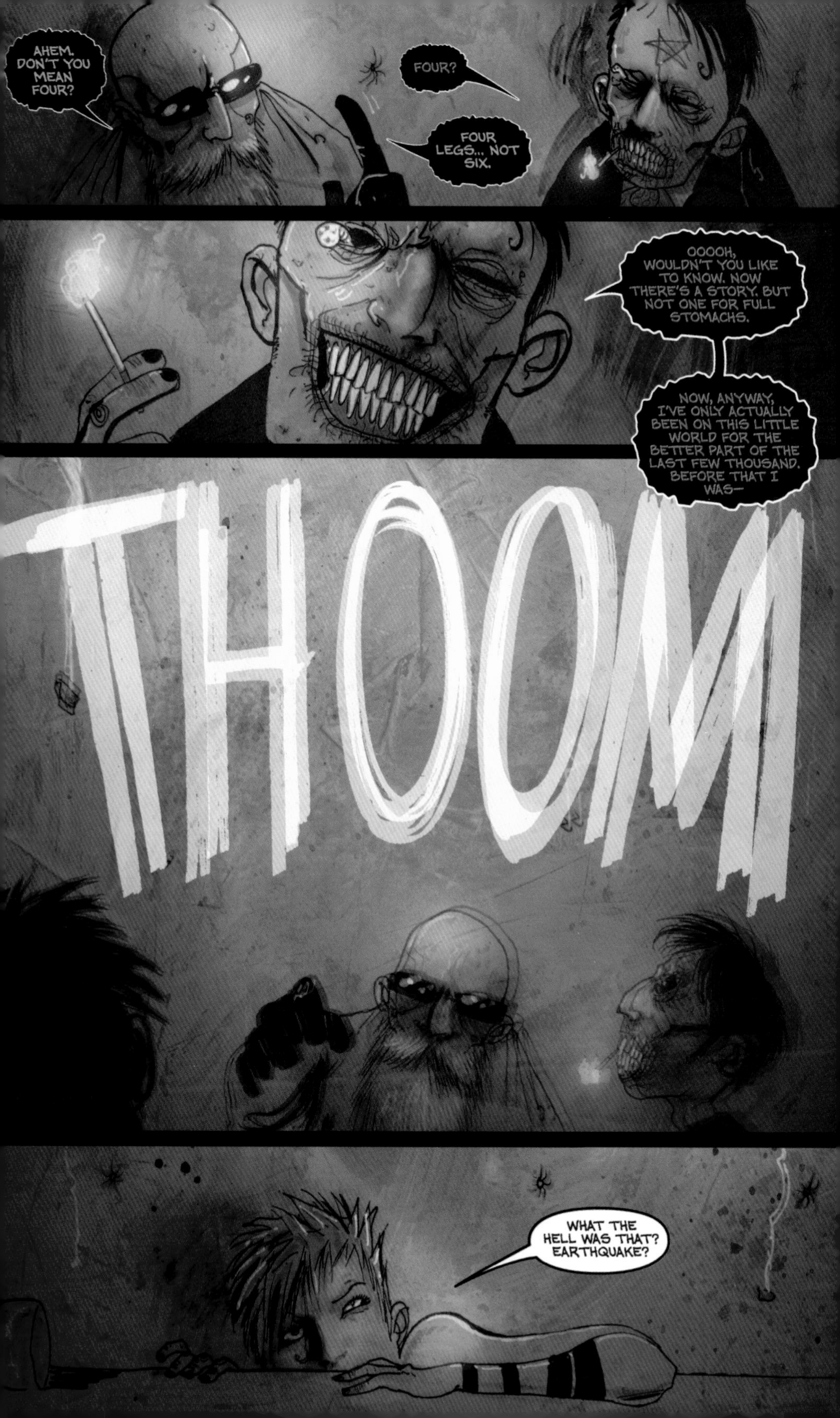
AHEM. DON'T YOU MEAN FOUR?
FOUR?
FOUR LEGS... NOT SIX.
OOOOH, WOULDN'T YOU LIKE TO KNOW. NOW THERE'S A STORY. BUT NOT ONE FOR FULL STOMACHS.
NOW, ANYWAY, I'VE ONLY ACTUALLY BEEN ON THIS LITTLE WORLD FOR THE BETTER PART OF THE LAST FEW THOUSAND. BEFORE THAT I WAS—
THOOM
WHAT THE HELL WAS THAT? EARTHQUAKE?

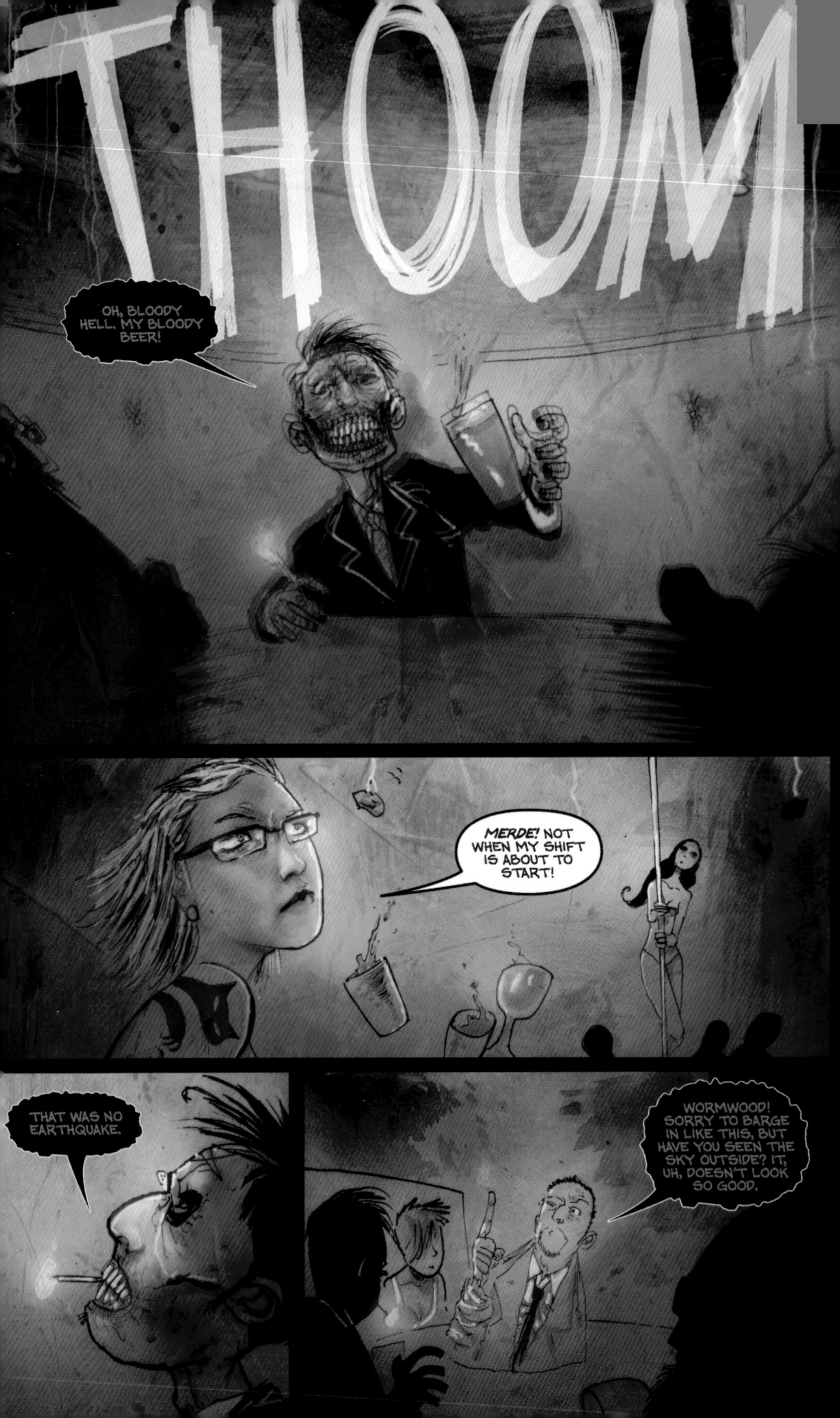
THOOM
OH, BLOODY HELL. MY BLOODY BEER!
MERDE! NOT WHEN MY SHIFT IS ABOUT TO START!
THAT WAS NO EARTHQUAKE.
WORMWOOD! SORRY TO BARGE IN LIKE THIS, BUT HAVE YOU SEEN THE SKY OUTSIDE? IT, UH, DOESN'T LOOK SO GOOD.

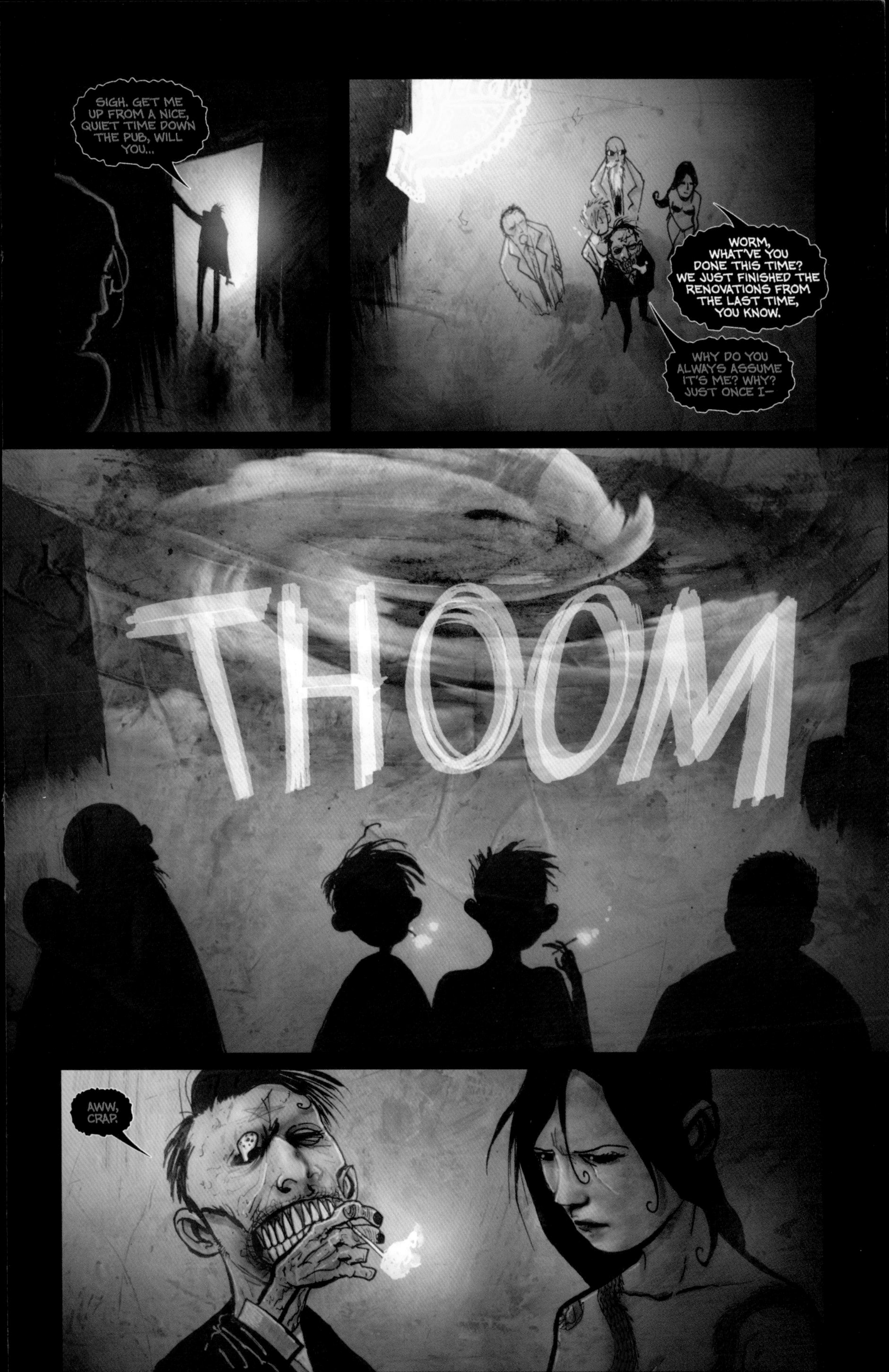
SIGH. GET ME UP FROM A NICE, QUIET TIME DOWN THE PUB, WILL YOU...
WORM, WHAT'VE YOU DONE THIS TIME? WE JUST FINISHED THE RENOVATIONS FROM THE LAST TIME, YOU KNOW.
WHY DO YOU ALWAYS ASSUME IT'S ME? WHY? JUST ONCE I—
THOOM
AWW, CRAP.

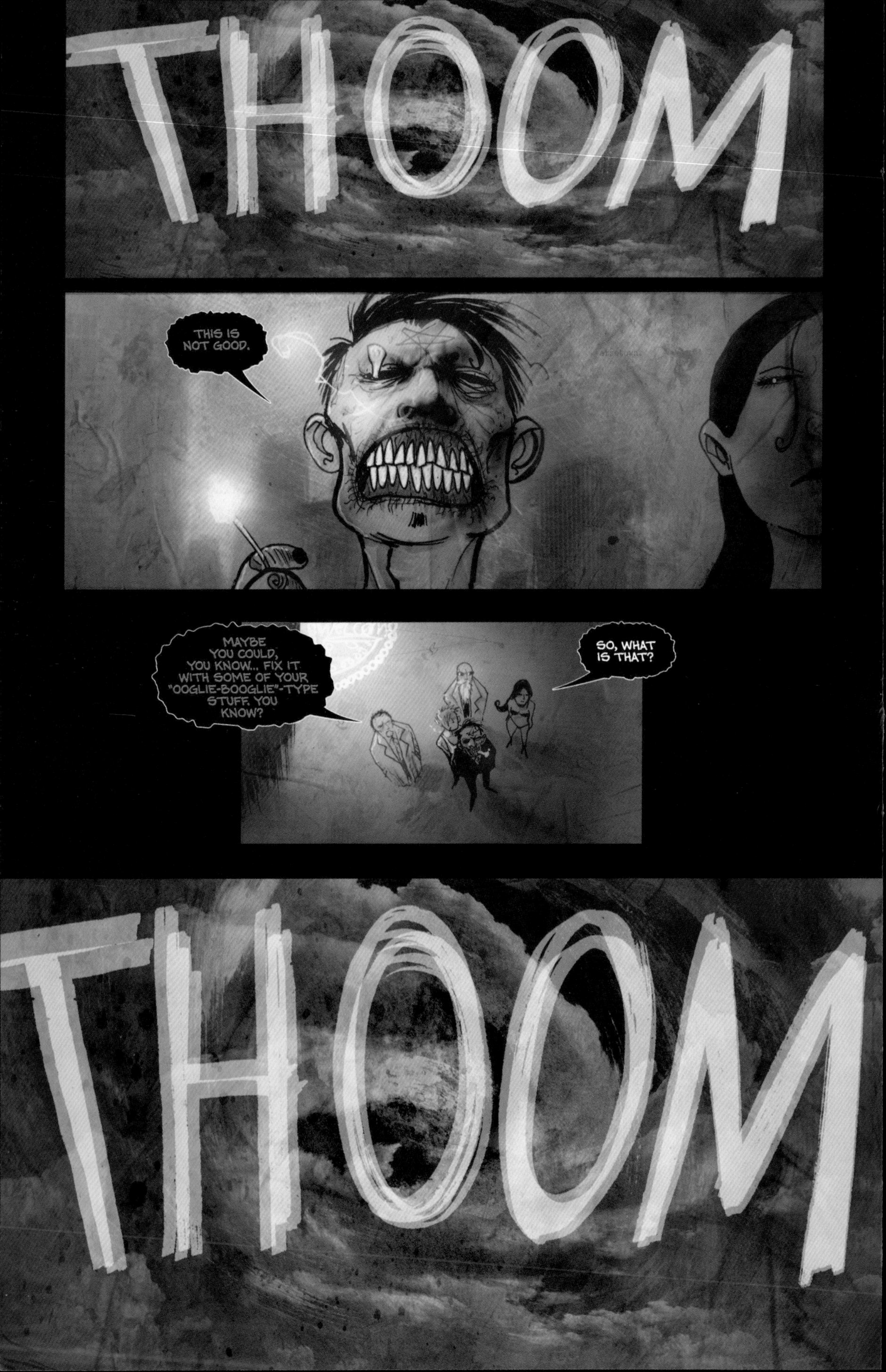
THOOM
THIS IS NOT GOOD.
MAYBE YOU COULD, YOU KNOW... FIX IT WITH SOME OF YOUR "OOGLIE-BOOGLIE"-TYPE STUFF. YOU KNOW?
SO, WHAT IS THAT?
THOOM

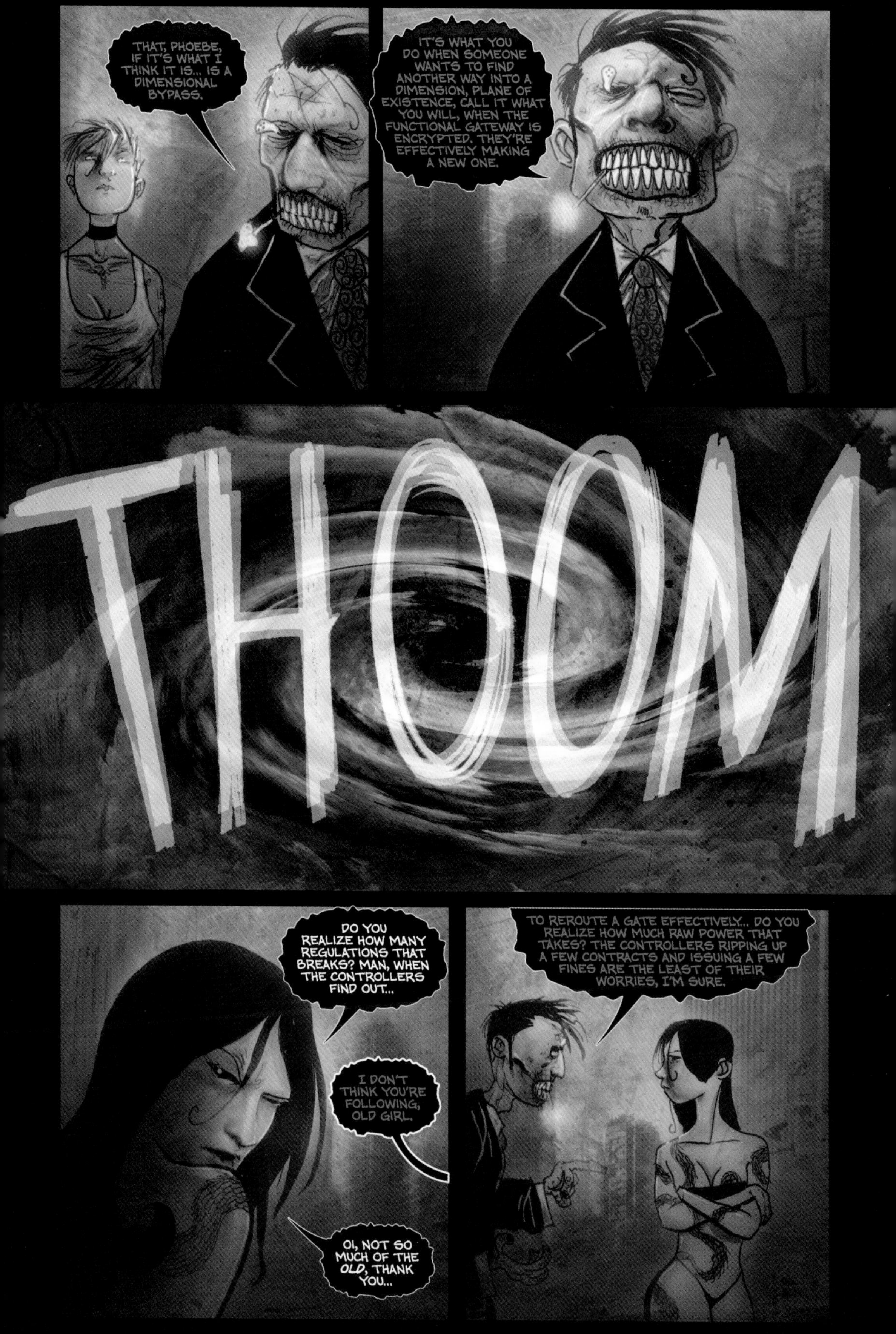
THAT, PHOEBE, IF IT'S WHAT I THINK IT IS... IS A DIMENSIONAL BYPASS.
IT'S WHAT YOU DO WHEN SOMEONE WANTS TO FIND ANOTHER WAY INTO A DIMENSION, PLANE OF EXISTENCE, CALL IT WHAT YOU WILL, WHEN THE FUNCTIONAL GATEWAY IS ENCRYPTED. THEY'RE EFFECTIVELY MAKING A NEW ONE.
THOOM
DO YOU REALIZE HOW MANY REGULATIONS THAT BREAKS? MAN, WHEN THE CONTROLLERS FIND OUT...
I DON'T THINK YOU'RE FOLLOWING, OLD GIRL.
OI, NOT SO MUCH OF THE OLD, THANK YOU...
TO REROUTE A GATE EFFECTIVELY... DO YOU REALIZE HOW MUCH RAW POWER THAT TAKES? THE CONTROLLERS RIPPING UP A FEW CONTRACTS AND ISSUING A FEW FINES ARE THE LEAST OF THEIR WORRIES, I'M SURE.

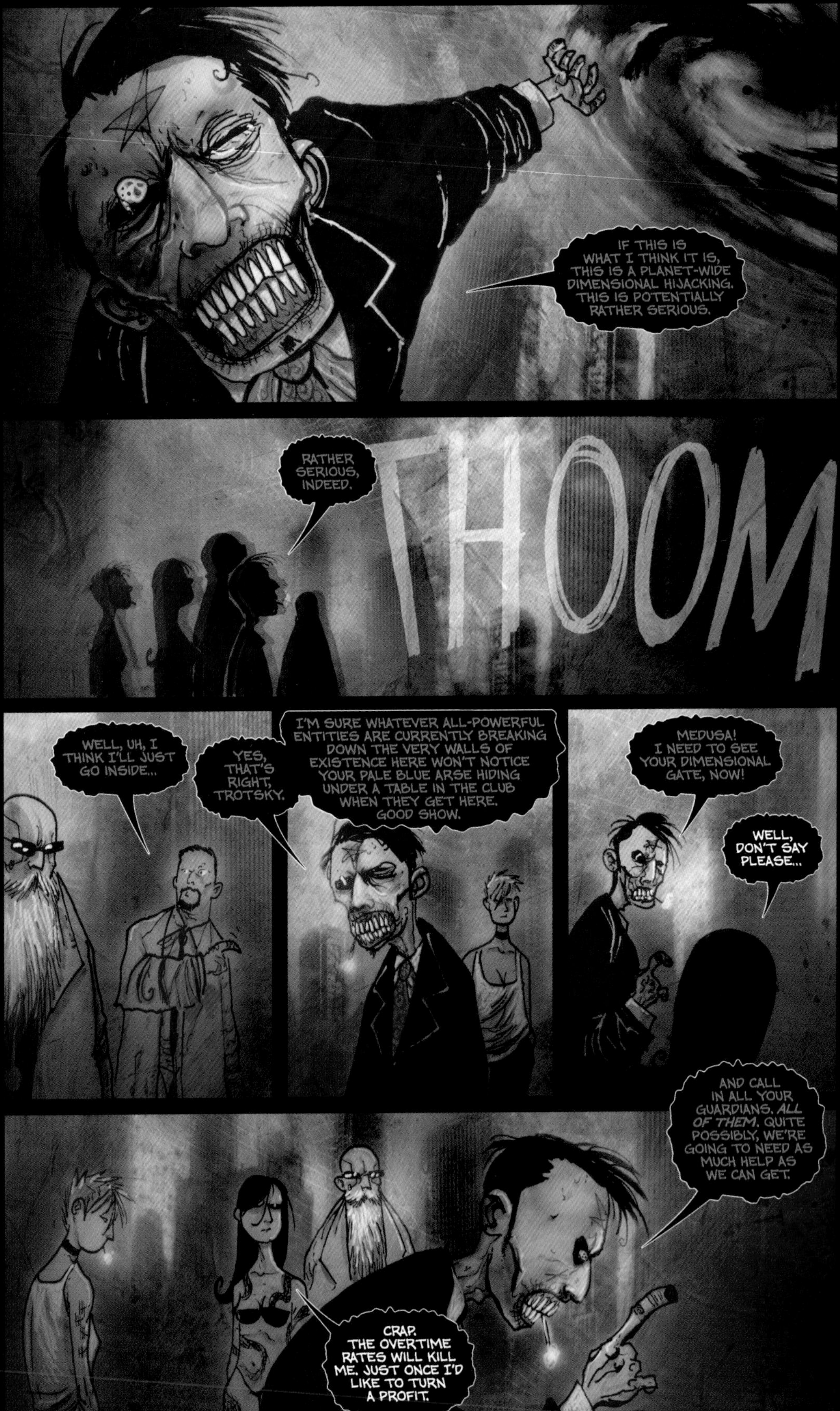
IF THIS IS WHAT I THINK IT IS, THIS IS A PLANET-WIDE DIMENSIONAL HIJACKING. THIS IS POTENTIALLY RATHER SERIOUS.
RATHER SERIOUS, INDEED.
THOOM
WELL, UH, I THINK I'LL JUST GO INSIDE...
YES, THAT'S RIGHT, TROTSKY.
I'M SURE WHATEVER ALL-POWERFUL ENTITIES ARE CURRENTLY BREAKING DOWN THE VERY WALLS OF EXISTENCE HERE WON'T NOTICE YOUR PALE BLUE ARSE HIDING UNDER A TABLE IN THE CLUB WHEN THEY GET HERE. GOOD SHOW.
MEDUSA! I NEED TO SEE YOUR DIMENSIONAL GATE, NOW!
WELL, DON'T SAY PLEASE...
AND CALL IN ALL YOUR GUARDIANS. *ALL OF THEM.* QUITE POSSIBLY, WE'RE GOING TO NEED AS MUCH HELP AS WE CAN GET.
CRAP. THE OVERTIME RATES WILL KILL ME. JUST ONCE I'D LIKE TO TURN A PROFIT.

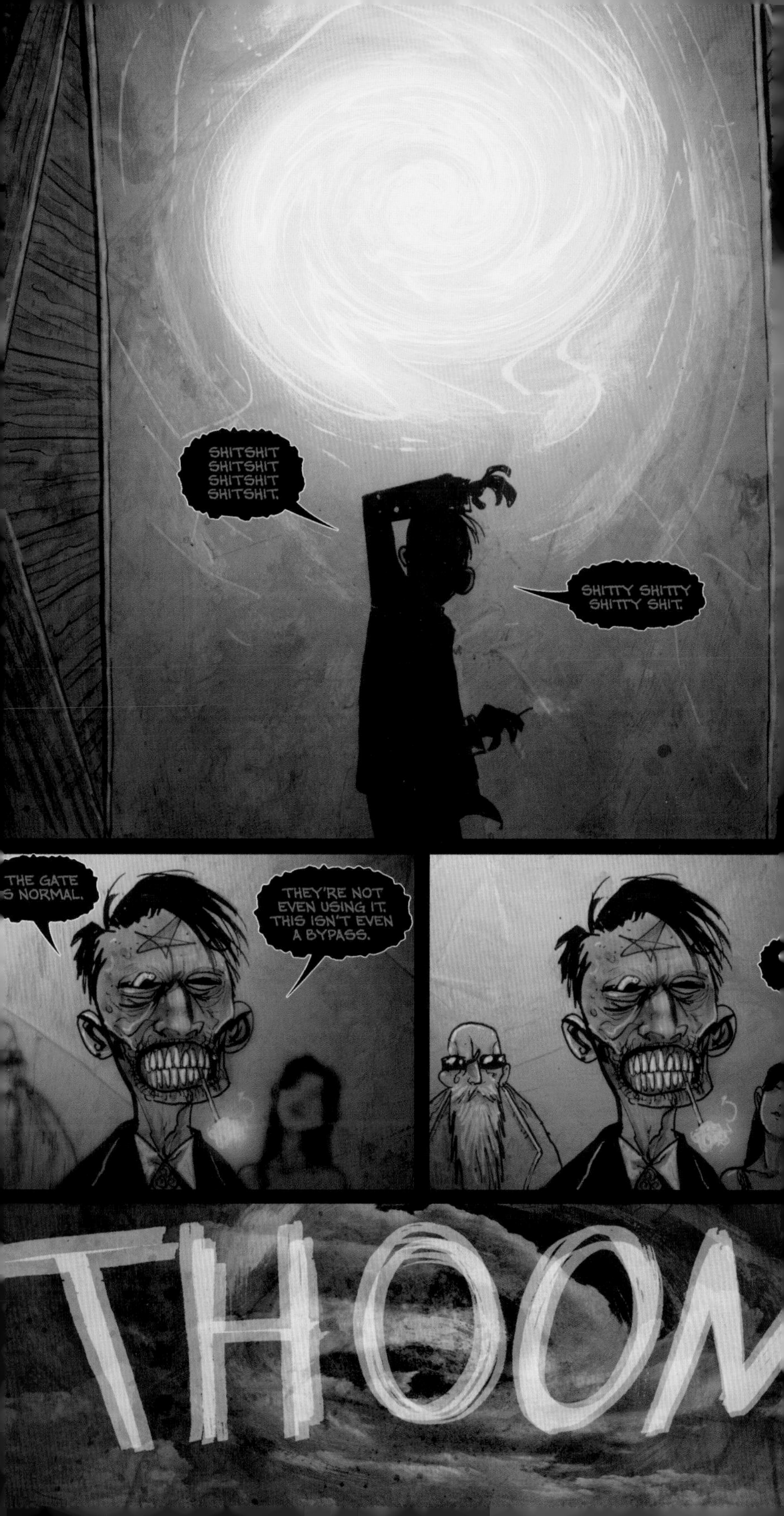
SHITSHIT SHITSHIT SHITSHIT SHITSHIT.
SHITTY SHITTY SHITTY SHIT.
THE GATE S NORMAL.
THEY'RE NOT EVEN USING IT. THIS ISN'T EVEN A BYPASS.
THOOM

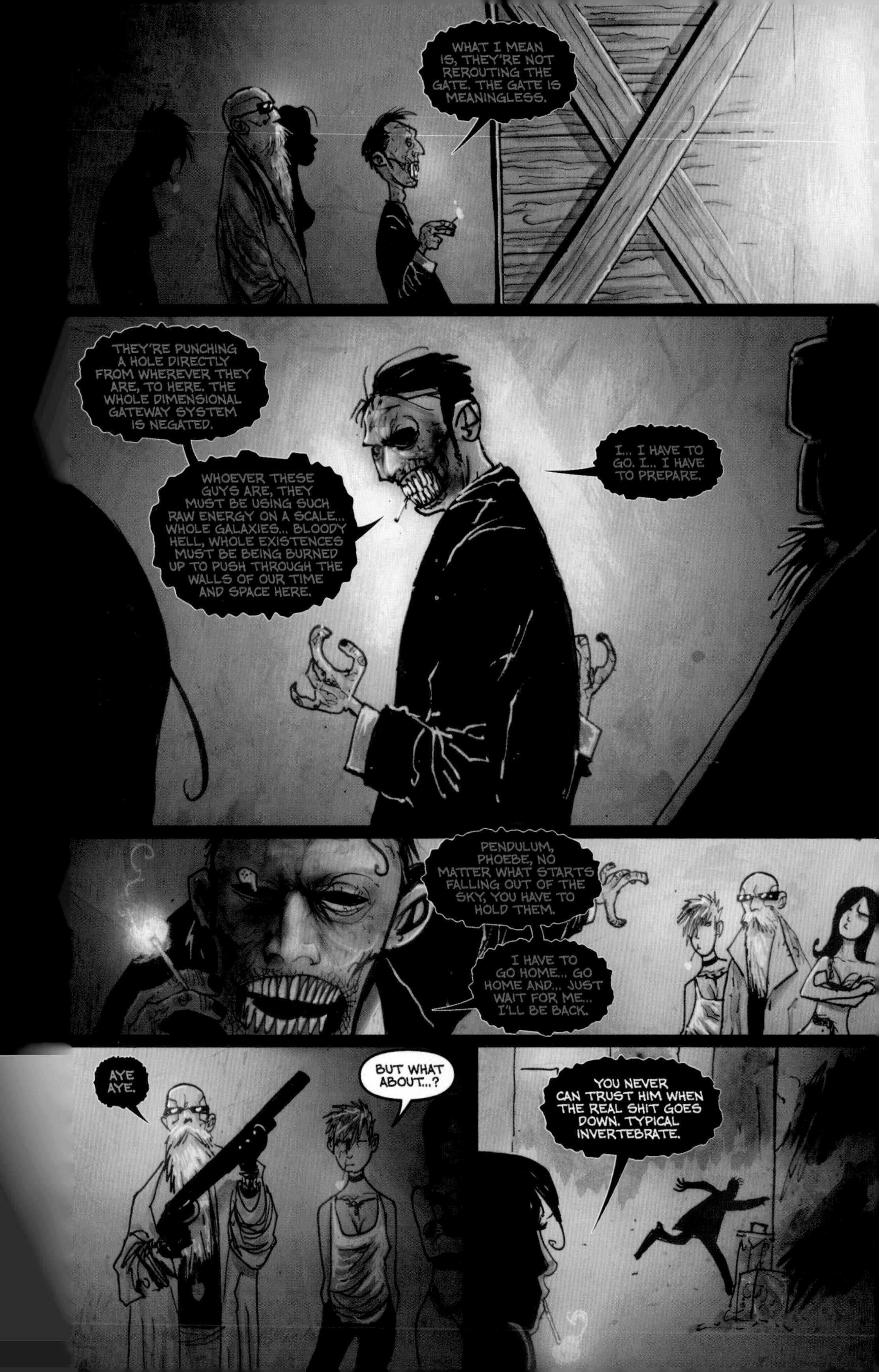

WHAT I MEAN IS, THEY'RE NOT REROUTING THE GATE. THE GATE IS MEANINGLESS.
THEY'RE PUNCHING A HOLE DIRECTLY FROM WHEREVER THEY ARE, TO HERE. THE WHOLE DIMENSIONAL GATEWAY SYSTEM IS NEGATED.
WHOEVER THESE GUYS ARE, THEY MUST BE USING SUCH RAW ENERGY ON A SCALE... WHOLE GALAXIES... BLOODY HELL, WHOLE EXISTENCES MUST BE BEING BURNED UP TO PUSH THROUGH THE WALLS OF OUR TIME AND SPACE HERE.
I... I HAVE TO GO. I... I HAVE TO PREPARE.
PENDULUM, PHOEBE, NO MATTER WHAT STARTS FALLING OUT OF THE SKY, YOU HAVE TO HOLD THEM.
I HAVE TO GO HOME... GO HOME AND... JUST WAIT FOR ME... I'LL BE BACK.
AYE AYE.
BUT WHAT ABOUT...?
YOU NEVER CAN TRUST HIM WHEN THE REAL SHIT GOES DOWN. TYPICAL INVERTEBRATE.

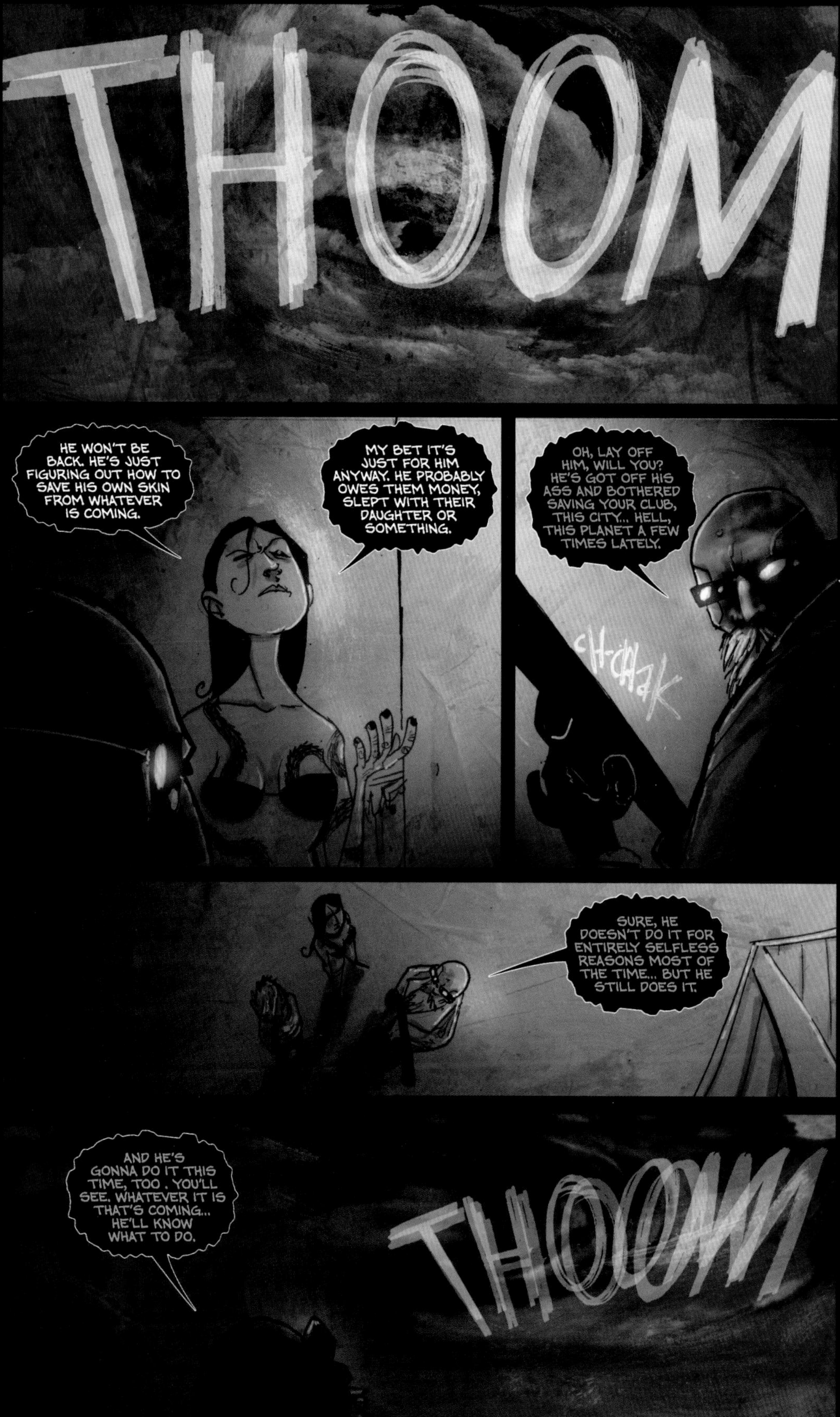
THOOM
HE WON'T BE BACK. HE'S JUST FIGURING OUT HOW TO SAVE HIS OWN SKIN FROM WHATEVER IS COMING.
MY BET IT'S JUST FOR HIM ANYWAY. HE PROBABLY OWES THEM MONEY, SLEPT WITH THEIR DAUGHTER OR SOMETHING.
OH, LAY OFF HIM, WILL YOU? HE'S GOT OFF HIS ASS AND BOTHERED SAVING YOUR CLUB, THIS CITY... HELL, THIS PLANET A FEW TIMES LATELY.
SURE, HE DOESN'T DO IT FOR ENTIRELY SELFLESS REASONS MOST OF THE TIME... BUT HE STILL DOES IT.
AND HE'S GONNA DO IT THIS TIME, TOO . YOU'LL SEE. WHATEVER IT IS THAT'S COMING... HE'LL KNOW WHAT TO DO.
THOOM

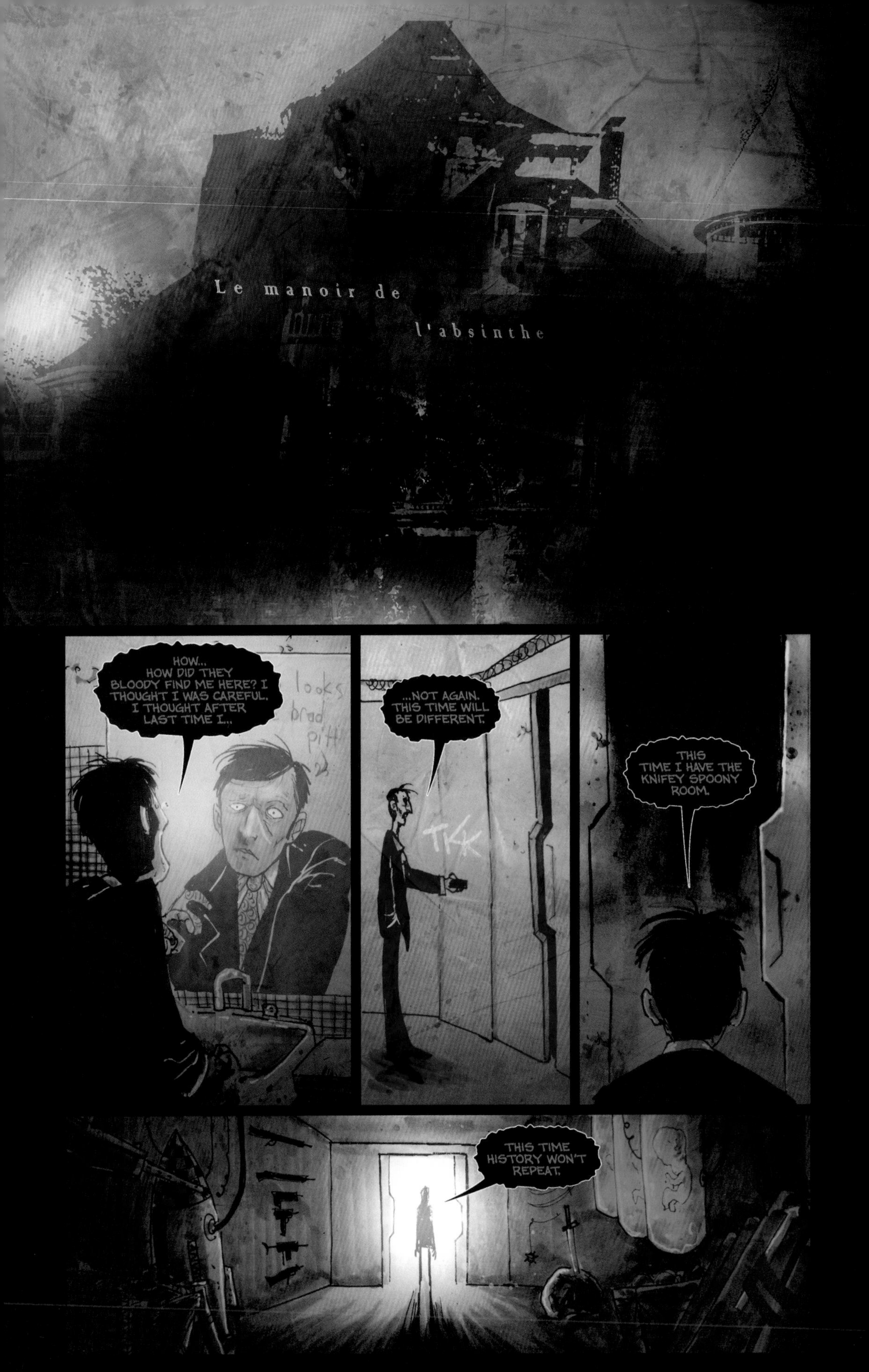
Le manoir de l'absinthe
HOW... HOW DID THEY BLOODY FIND ME HERE? I THOUGHT I WAS CAREFUL. I THOUGHT AFTER LAST TIME I...
looks brad pitt
...NOT AGAIN. THIS TIME WILL BE DIFFERENT.
TKK
THIS TIME I HAVE THE KNIFEY SPOONY ROOM.
THIS TIME HISTORY WON'T REPEAT.

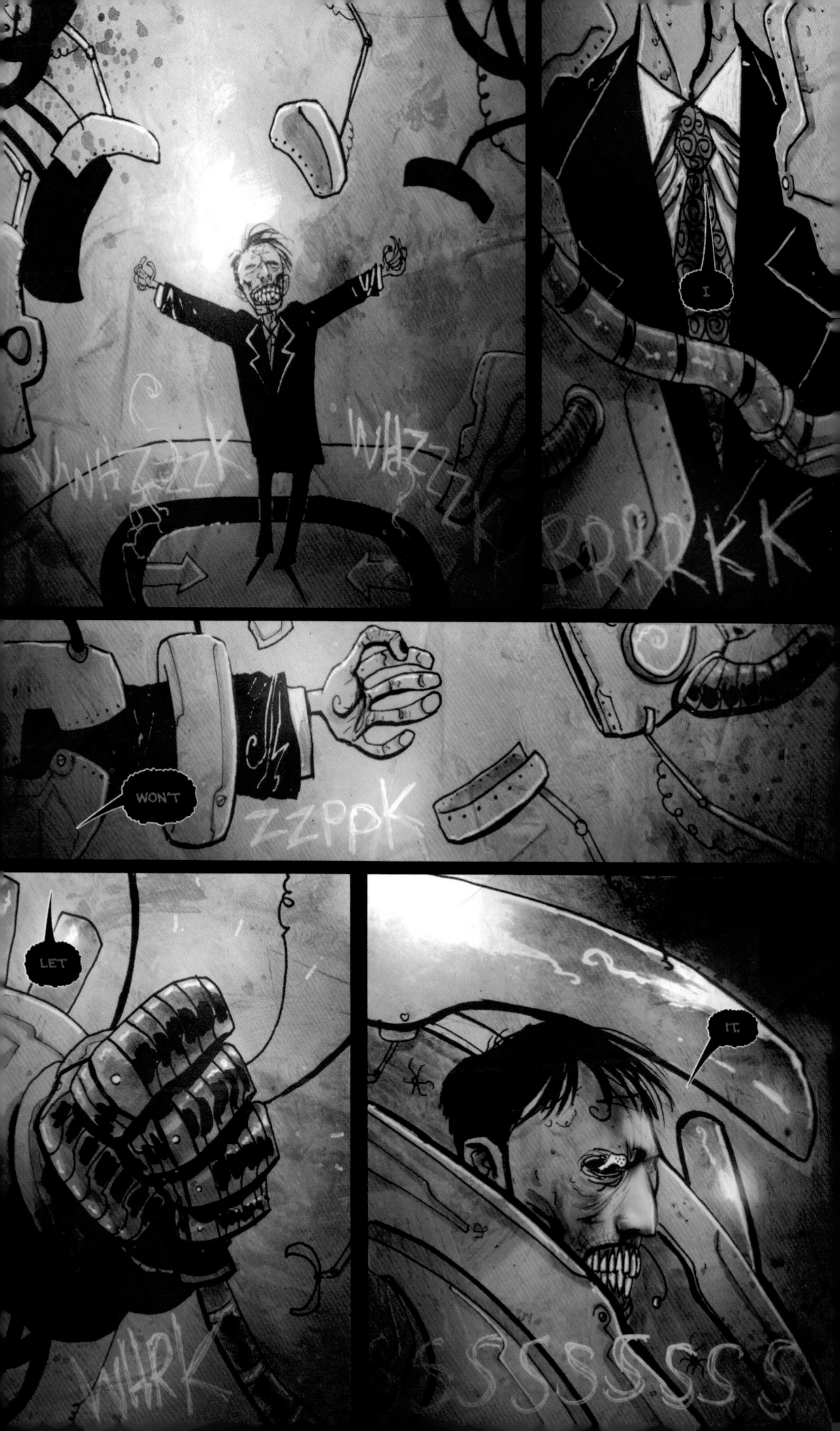
WHZZZZK
WHZZZZK
I
RRRRKK
WON'T
ZZPPK
LET
WHRK
IT.
SSSSSSSSS

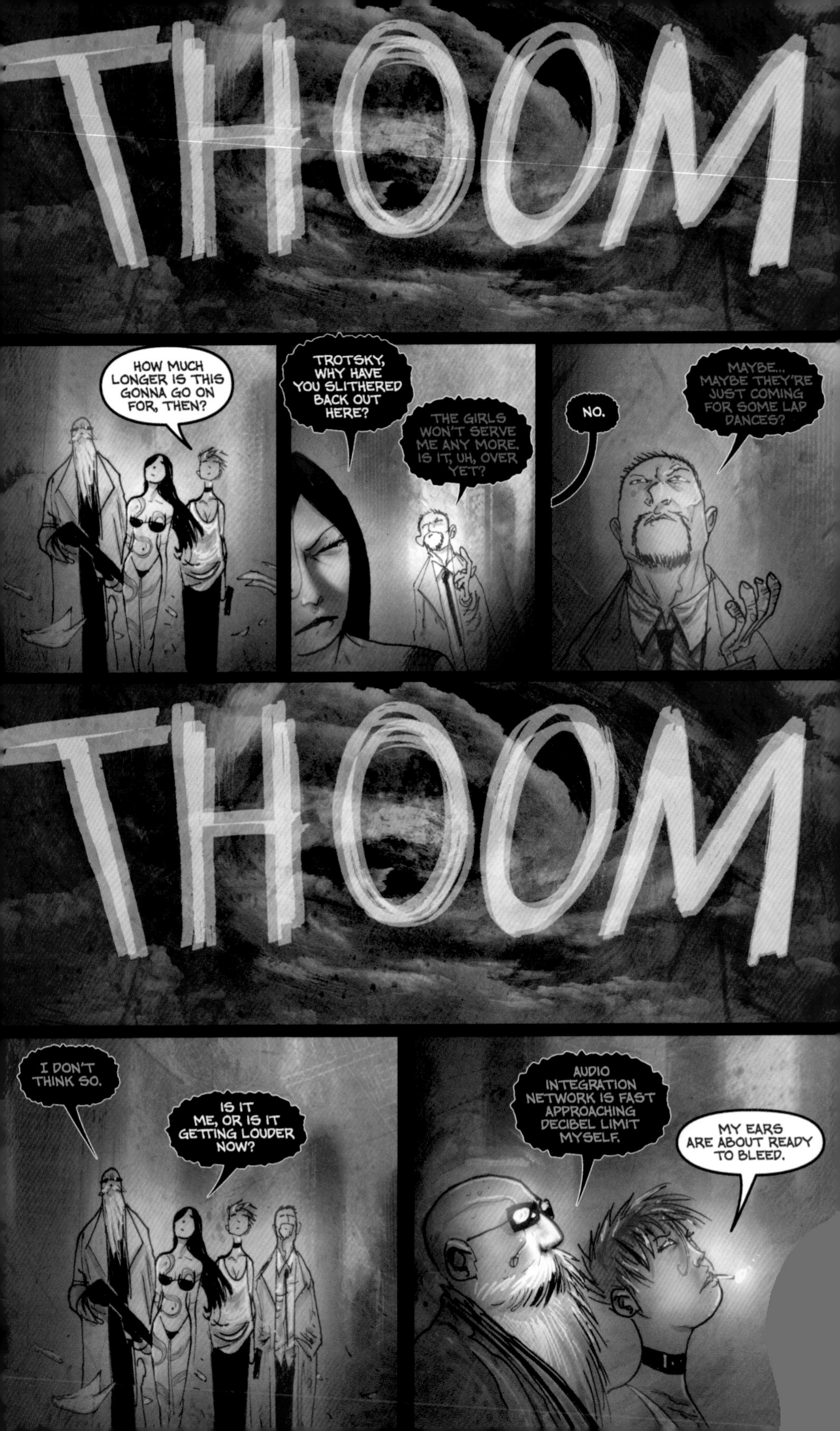
THOOM
HOW MUCH LONGER IS THIS GONNA GO ON FOR, THEN?
TROTSKY, WHY HAVE YOU SLITHERED BACK OUT HERE?
THE GIRLS WON'T SERVE ME ANY MORE. IS IT, UH, OVER YET?
NO.
MAYBE... MAYBE THEY'RE JUST COMING FOR SOME LAP DANCES?
THOOM
I DON'T THINK SO.
IS IT ME, OR IS IT GETTING LOUDER NOW?
AUDIO INTEGRATION NETWORK IS FAST APPROACHING DECIBEL LIMIT MYSELF.
MY EARS ARE ABOUT READY TO BLEED.

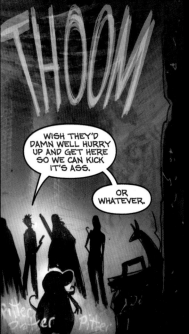

THOOM
WISH THEY'D DAMN WELL HURRY UP AND GET HERE SO WE CAN KICK IT'S ASS.
OR WHATEVER.
Pitter Patter Pitter
Pretty!
I HAD ALMOST FORGOTTEN HOW MUCH I LOATHE YOU. THANKS.
GOOD, GIRLS, YOU CAME. I TRUST EVERYONE BROUGHT A WEAPON OR TWO? KITTY, KNIVES? WHERE'S JEANNE? SHE'D BETTER BRING THE FLAME-THROWER SHE BORROWED LAST WEEK. THERE'S GOING TO BE A RUCKUS.
THOOM
THOOM
I THINK IT'S OPENING.

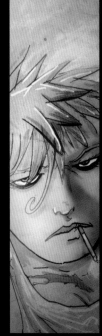

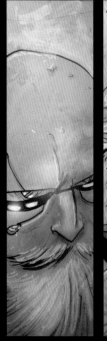

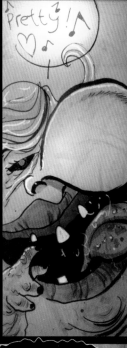

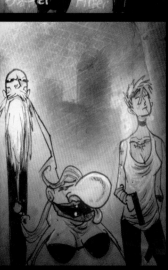

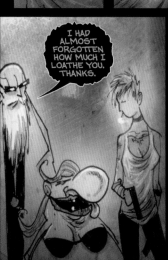

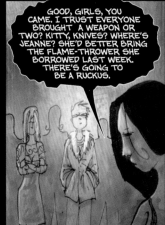

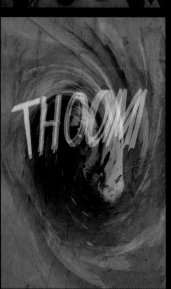

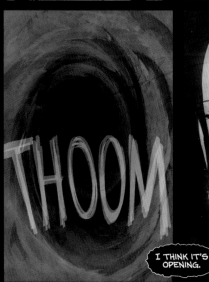

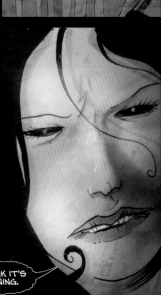

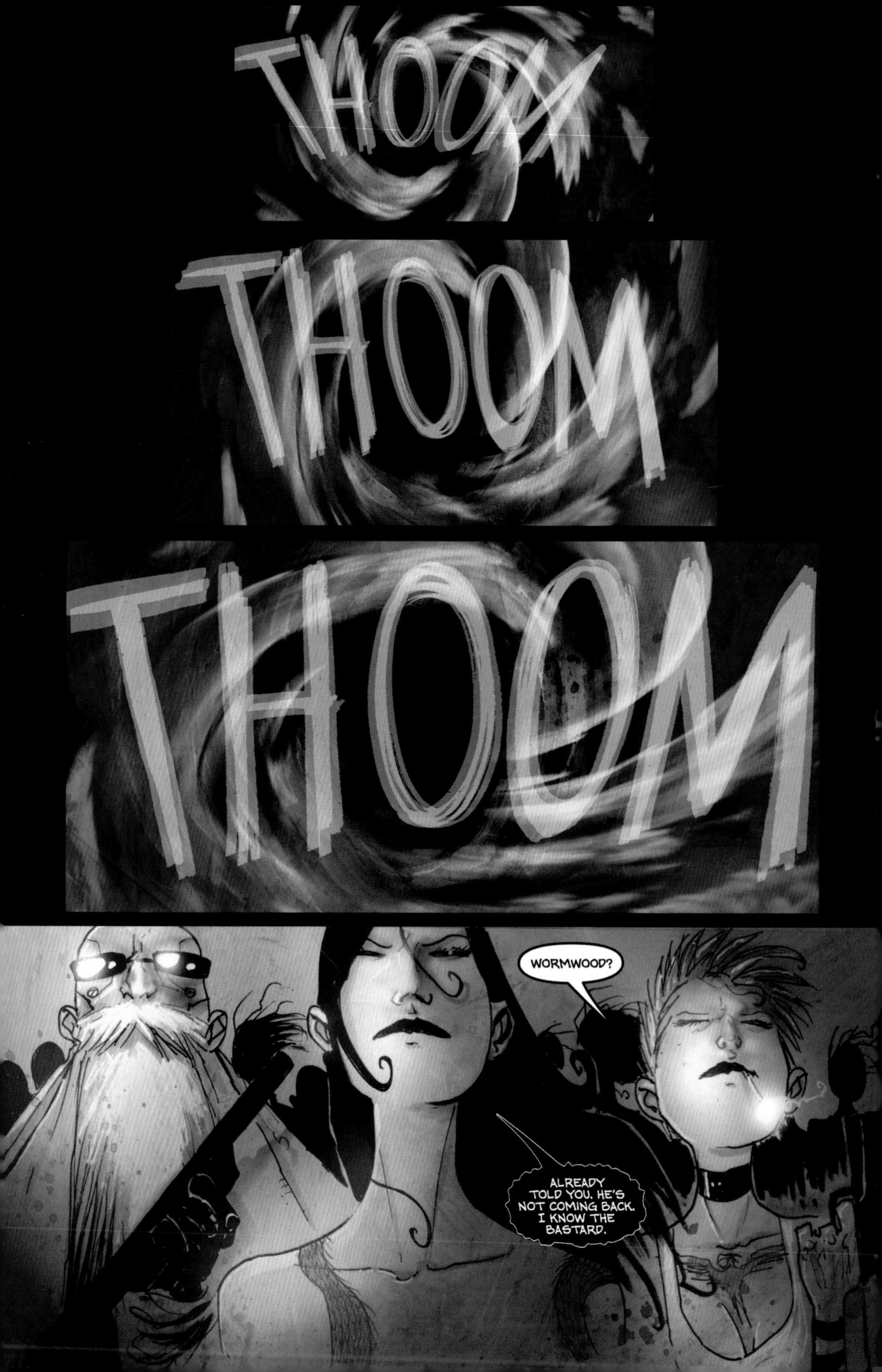
THOOM
THOOM
THOOM
WORMWOOD?
ALREADY TOLD YOU. HE'S NOT COMING BACK. I KNOW THE BASTARD.

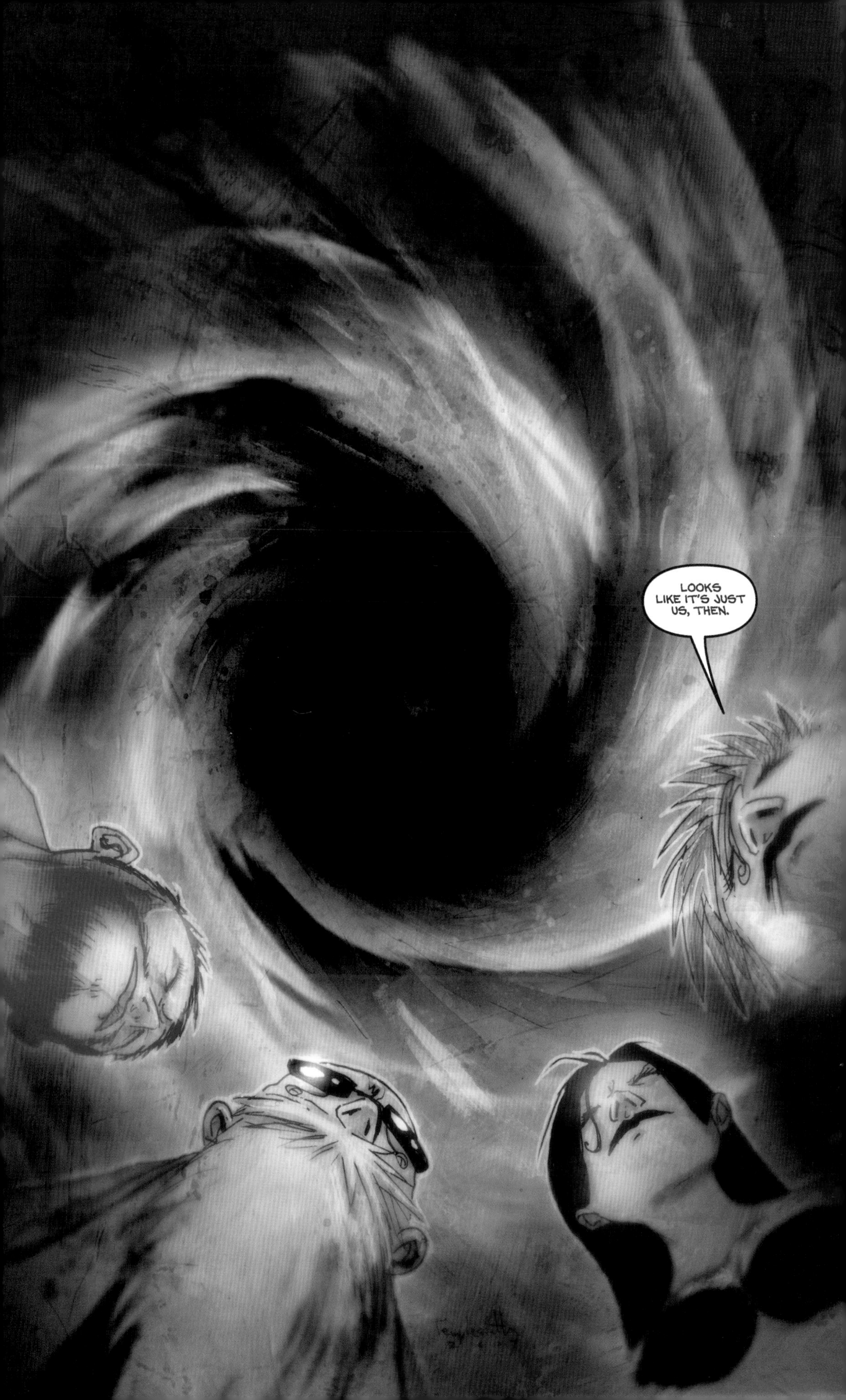
LOOKS LIKE IT'S JUST US, THEN.

Chapter 2

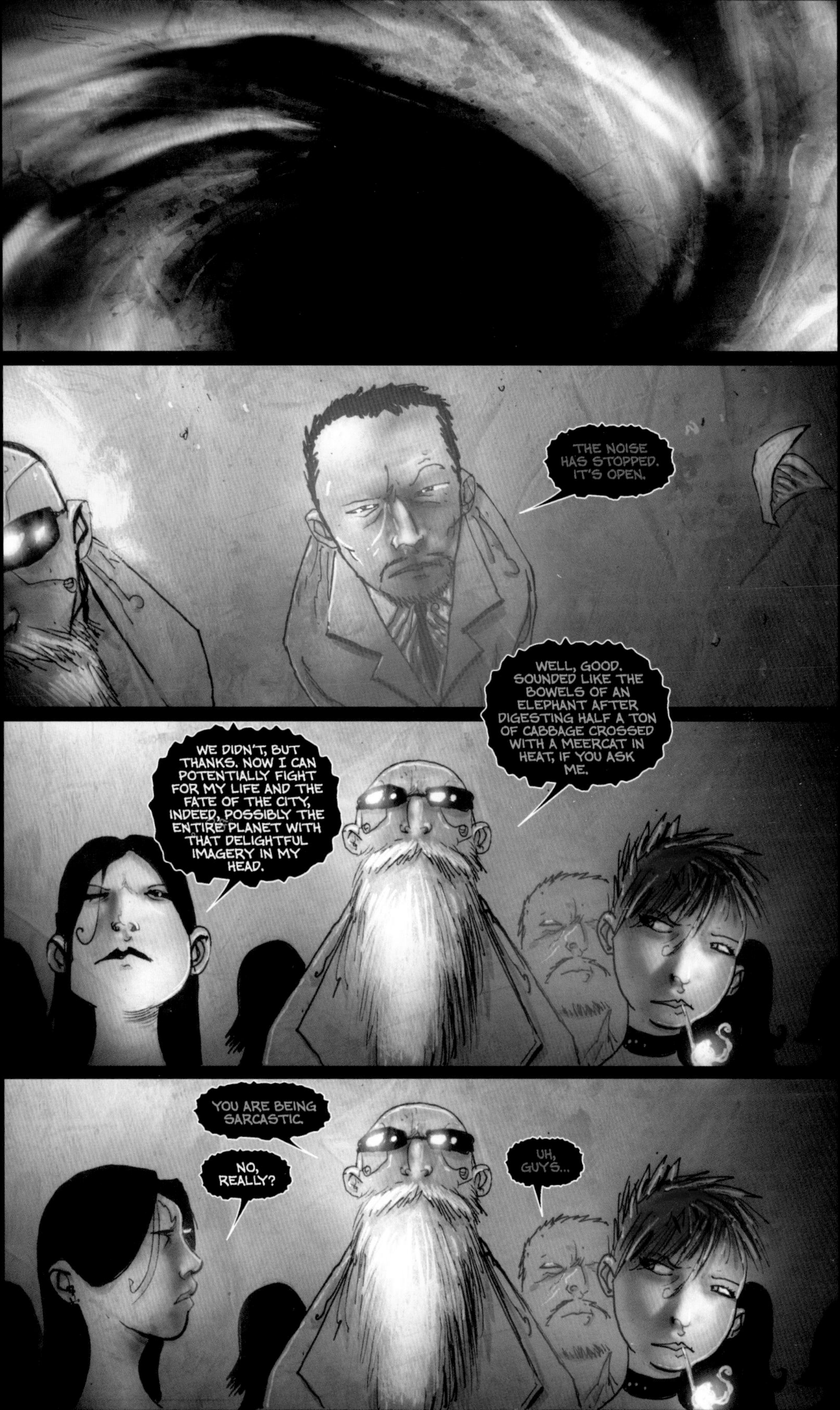
THE NOISE HAS STOPPED. IT'S OPEN.
WELL, GOOD. SOUNDED LIKE THE BOWELS OF AN ELEPHANT AFTER DIGESTING HALF A TON OF CABBAGE CROSSED WITH A MEERCAT IN HEAT, IF YOU ASK ME.
WE DIDN'T, BUT THANKS. NOW I CAN POTENTIALLY FIGHT FOR MY LIFE AND THE FATE OF THE CITY, INDEED, POSSIBLY THE ENTIRE PLANET WITH THAT DELIGHTFUL IMAGERY IN MY HEAD.
YOU ARE BEING SARCASTIC.
NO, REALLY?
UH, GUYS...

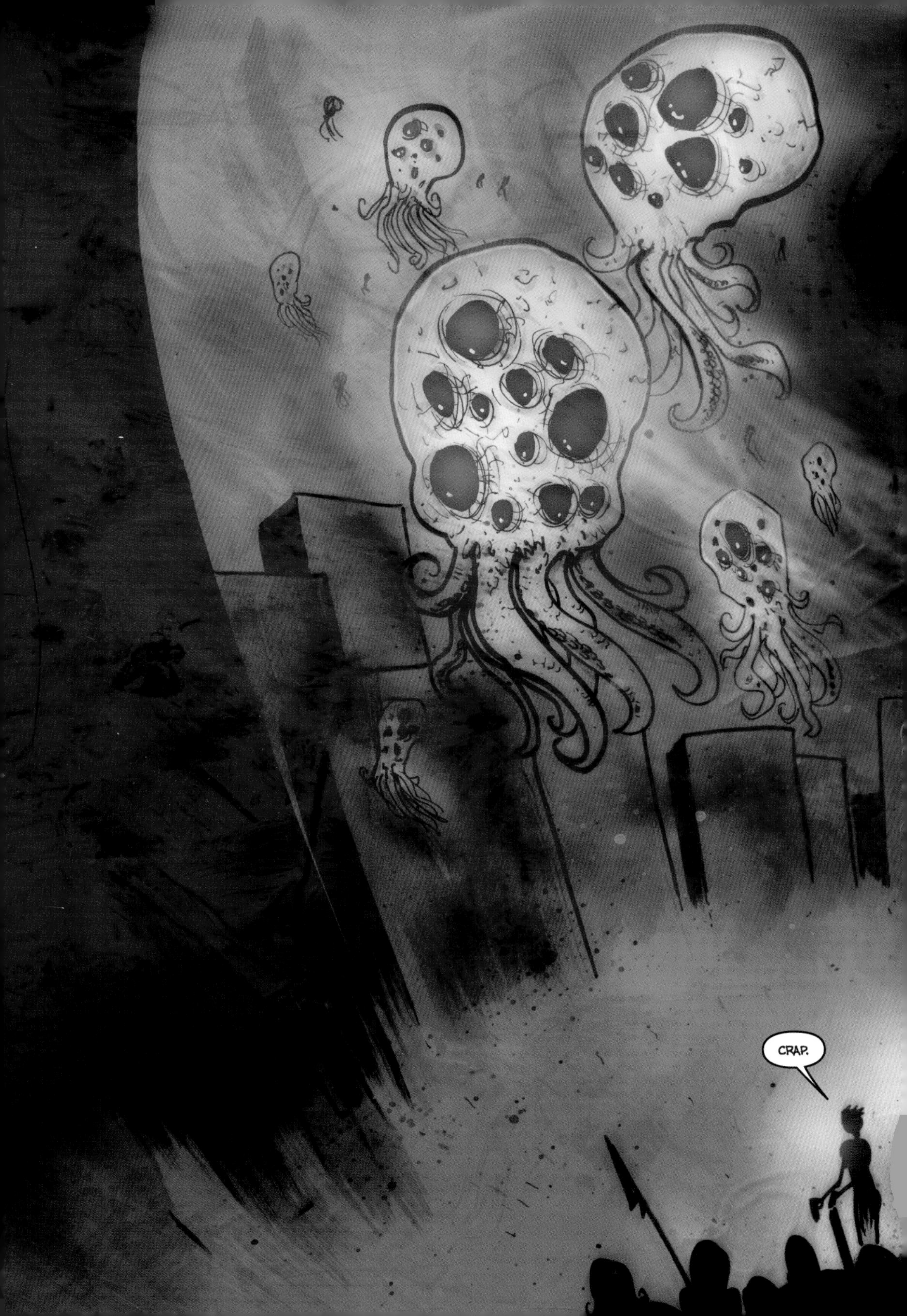
CRAP.

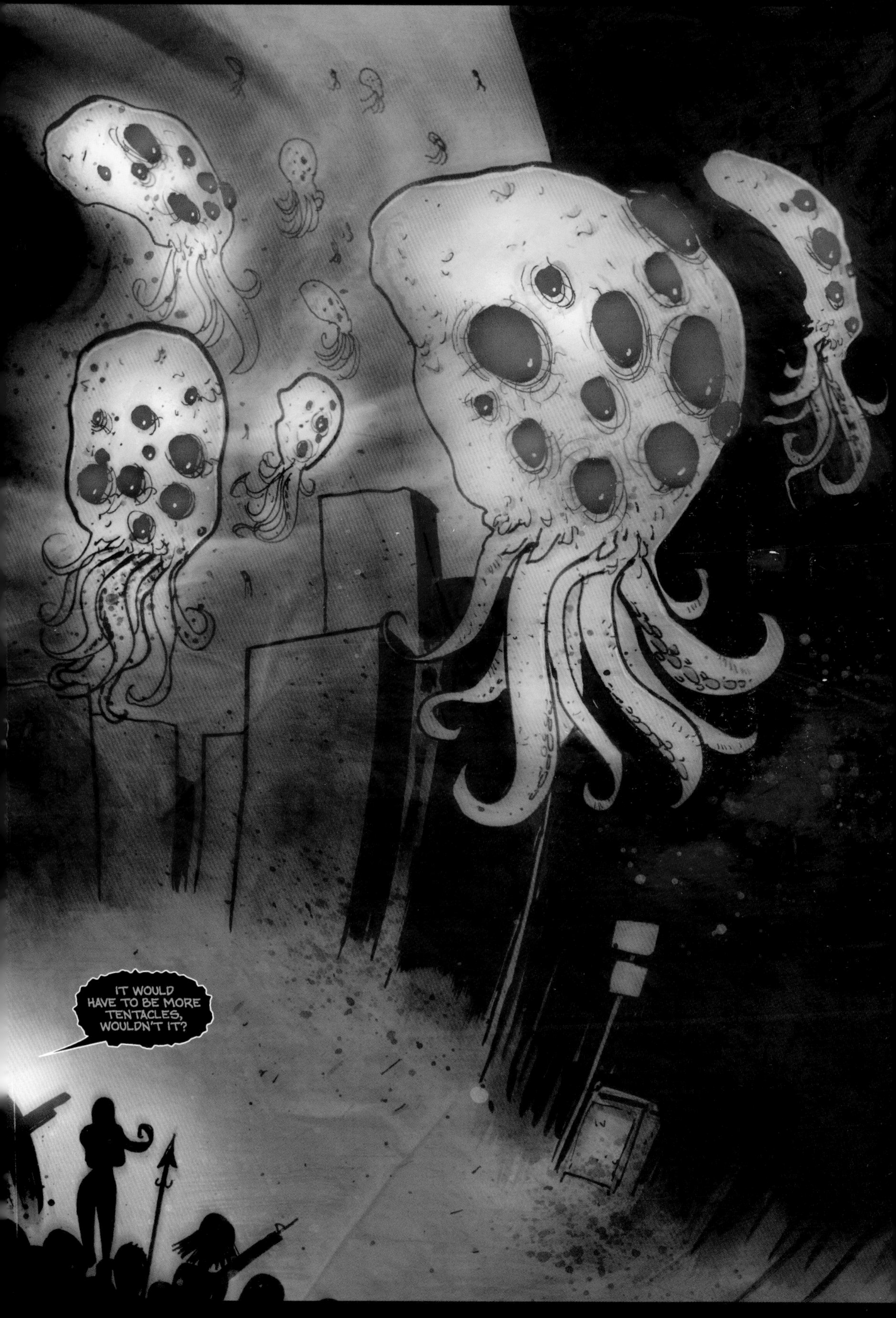
IT WOULD HAVE TO BE MORE TENTACLES, WOULDN'T IT?

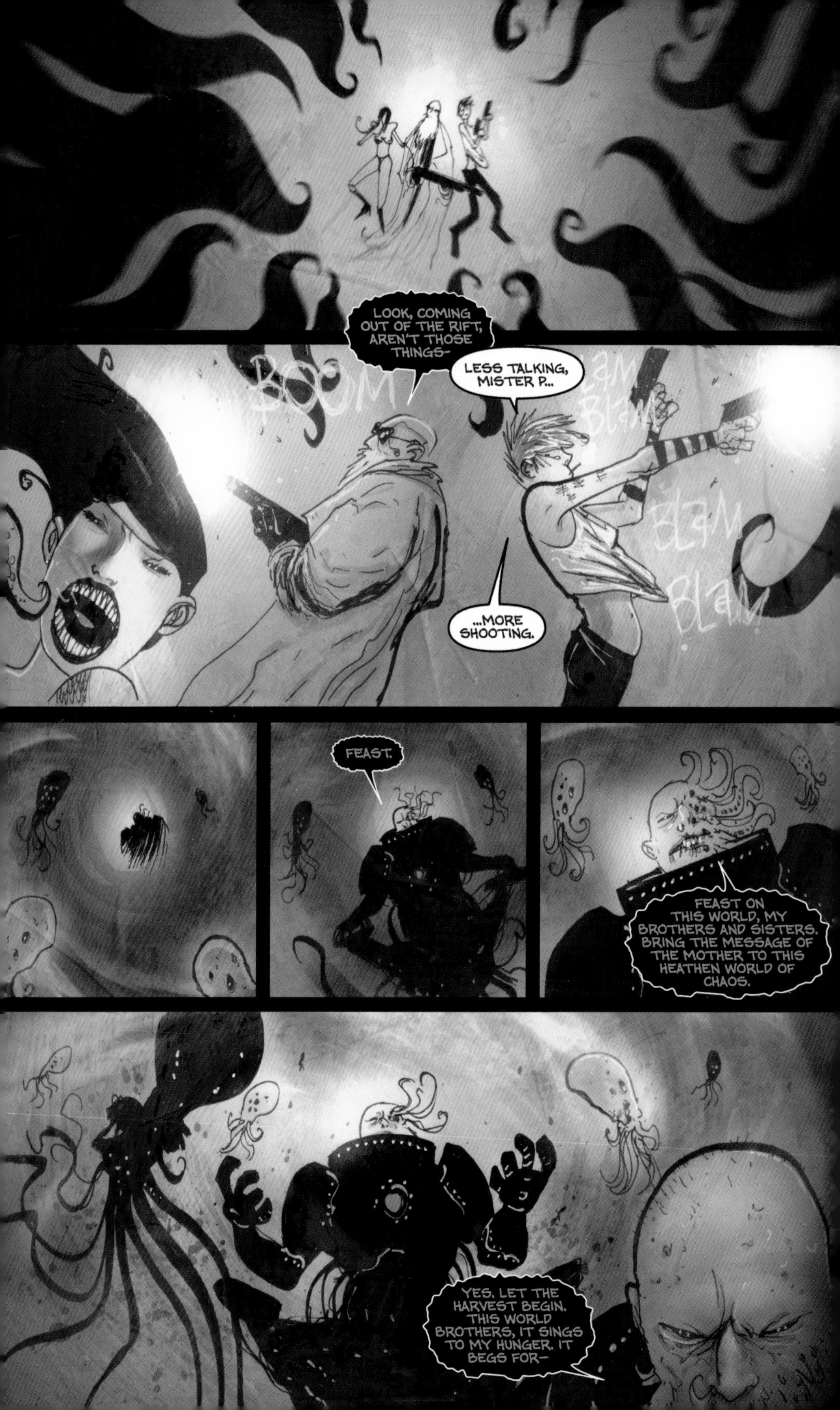
LOOK, COMING OUT OF THE RIFT, AREN'T THOSE THINGS-
BOOM
LESS TALKING, MISTER P...
BLAM BLAM
BLAM
BLAM
...MORE SHOOTING.
FEAST.
FEAST ON THIS WORLD, MY BROTHERS AND SISTERS. BRING THE MESSAGE OF THE MOTHER TO THIS HEATHEN WORLD OF CHAOS.
YES. LET THE HARVEST BEGIN. THIS WORLD BROTHERS, IT SINGS TO MY HUNGER. IT BEGS FOR-

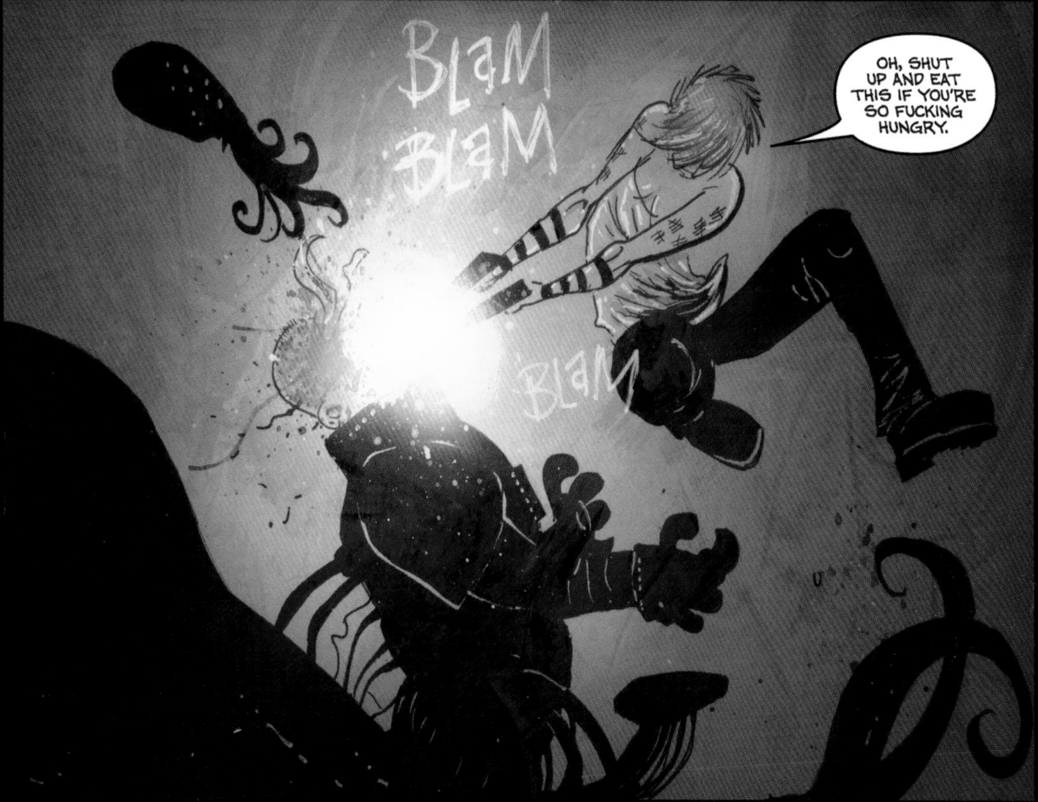
BLAM
BLAM
OH, SHUT UP AND EAT THIS IF YOU'RE SO FUCKING HUNGRY.
BLAM

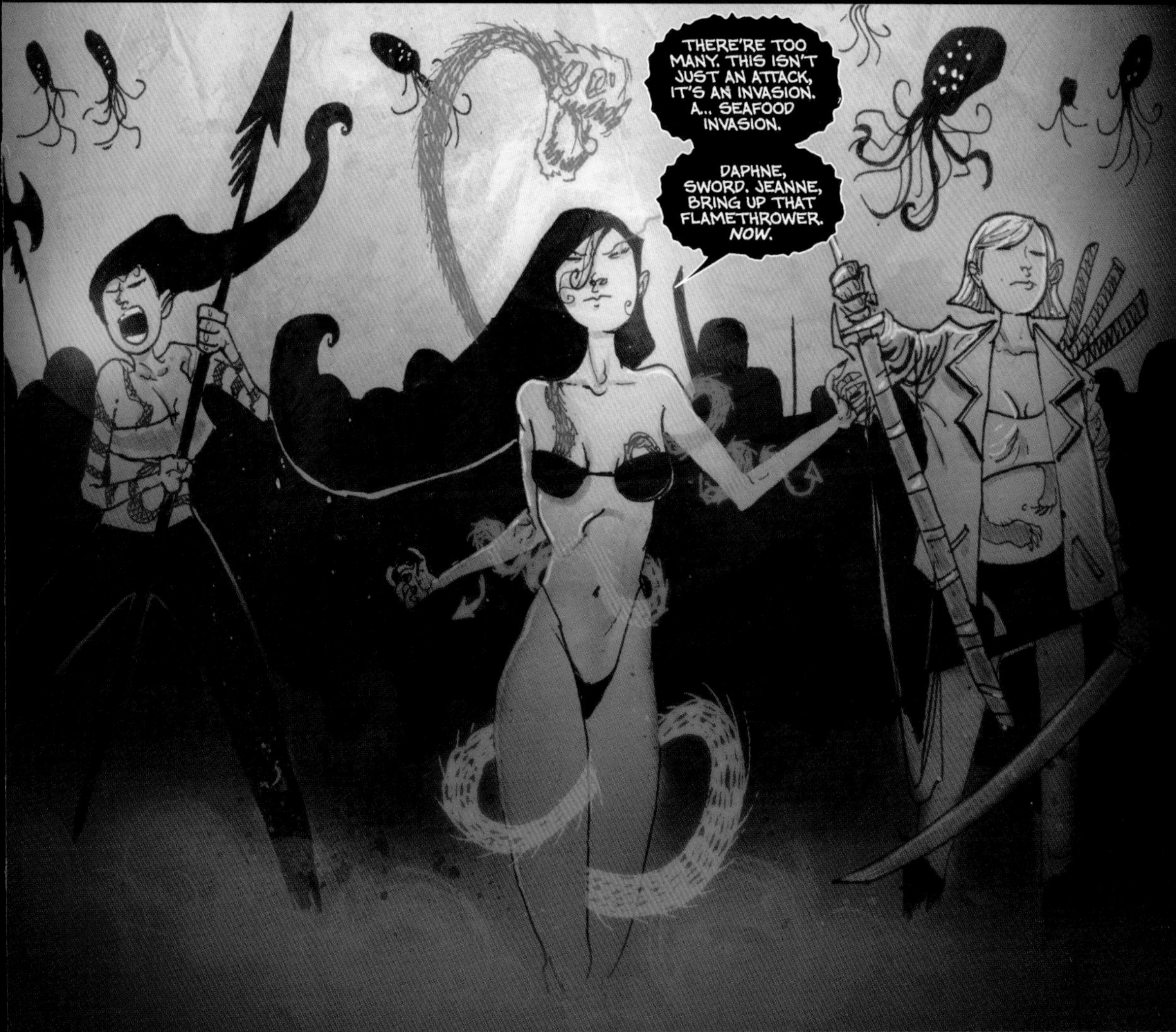
THERE'RE TOO MANY. THIS ISN'T JUST AN ATTACK, IT'S AN INVASION. A... SEAFOOD INVASION.
DAPHNE, SWORD. JEANNE, BRING UP THAT FLAMETHROWER. NOW.

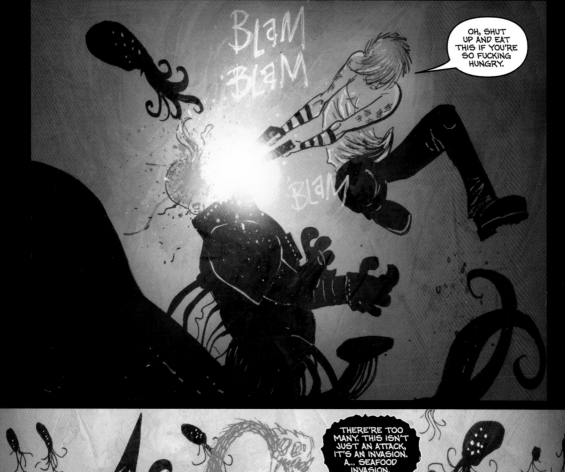

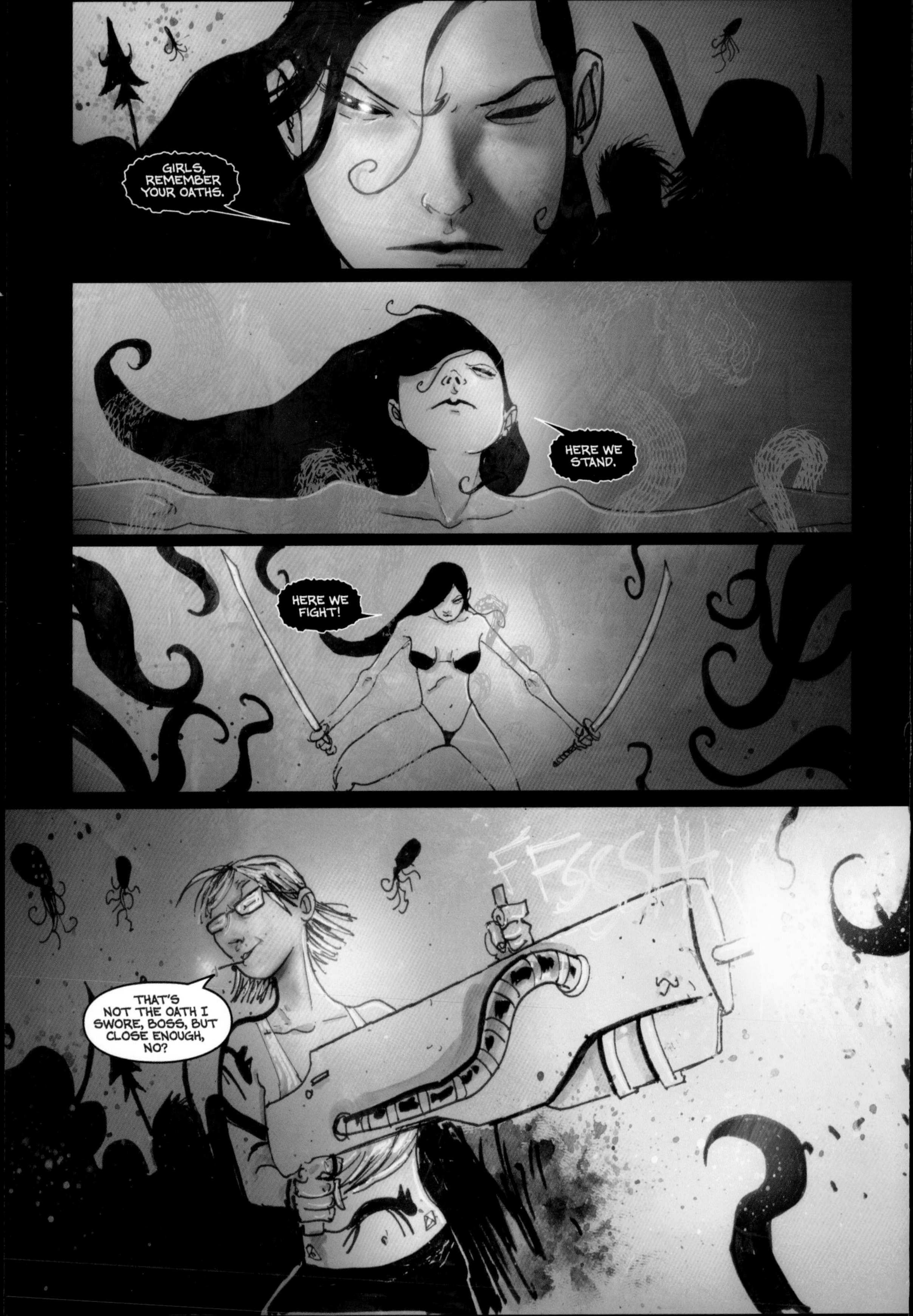
GIRLS, REMEMBER YOUR OATHS.
HERE WE STAND.
HERE WE FIGHT!
FFSSCHHH
THAT'S NOT THE OATH I SWORE, BOSS, BUT CLOSE ENOUGH, NO?

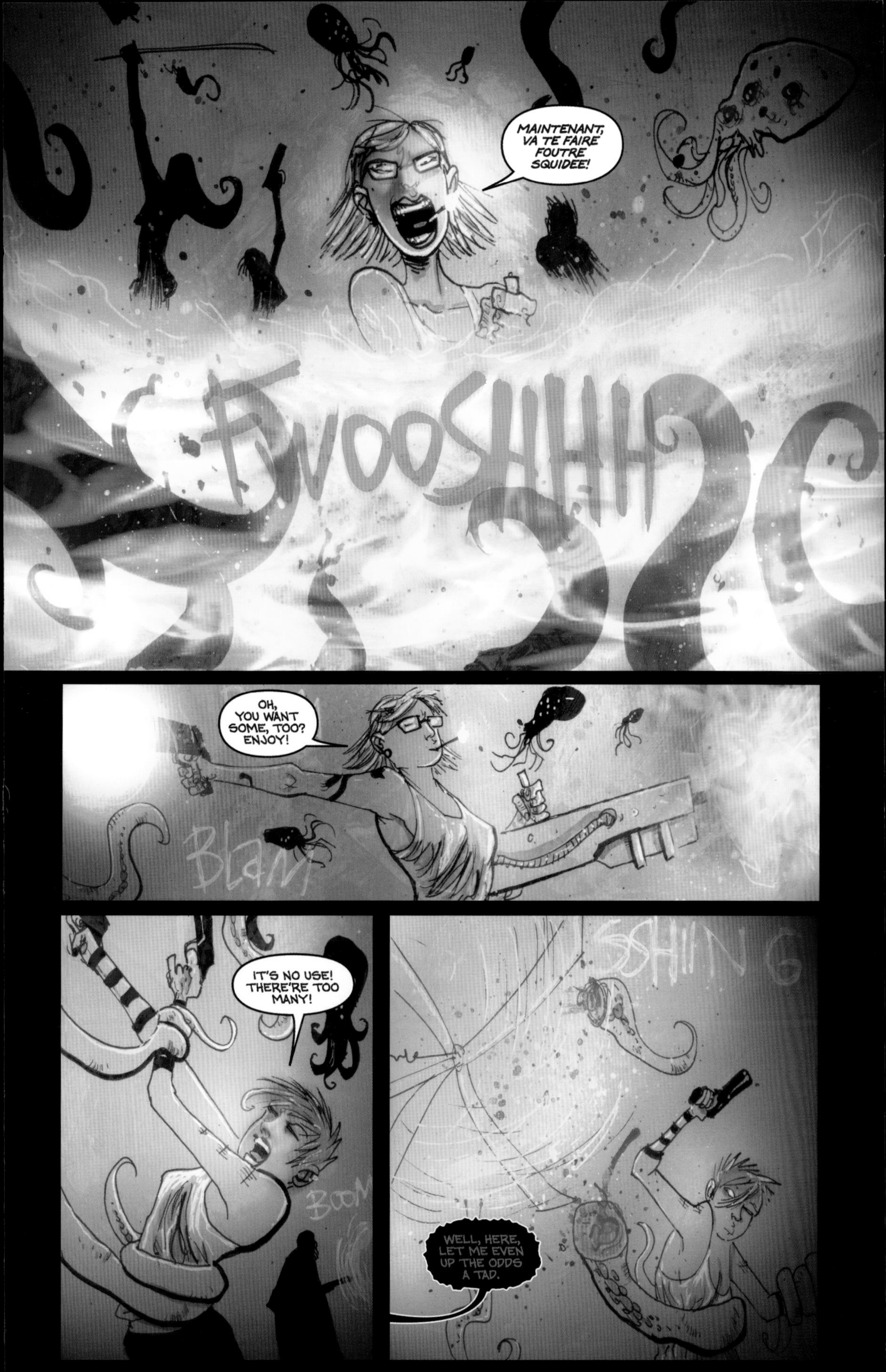
MAINTENANT, VA TE FAIRE FOUTRE SQUIDEE!
FWOOSHHH
OH, YOU WANT SOME, TOO? ENJOY!
BLAM
IT'S NO USE! THERE'RE TOO MANY!
BOOM
SSHING
WELL, HERE, LET ME EVEN UP THE ODDS A TAD.

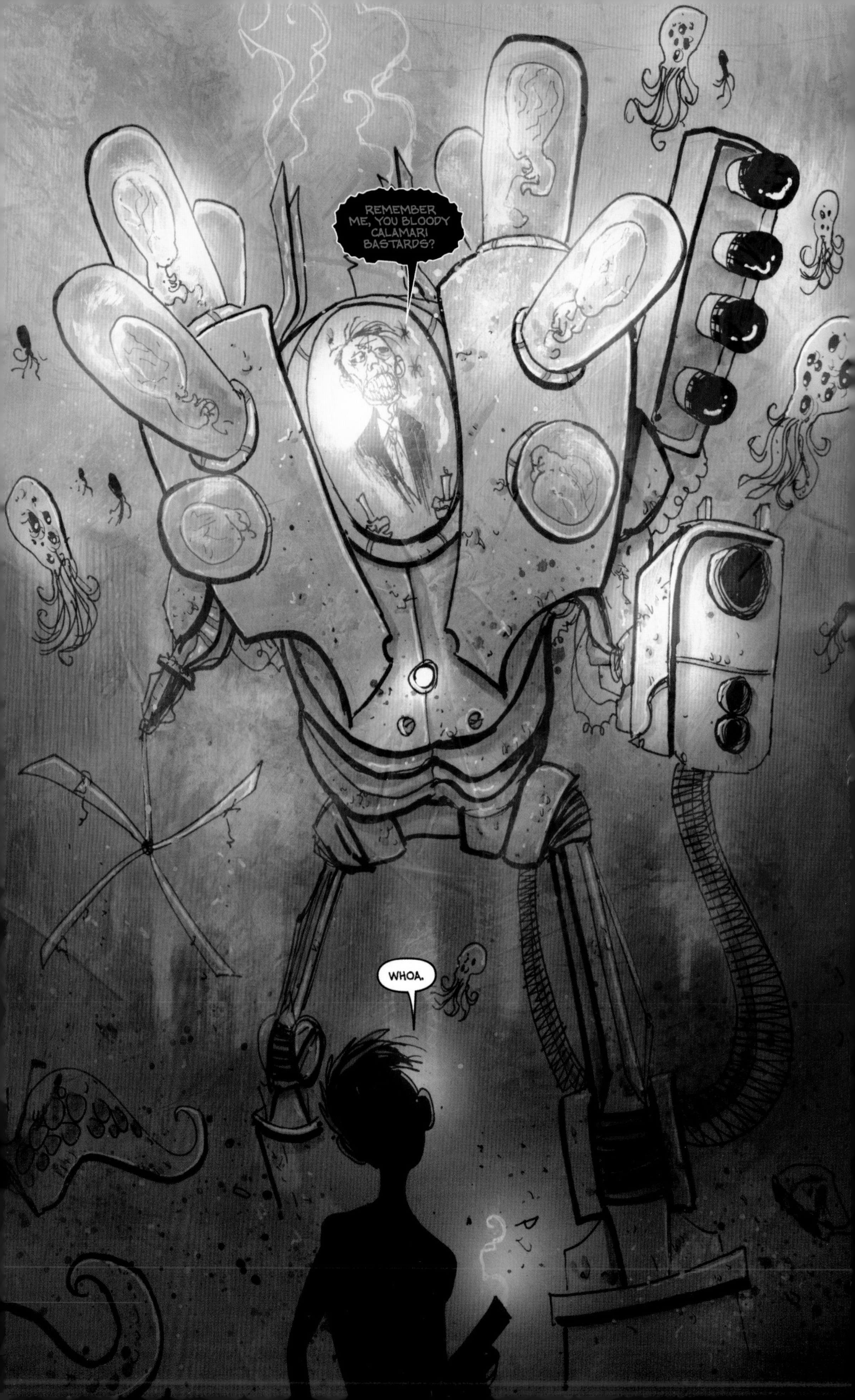
REMEMBER ME, YOU BLOODY CALAMARI BASTARDS?
WHOA.

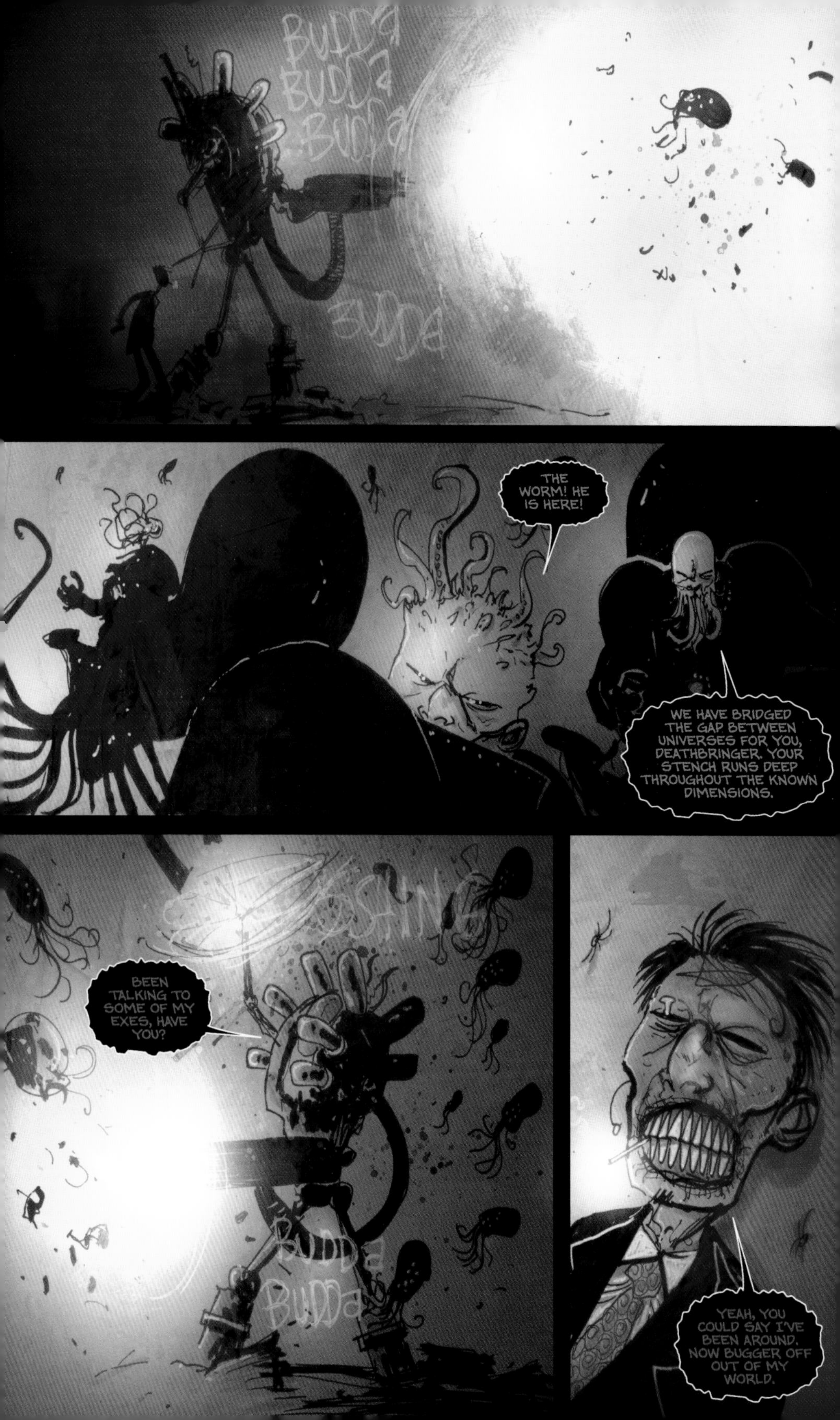

BUDDA BUDDA BUDDA
BUDDA
THE WORM! HE IS HERE!
WE HAVE BRIDGED THE GAP BETWEEN UNIVERSES FOR YOU, DEATHBRINGER. YOUR STENCH RUNS DEEP THROUGHOUT THE KNOWN DIMENSIONS.
BEEN TALKING TO SOME OF MY EXES, HAVE YOU?
BUDDA BUDDA
YEAH, YOU COULD SAY I'VE BEEN AROUND. NOW BUGGER OFF OUT OF MY WORLD.

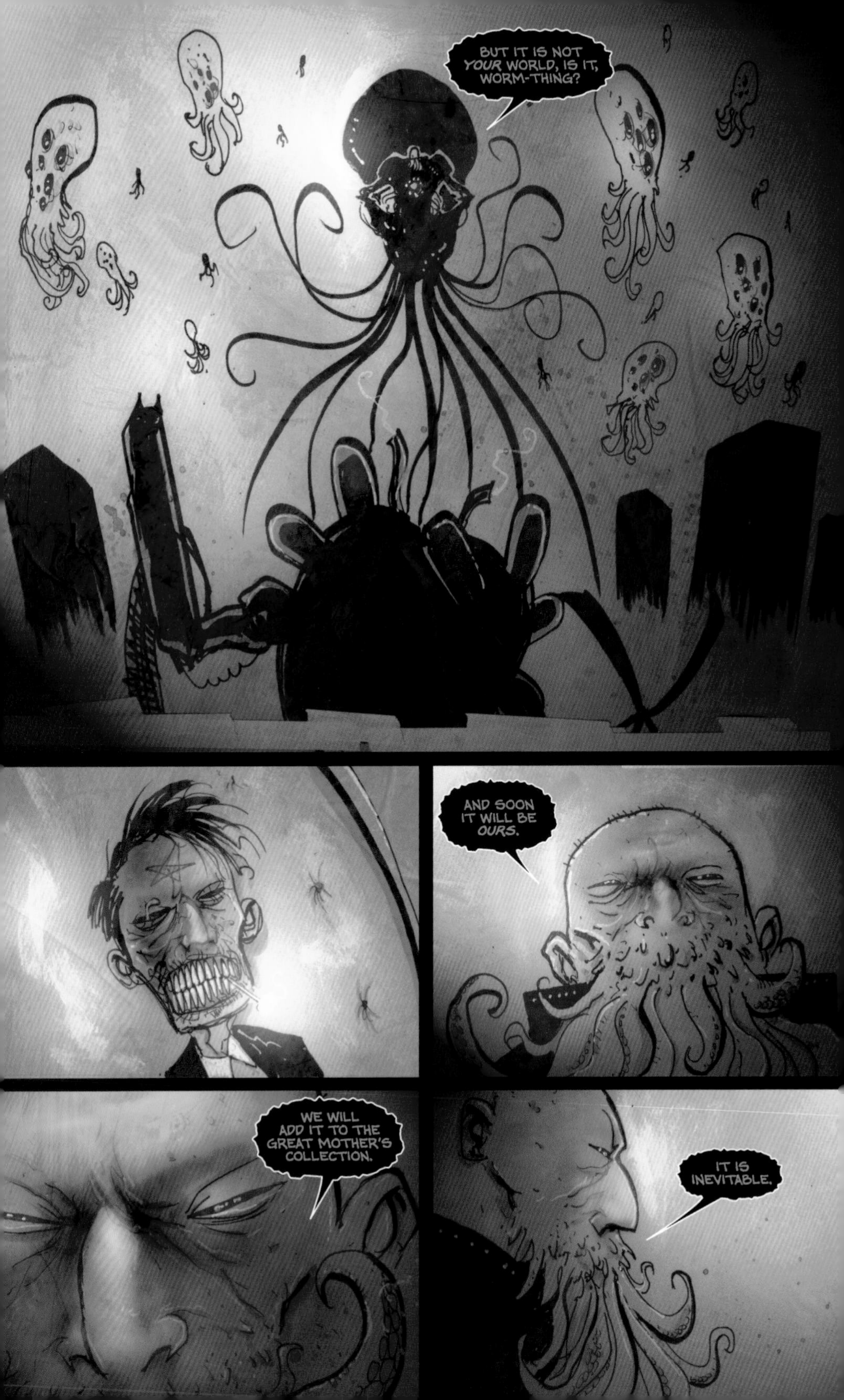
BUT IT IS NOT *YOUR* WORLD, IS IT, WORM-THING?
AND SOON IT WILL BE *OURS*.
WE WILL ADD IT TO THE GREAT MOTHER'S COLLECTION.
IT IS INEVITABLE.

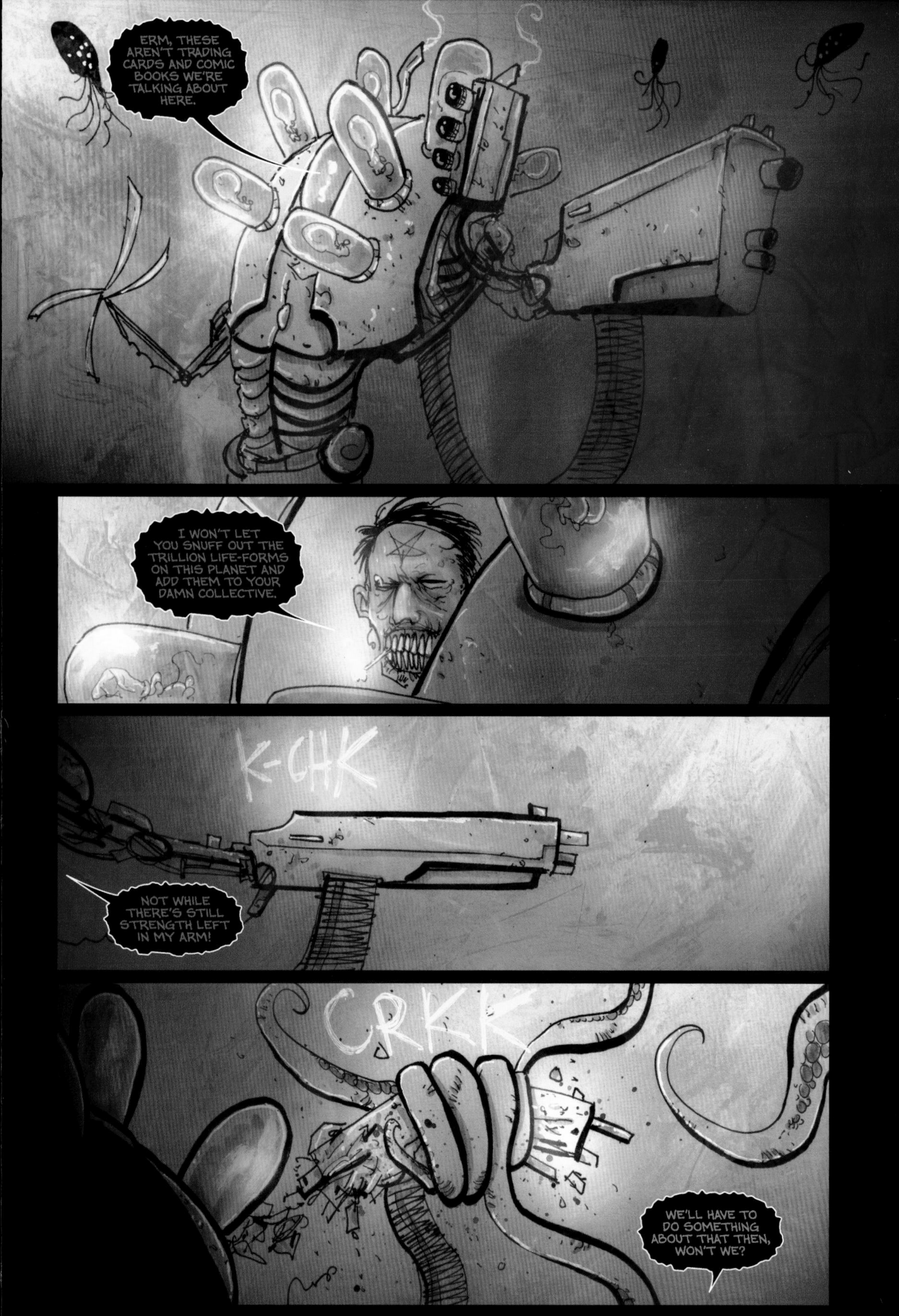
ERM, THESE AREN'T TRADING CARDS AND COMIC BOOKS WE'RE TALKING ABOUT HERE.
I WON'T LET YOU SNUFF OUT THE TRILLION LIFE-FORMS ON THIS PLANET AND ADD THEM TO YOUR DAMN COLLECTIVE.
K-CHK
NOT WHILE THERE'S STILL STRENGTH LEFT IN MY ARM!
CRKK
WE'LL HAVE TO DO SOMETHING ABOUT THAT THEN, WON'T WE?

BUGGER.

AH, PENDULUM, GOOD CHAP.

I BELIEVE THIS WAS THE SORT OF RESPONSE YOU WERE TRYING TO COMMUNICATE WITH THEM, NO?

BOOM

NICE OUTFIT, WORM. I'M JEALOUS.

THANKS.

MADE IT SOON AFTER I BUILT YOU, ACTUALLY. SAME PARTS IN SOME PLACES. YOU COULD SAY I'M WEARING YOUR HALF-BROTHER.

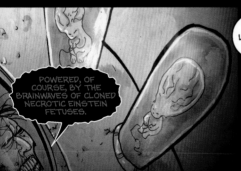

POWERED, OF COURSE, BY THE BRAINWAVES OF CLONED NECROTIC EINSTEIN FETUSES.

THAT'S A WHOLE NEW LEVEL I DIDN'T NEED TO GO TO.

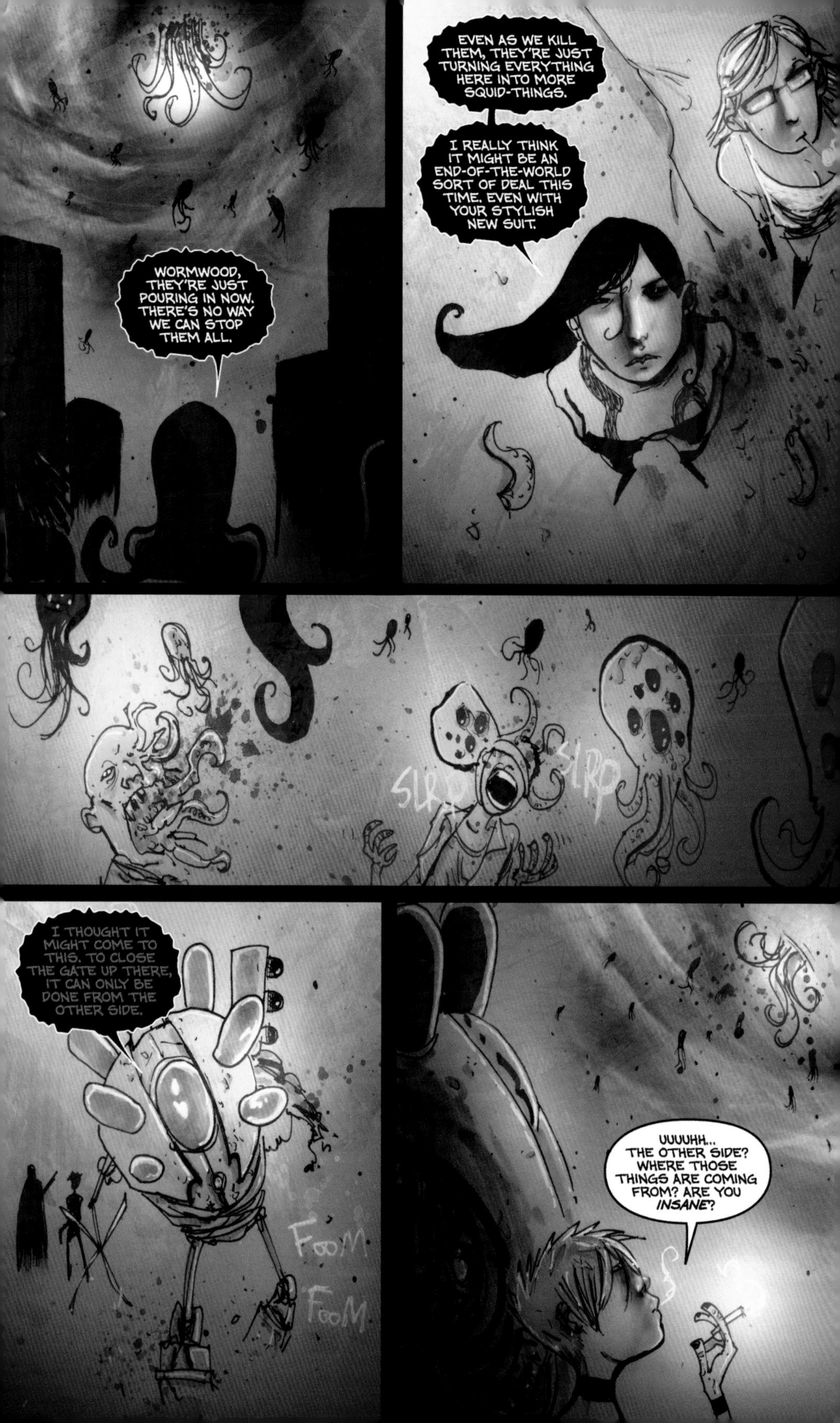
WORMWOOD, THEY'RE JUST POURING IN NOW. THERE'S NO WAY WE CAN STOP THEM ALL.
EVEN AS WE KILL THEM, THEY'RE JUST TURNING EVERYTHING HERE INTO MORE SQUID-THINGS.
I REALLY THINK IT MIGHT BE AN END-OF-THE-WORLD SORT OF DEAL THIS TIME. EVEN WITH YOUR STYLISH NEW SUIT.
SLRP
SLRP
I THOUGHT IT MIGHT COME TO THIS. TO CLOSE THE GATE UP THERE, IT CAN ONLY BE DONE FROM THE OTHER SIDE.
FOOM
FOOM
UUUUHH... THE OTHER SIDE? WHERE THOSE THINGS ARE COMING FROM? ARE YOU *INSANE*?

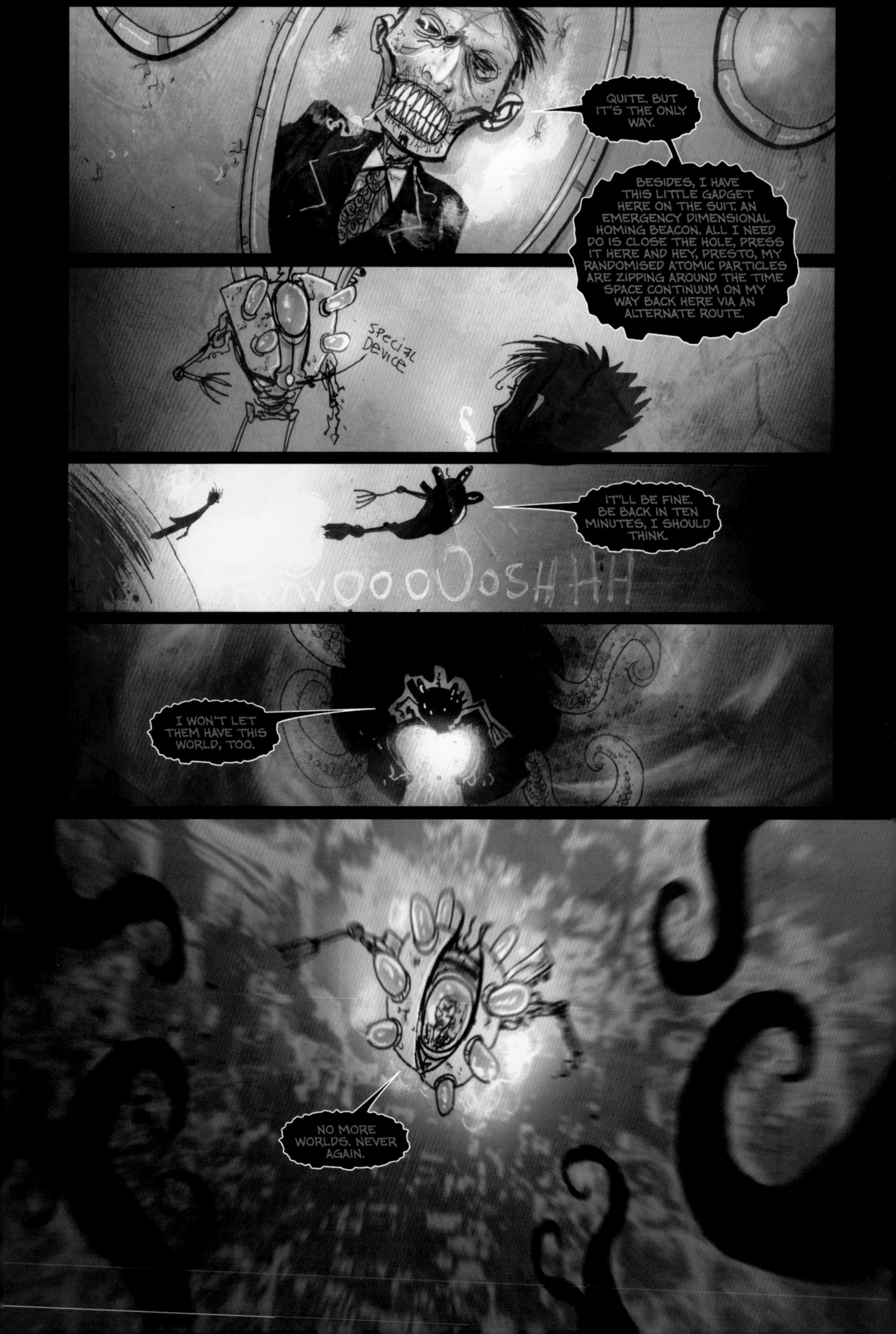
QUITE. BUT IT'S THE ONLY WAY.
BESIDES, I HAVE THIS LITTLE GADGET HERE ON THE SUIT. AN EMERGENCY DIMENSIONAL HOMING BEACON. ALL I NEED DO IS CLOSE THE HOLE, PRESS IT HERE AND HEY, PRESTO, MY RANDOMISED ATOMIC PARTICLES ARE ZIPPING AROUND THE TIME SPACE CONTINUUM ON MY WAY BACK HERE VIA AN ALTERNATE ROUTE.
SPECIAL DEVICE
IT'LL BE FINE. BE BACK IN TEN MINUTES, I SHOULD THINK.
WOOOOOOSHHH
I WON'T LET THEM HAVE THIS WORLD, TOO.
NO MORE WORLDS. NEVER AGAIN.

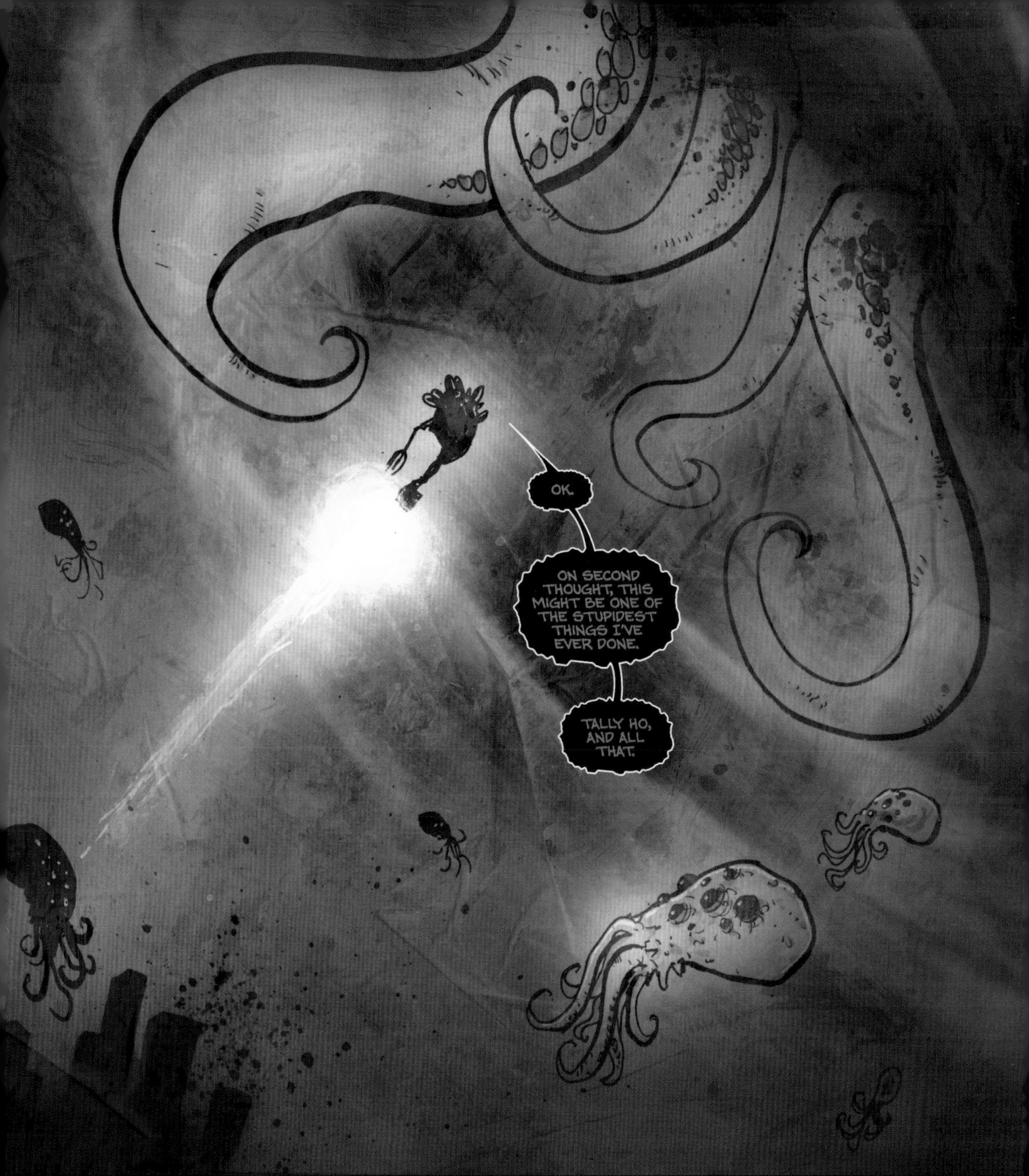
OK.
ON SECOND THOUGHT, THIS MIGHT BE ONE OF THE STUPIDEST THINGS I'VE EVER DONE.
TALLY HO, AND ALL THAT.

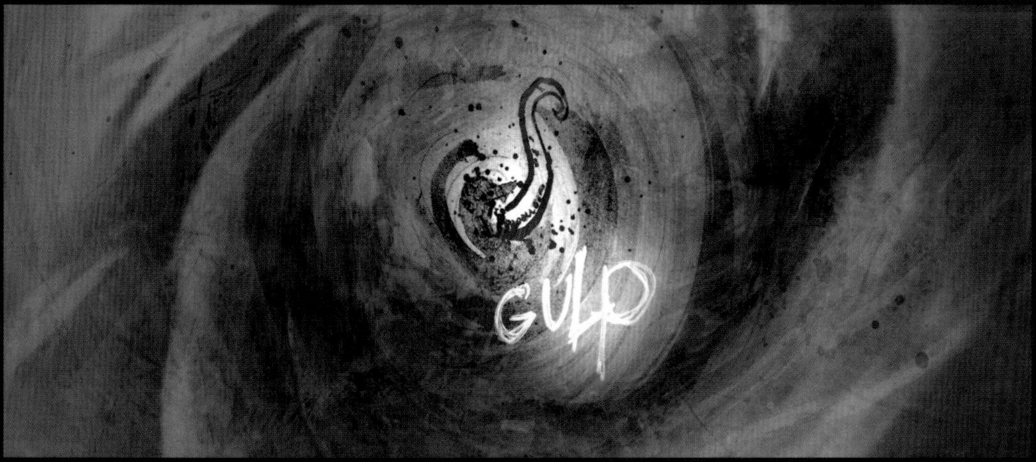
GULP

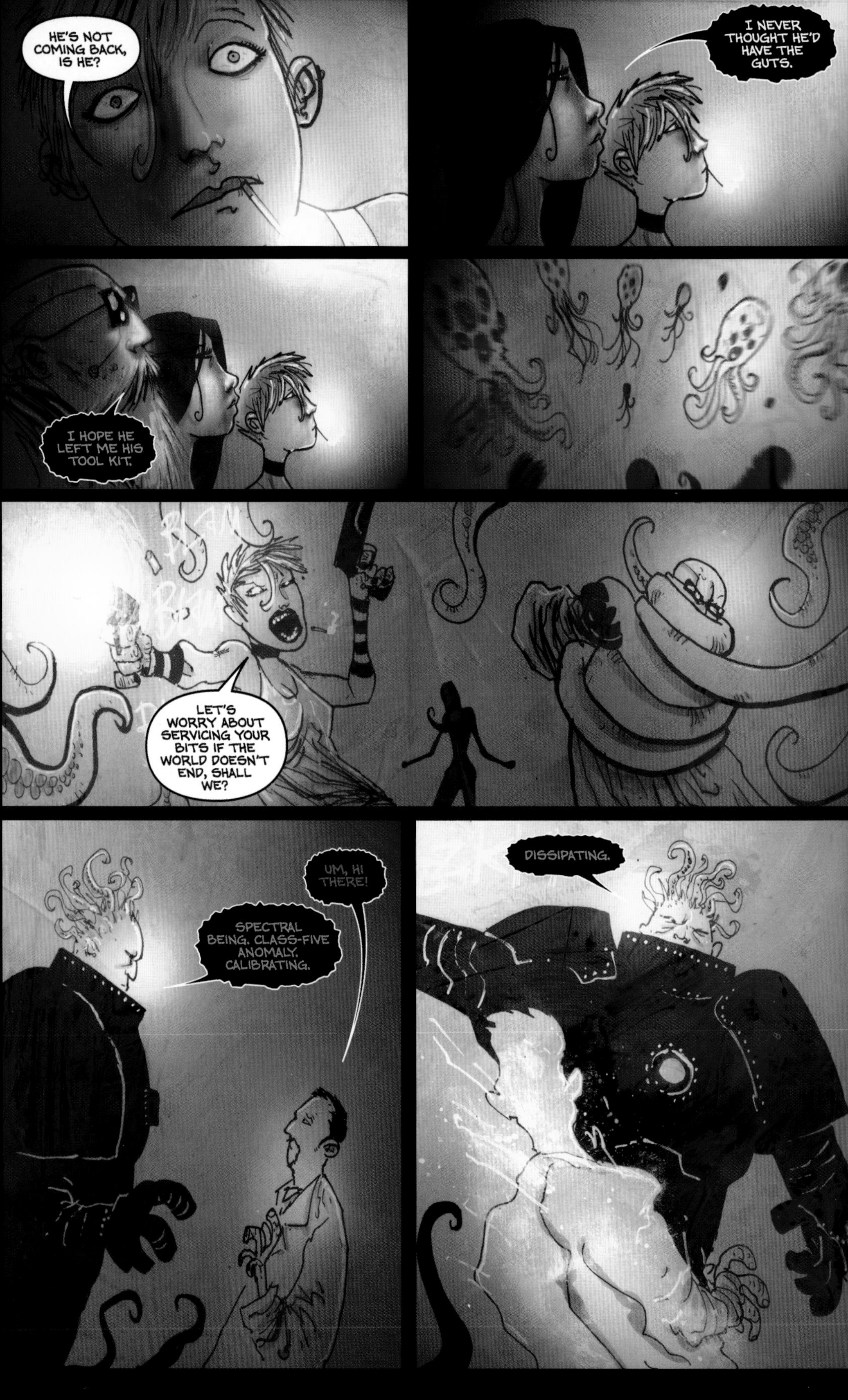
HE'S NOT COMING BACK, IS HE?
I NEVER THOUGHT HE'D HAVE THE GUTS.
I HOPE HE LEFT ME HIS TOOL KIT.
LET'S WORRY ABOUT SERVICING YOUR BITS IF THE WORLD DOESN'T END, SHALL WE?
SPECTRAL BEING. CLASS-FIVE ANOMALY. CALIBRATING.
UM, HI THERE!
DISSIPATING.

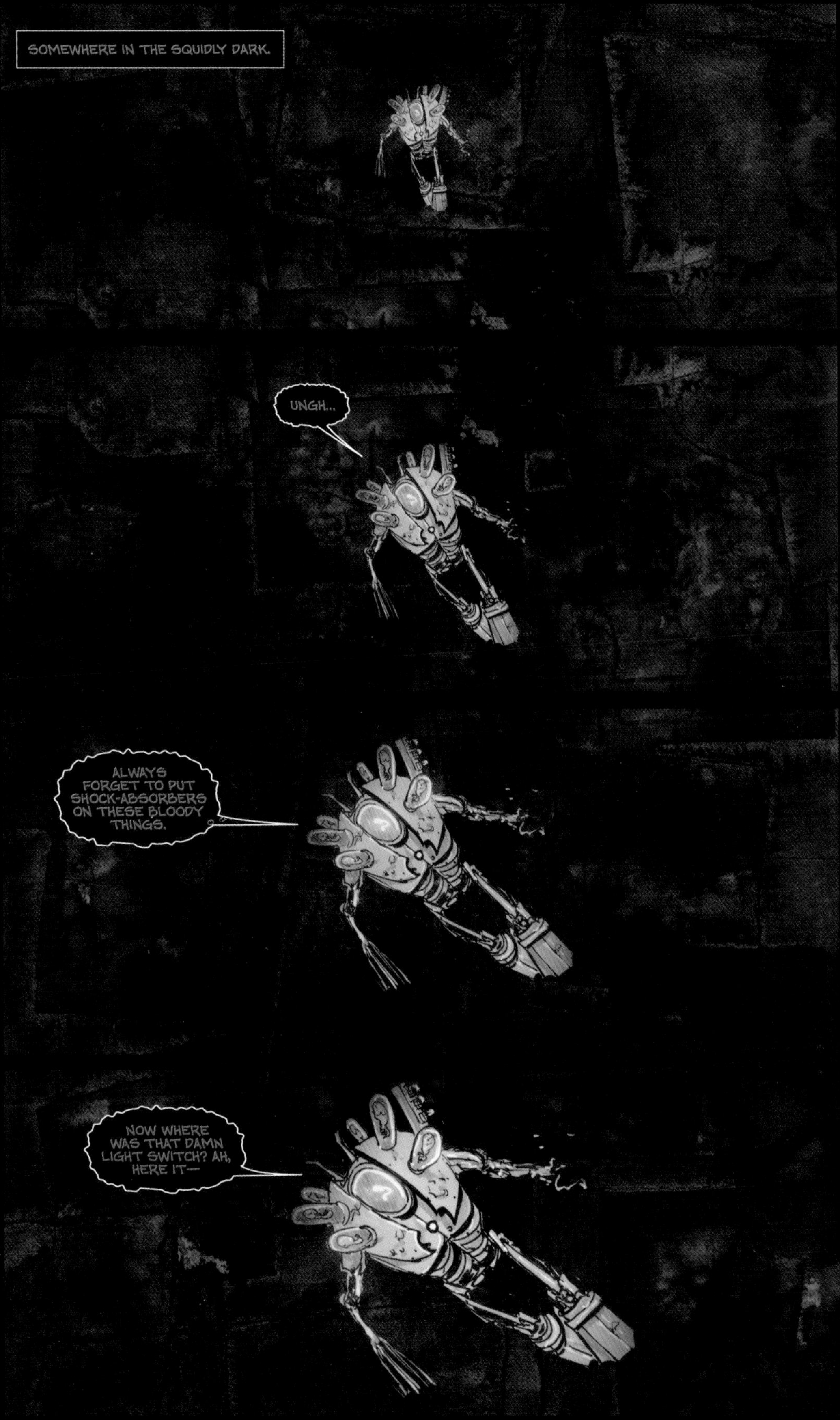
SOMEWHERE IN THE SQUIDLY DARK.
UNGH...
ALWAYS FORGET TO PUT SHOCK-ABSORBERS ON THESE BLOODY THINGS.
NOW WHERE WAS THAT DAMN LIGHT SWITCH? AH, HERE IT—

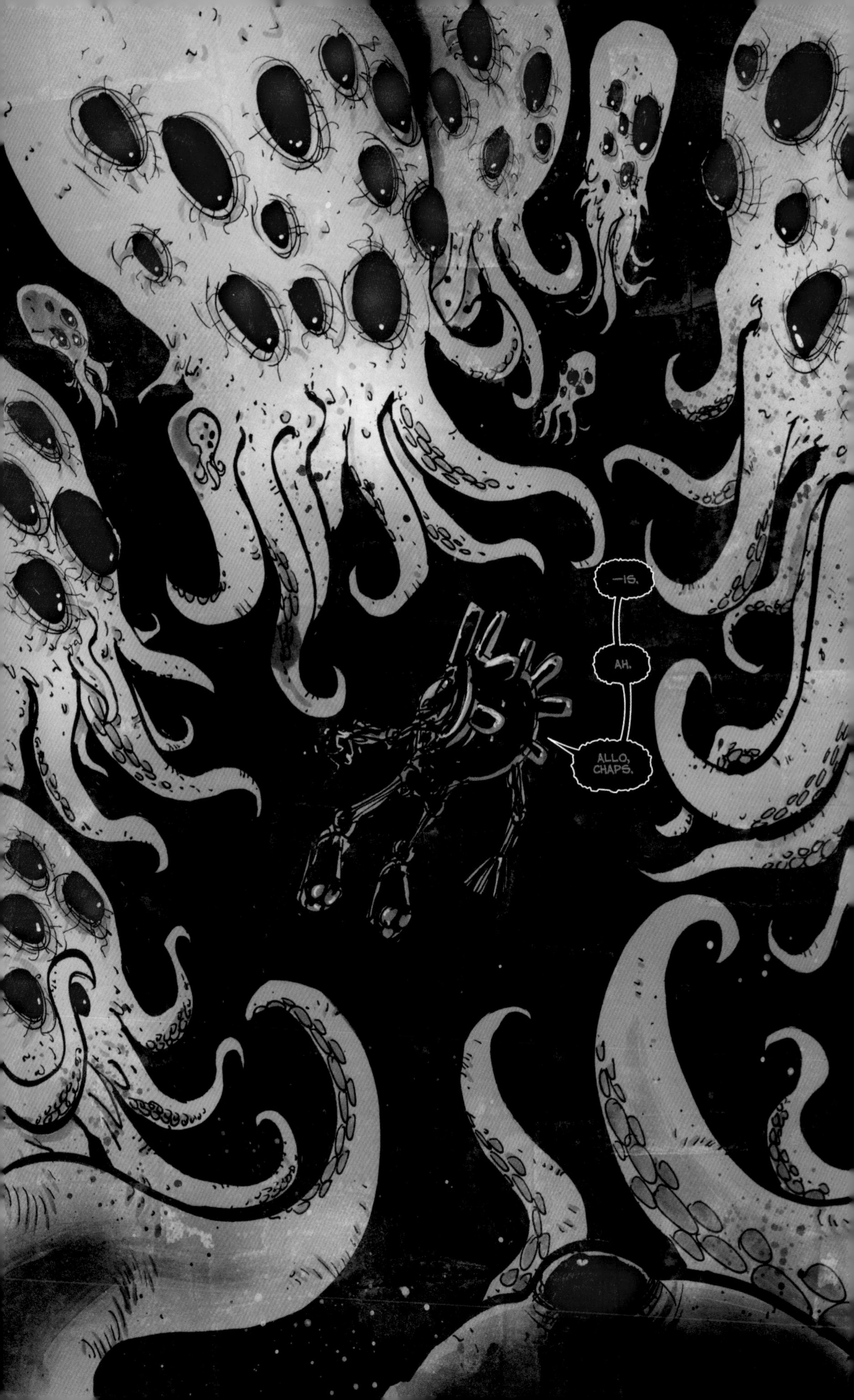
—IS.
AH.
ALLO, CHAPS.

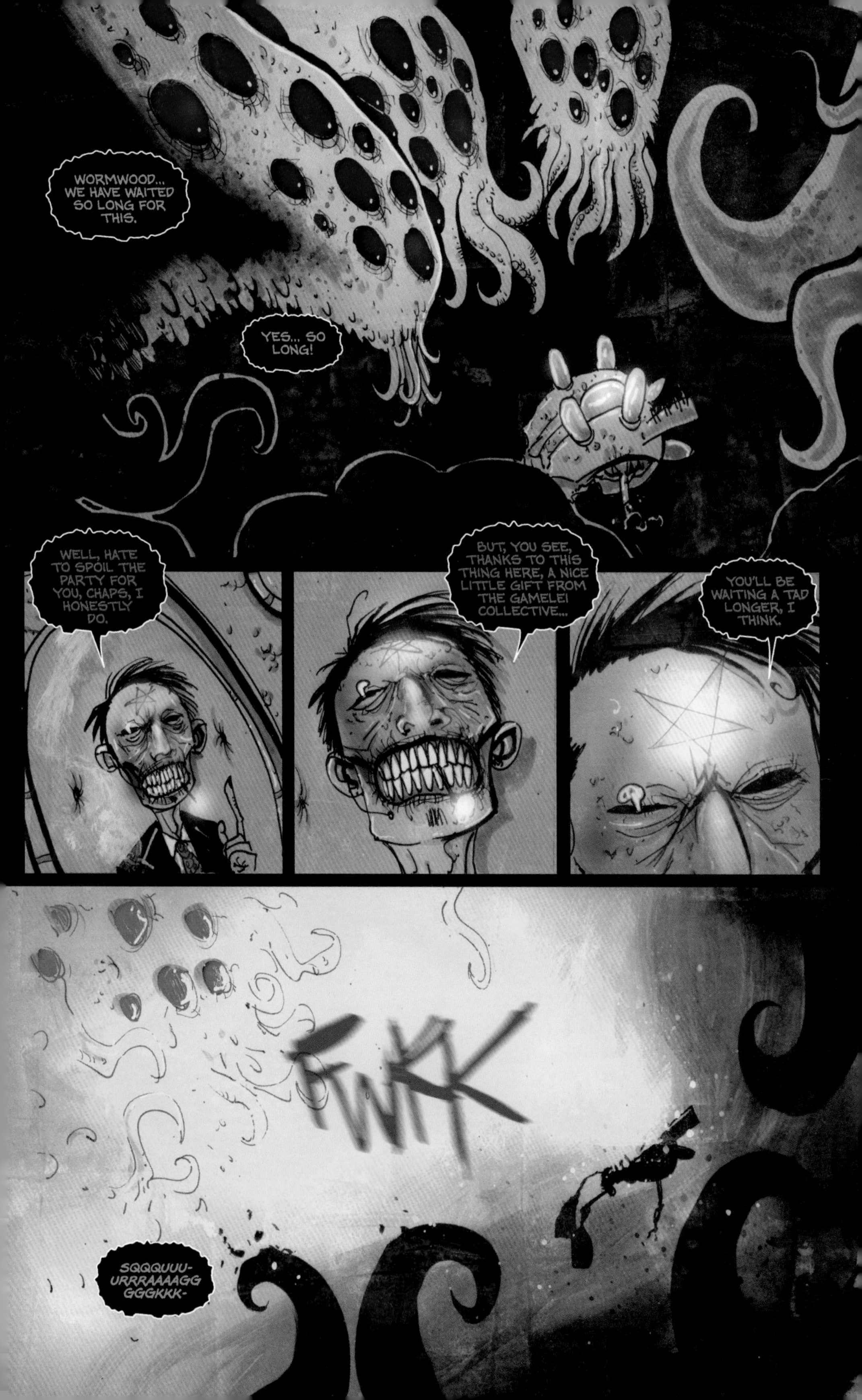
WORMWOOD... WE HAVE WAITED SO LONG FOR THIS.
YES... SO LONG!
WELL, HATE TO SPOIL THE PARTY FOR YOU, CHAPS, I HONESTLY DO.
BUT, YOU SEE, THANKS TO THIS THING HERE, A NICE LITTLE GIFT FROM THE GAMELEI COLLECTIVE...
YOU'LL BE WAITING A TAD LONGER, I THINK.
FWKK
SQQQUUU-URRRAAAAGG GGGKKK-

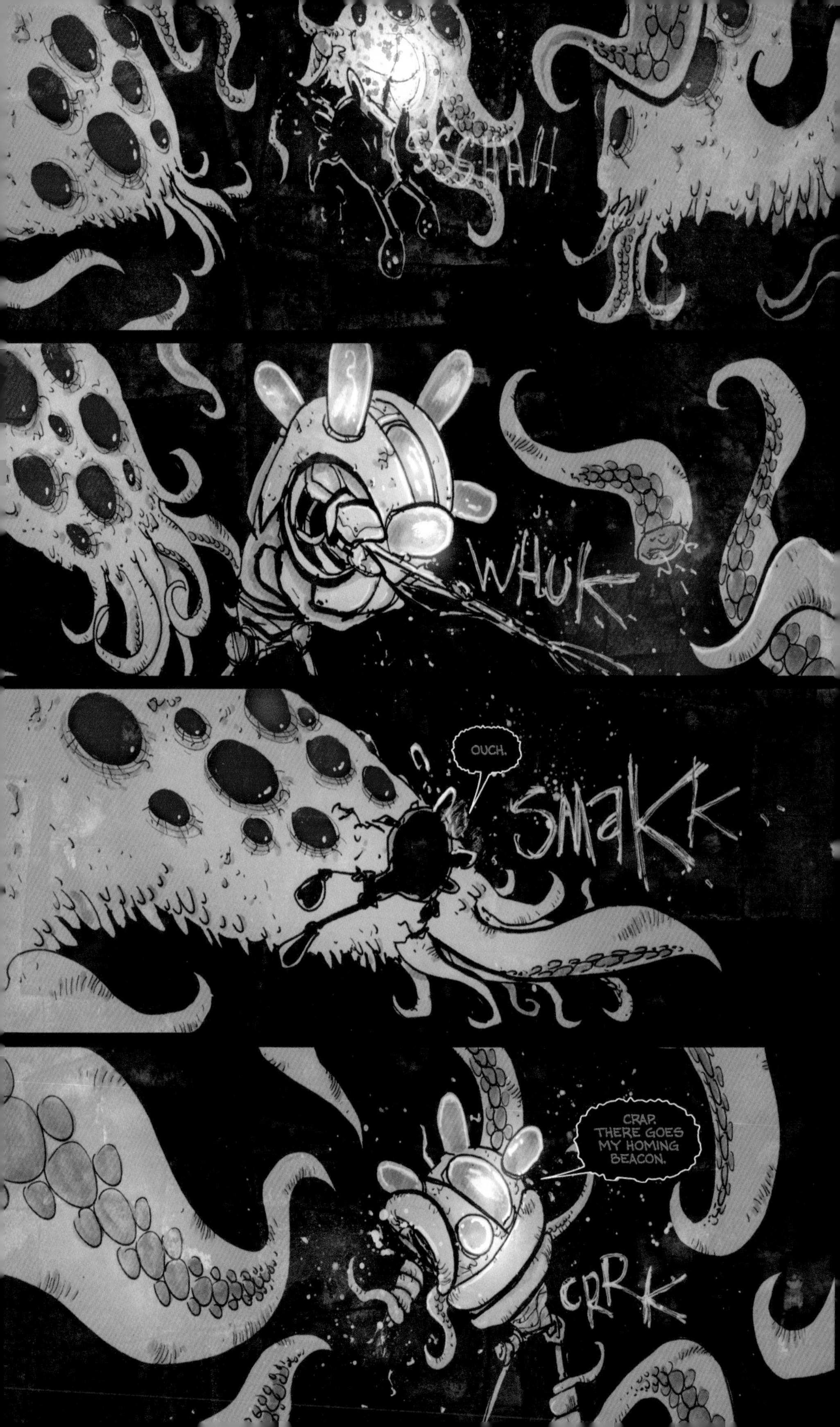
SSSHAH
WHUK
OUCH.
SMAKK
CRAP. THERE GOES MY HOMING BEACON.
CRRK

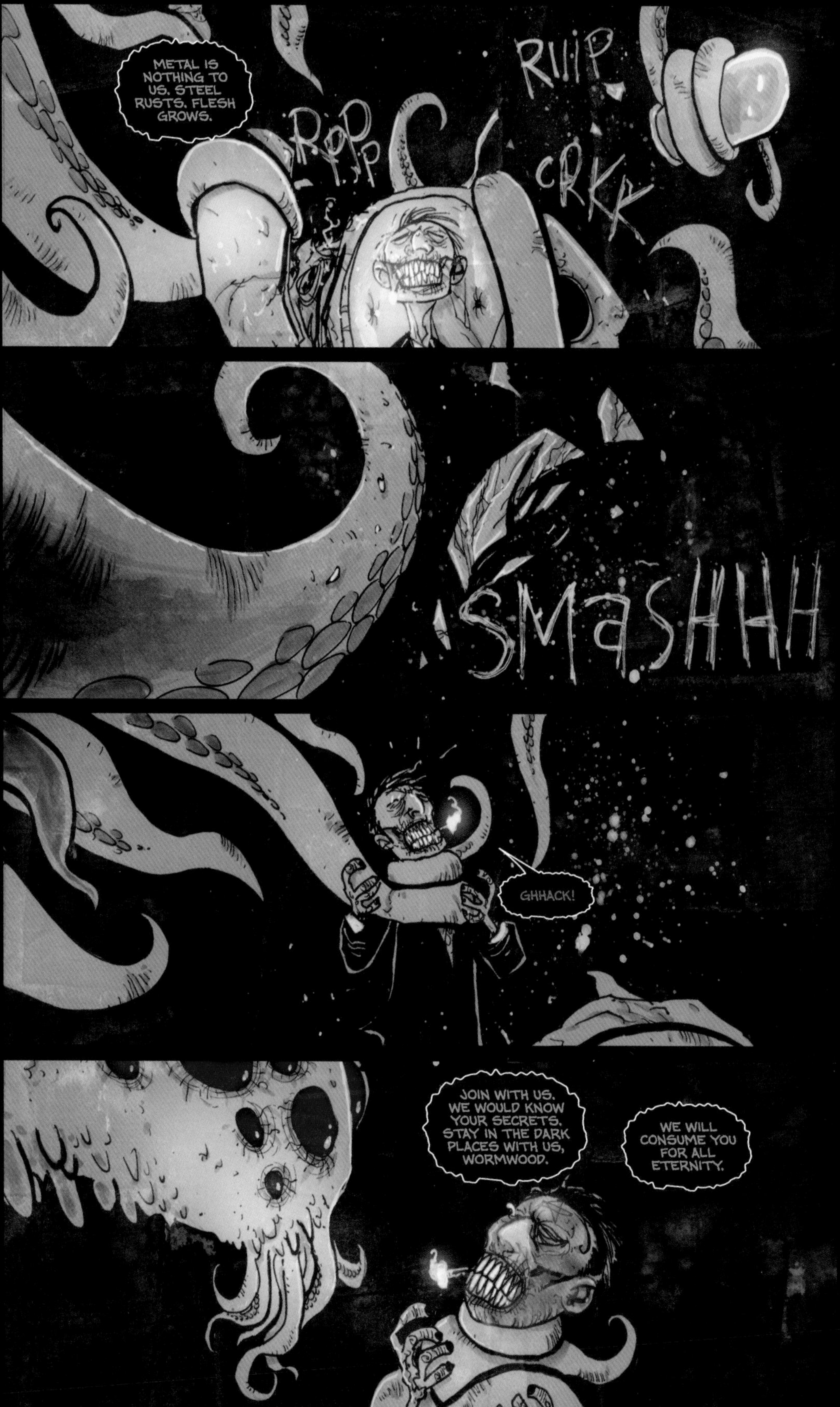
METAL IS NOTHING TO US. STEEL RUSTS. FLESH GROWS.
RIIIP
CRKK
SMASHHH
GHHACK!
JOIN WITH US. WE WOULD KNOW YOUR SECRETS. STAY IN THE DARK PLACES WITH US, WORMWOOD.
WE WILL CONSUME YOU FOR ALL ETERNITY.

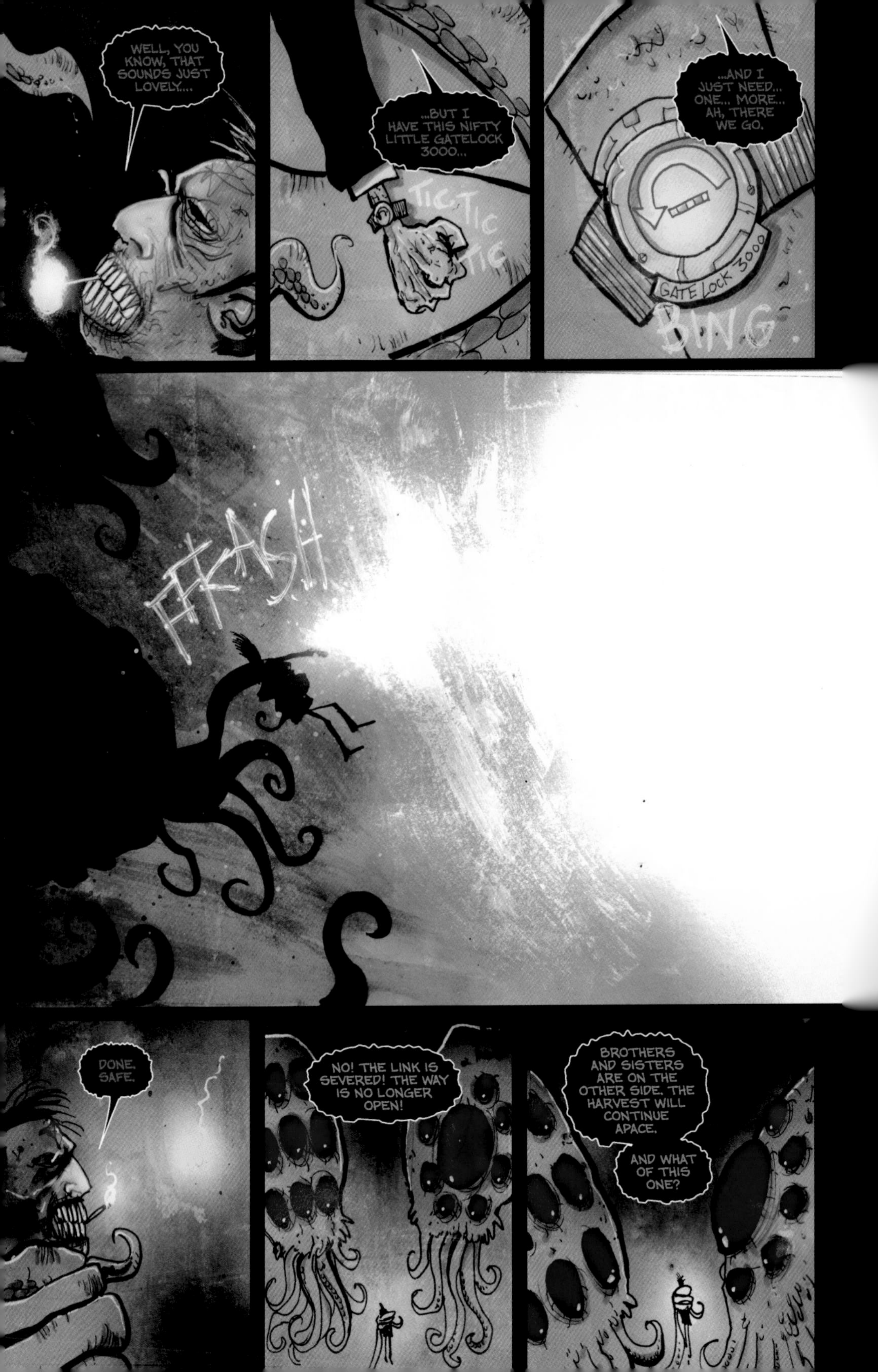

WELL, YOU KNOW, THAT SOUNDS JUST LOVELY....
...BUT I HAVE THIS NIFTY LITTLE GATELOCK 3000...
TIC, TIC TIC TIC
...AND I JUST NEED... ONE... MORE... AH, THERE WE GO.
GATE LOCK 3000
BING.
FFKASH
DONE. SAFE.
NO! THE LINK IS SEVERED! THE WAY IS NO LONGER OPEN!
BROTHERS AND SISTERS ARE ON THE OTHER SIDE. THE HARVEST WILL CONTINUE APACE.
AND WHAT OF THIS ONE?

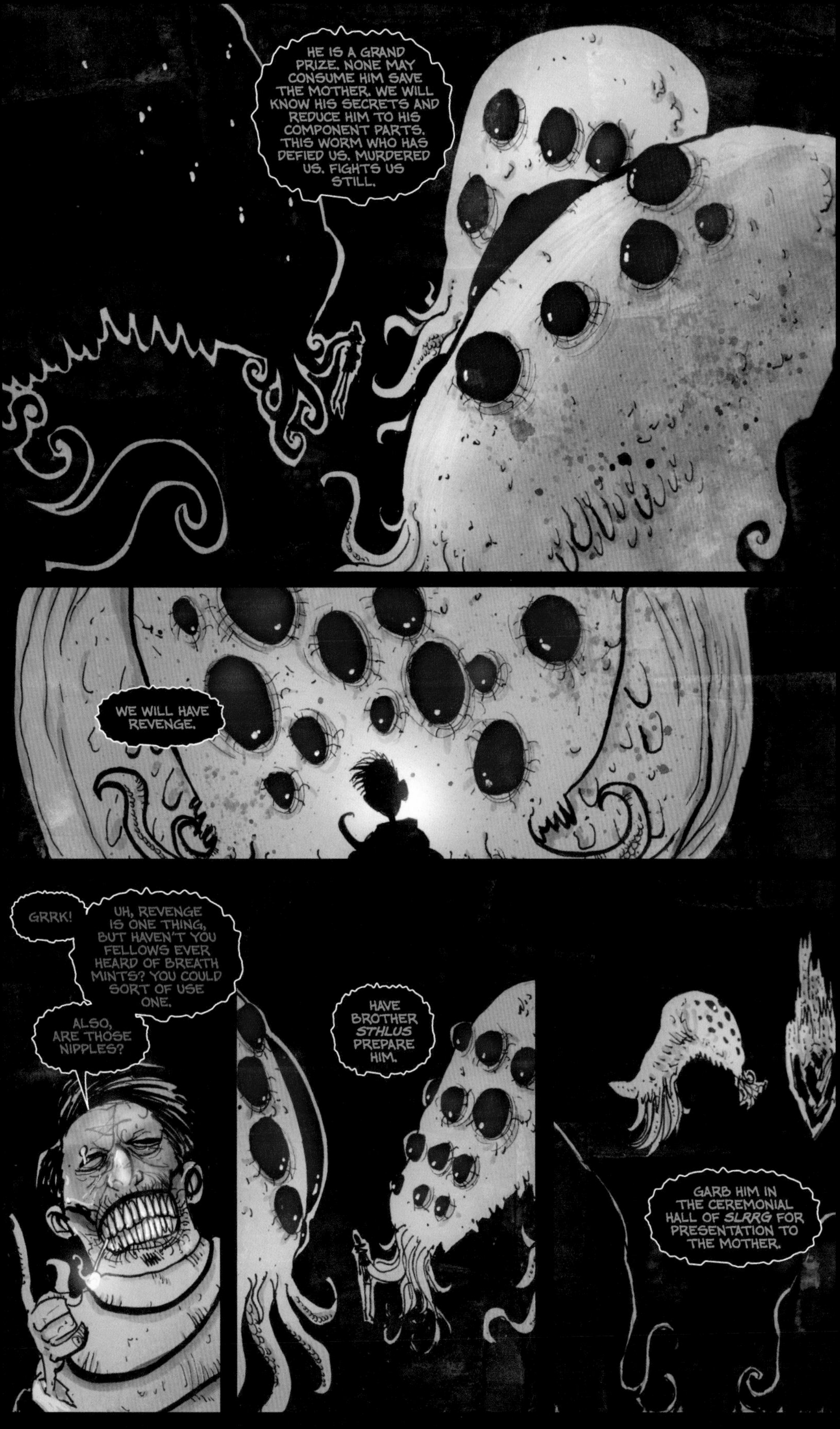
HE IS A GRAND PRIZE. NONE MAY CONSUME HIM SAVE THE MOTHER. WE WILL KNOW HIS SECRETS AND REDUCE HIM TO HIS COMPONENT PARTS. THIS WORM WHO HAS DEFIED US. MURDERED US. FIGHTS US STILL.
WE WILL HAVE REVENGE.
GRRK!
UH, REVENGE IS ONE THING, BUT HAVEN'T YOU FELLOWS EVER HEARD OF BREATH MINTS? YOU COULD SORT OF USE ONE.
ALSO, ARE THOSE NIPPLES?
HAVE BROTHER *STHLUS* PREPARE HIM.
GARB HIM IN THE CEREMONIAL HALL OF *SLRRG* FOR PRESENTATION TO THE MOTHER.

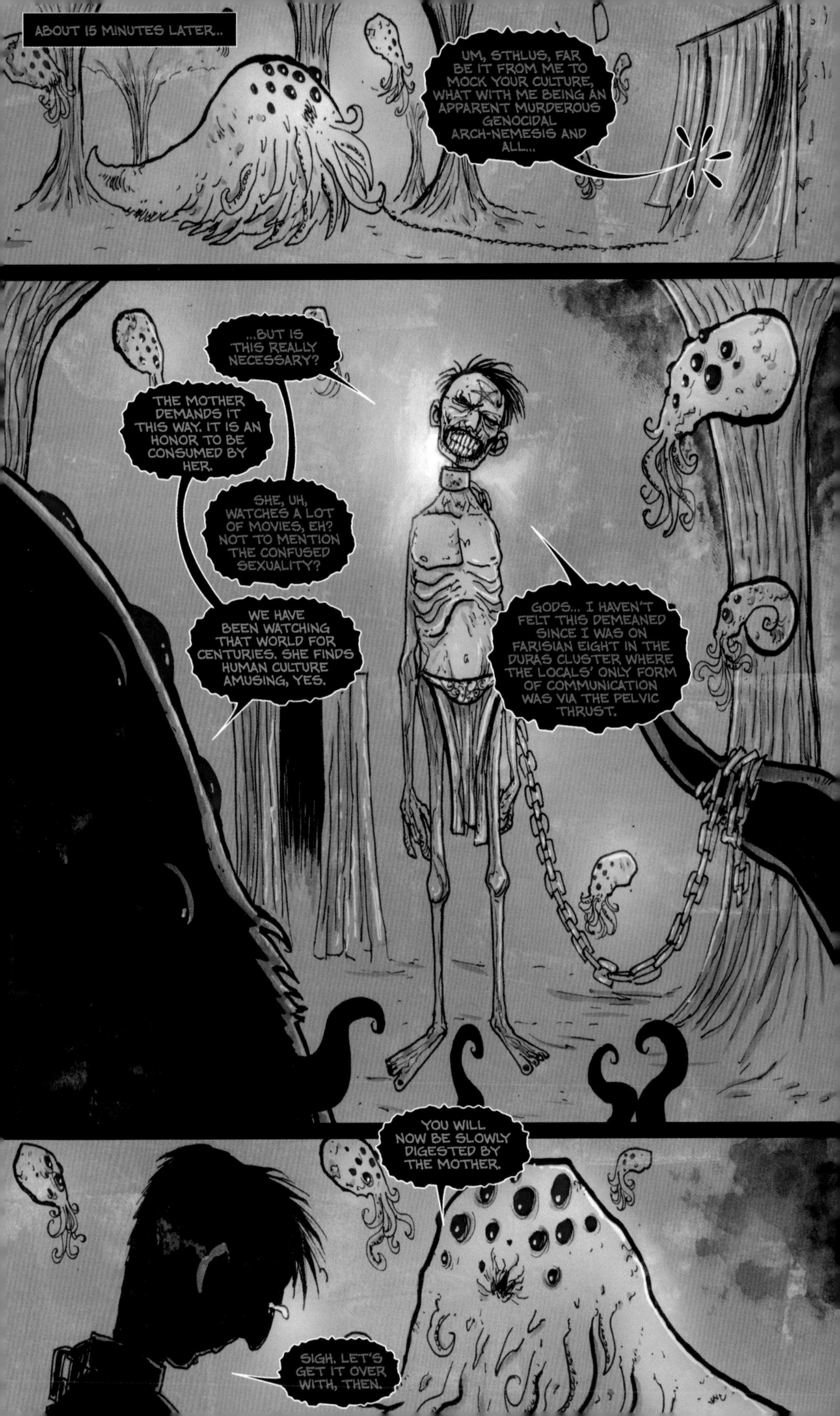
ABOUT 15 MINUTES LATER...
UM, STHLUS, FAR BE IT FROM ME TO MOCK YOUR CULTURE, WHAT WITH ME BEING AN APPARENT MURDEROUS GENOCIDAL ARCH-NEMESIS AND ALL...
...BUT IS THIS REALLY NECESSARY?
THE MOTHER DEMANDS IT THIS WAY. IT IS AN HONOR TO BE CONSUMED BY HER.
SHE, UH, WATCHES A LOT OF MOVIES, EH? NOT TO MENTION THE CONFUSED SEXUALITY?
WE HAVE BEEN WATCHING THAT WORLD FOR CENTURIES. SHE FINDS HUMAN CULTURE AMUSING, YES.
GODS... I HAVEN'T FELT THIS DEMEANED SINCE I WAS ON FARISIAN EIGHT IN THE DURAS CLUSTER WHERE THE LOCALS' ONLY FORM OF COMMUNICATION WAS VIA THE PELVIC THRUST.
YOU WILL NOW BE SLOWLY DIGESTED BY THE MOTHER.
SIGH. LET'S GET IT OVER WITH, THEN.

Chapter 3

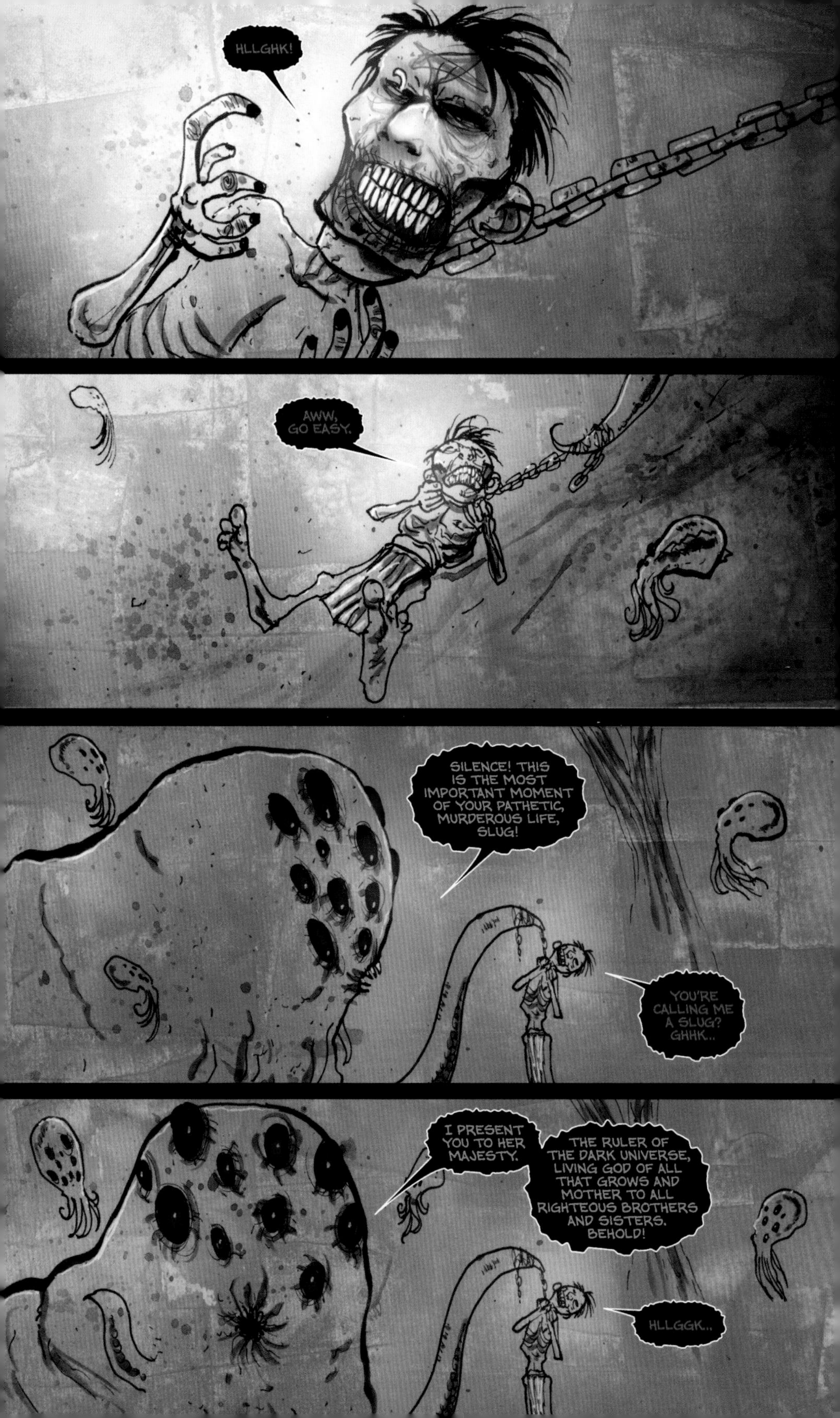
HLLGHK!
AWW, GO EASY.
SILENCE! THIS IS THE MOST IMPORTANT MOMENT OF YOUR PATHETIC, MURDEROUS LIFE, SLUG!
YOU'RE CALLING ME A SLUG? GHHK...
I PRESENT YOU TO HER MAJESTY.
THE RULER OF THE DARK UNIVERSE, LIVING GOD OF ALL THAT GROWS AND MOTHER TO ALL RIGHTEOUS BROTHERS AND SISTERS. BEHOLD!
HLLGGK...

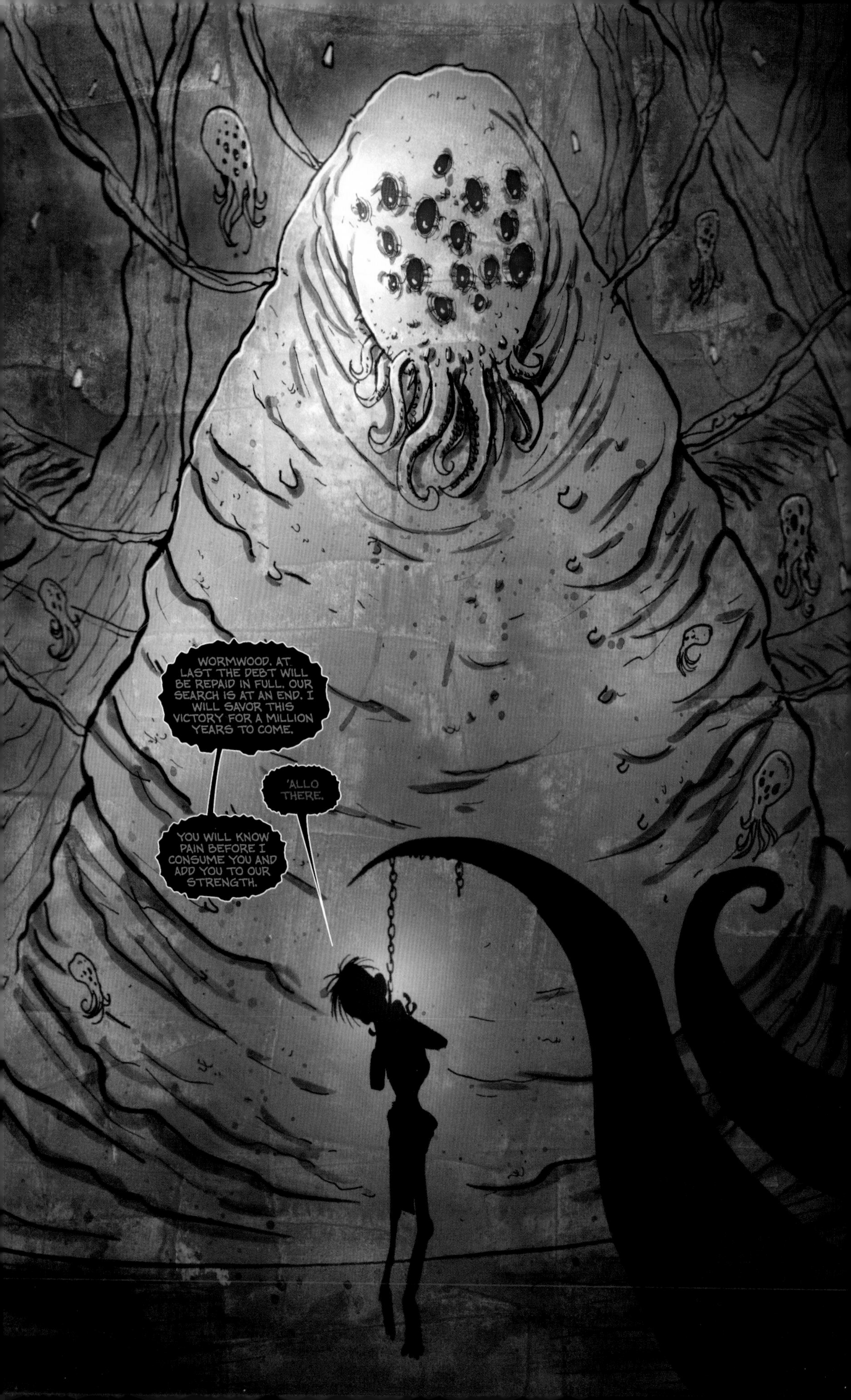
WORMWOOD. AT LAST THE DEBT WILL BE REPAID IN FULL. OUR SEARCH IS AT AN END. I WILL SAVOR THIS VICTORY FOR A MILLION YEARS TO COME.
YOU WILL KNOW PAIN BEFORE I CONSUME YOU AND ADD YOU TO OUR STRENGTH.
'ALLO THERE.

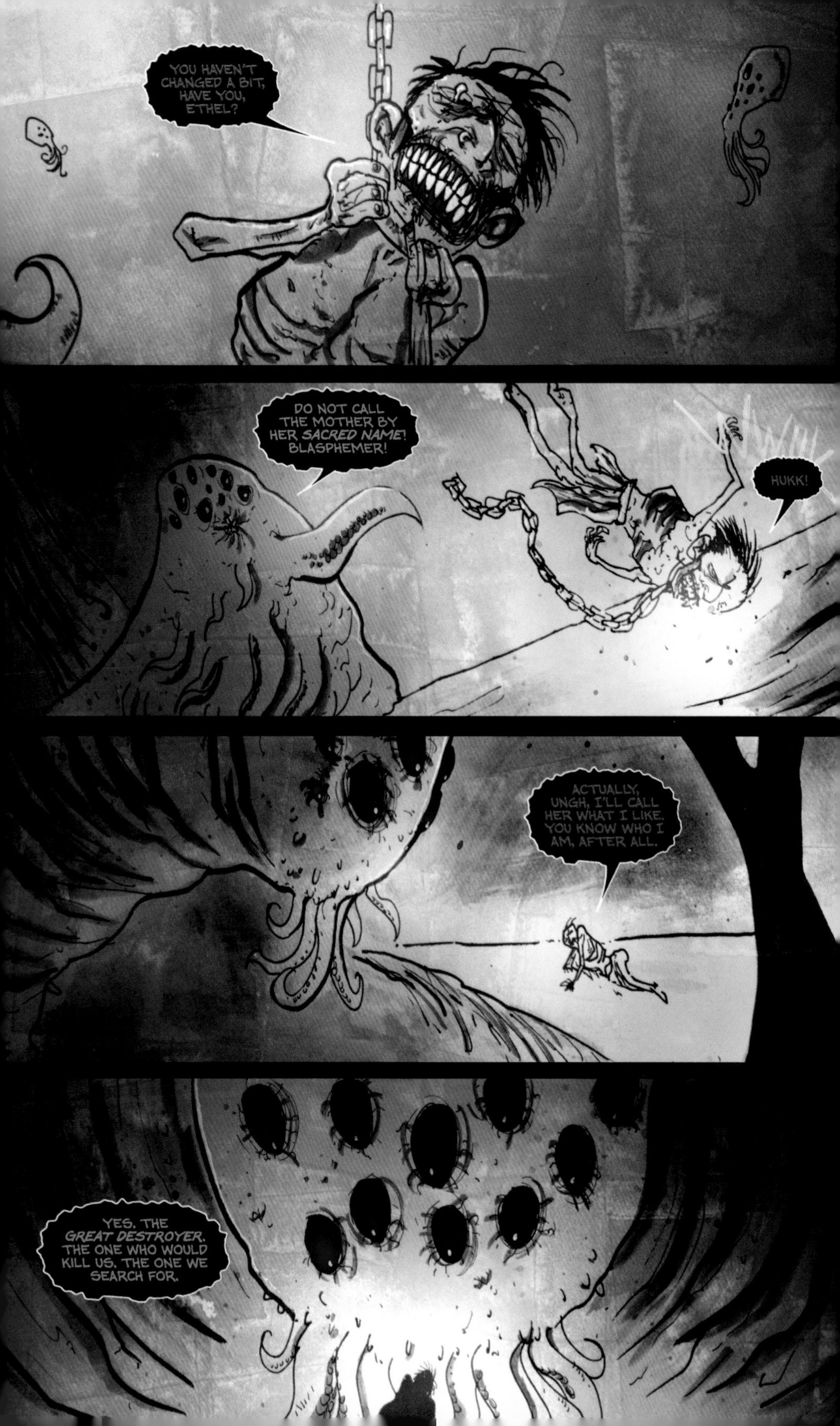
YOU HAVEN'T CHANGED A BIT, HAVE YOU, ETHEL?
DO NOT CALL THE MOTHER BY HER *SACRED NAME*! BLASPHEMER!
HUKK!
ACTUALLY, UNGH, I'LL CALL HER WHAT I LIKE. YOU KNOW WHO I AM, AFTER ALL.
YES. THE *GREAT DESTROYER*. THE ONE WHO WOULD KILL US. THE ONE WE SEARCH FOR.

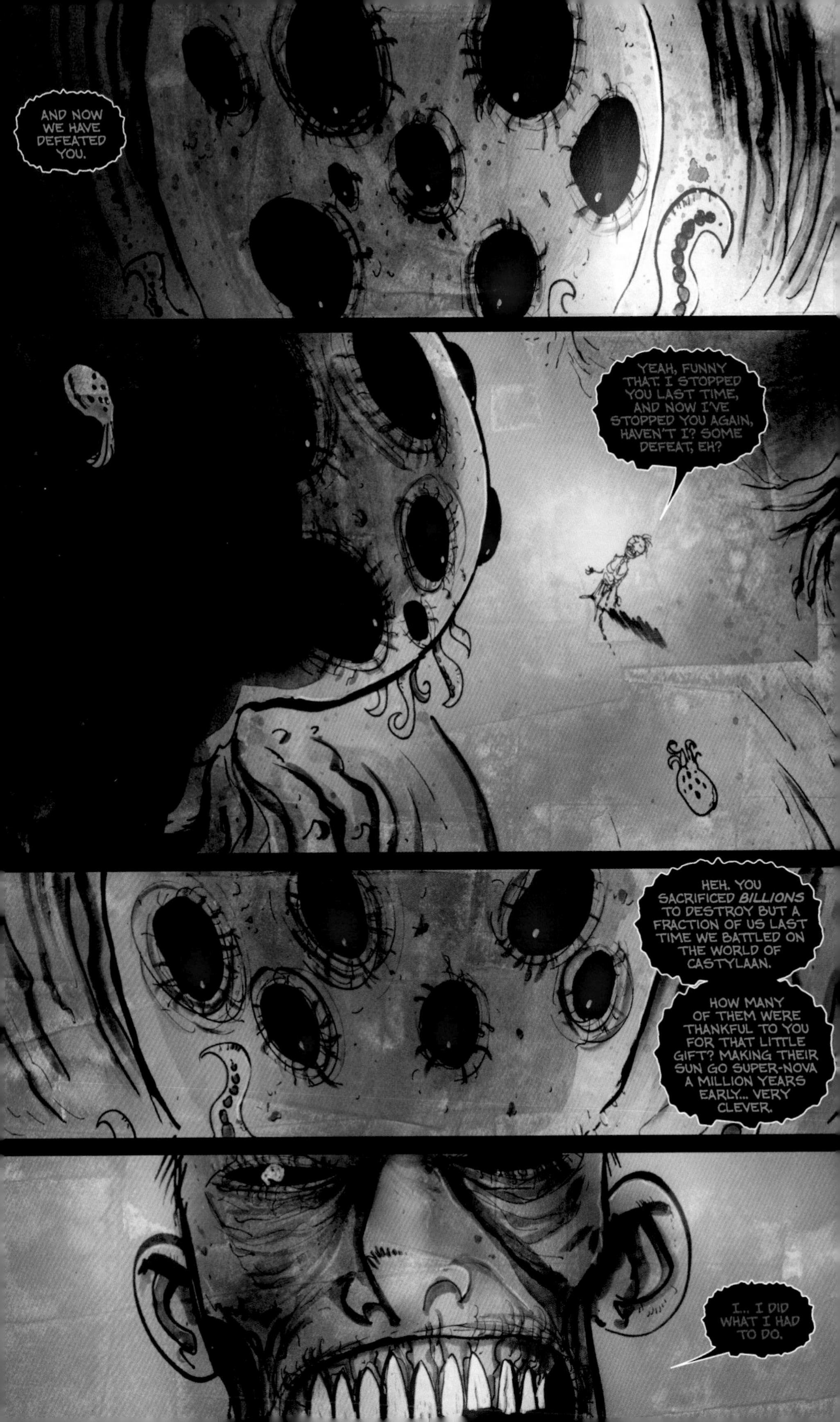
AND NOW WE HAVE DEFEATED YOU.
YEAH, FUNNY THAT. I STOPPED YOU LAST TIME, AND NOW I'VE STOPPED YOU AGAIN, HAVEN'T I? SOME DEFEAT, EH?
HEH. YOU SACRIFICED *BILLIONS* TO DESTROY BUT A FRACTION OF US LAST TIME WE BATTLED ON THE WORLD OF CASTYLAAN.
HOW MANY OF THEM WERE THANKFUL TO YOU FOR THAT LITTLE GIFT? MAKING THEIR SUN GO SUPER-NOVA A MILLION YEARS EARLY... VERY CLEVER.
I.. I DID WHAT I HAD TO DO.

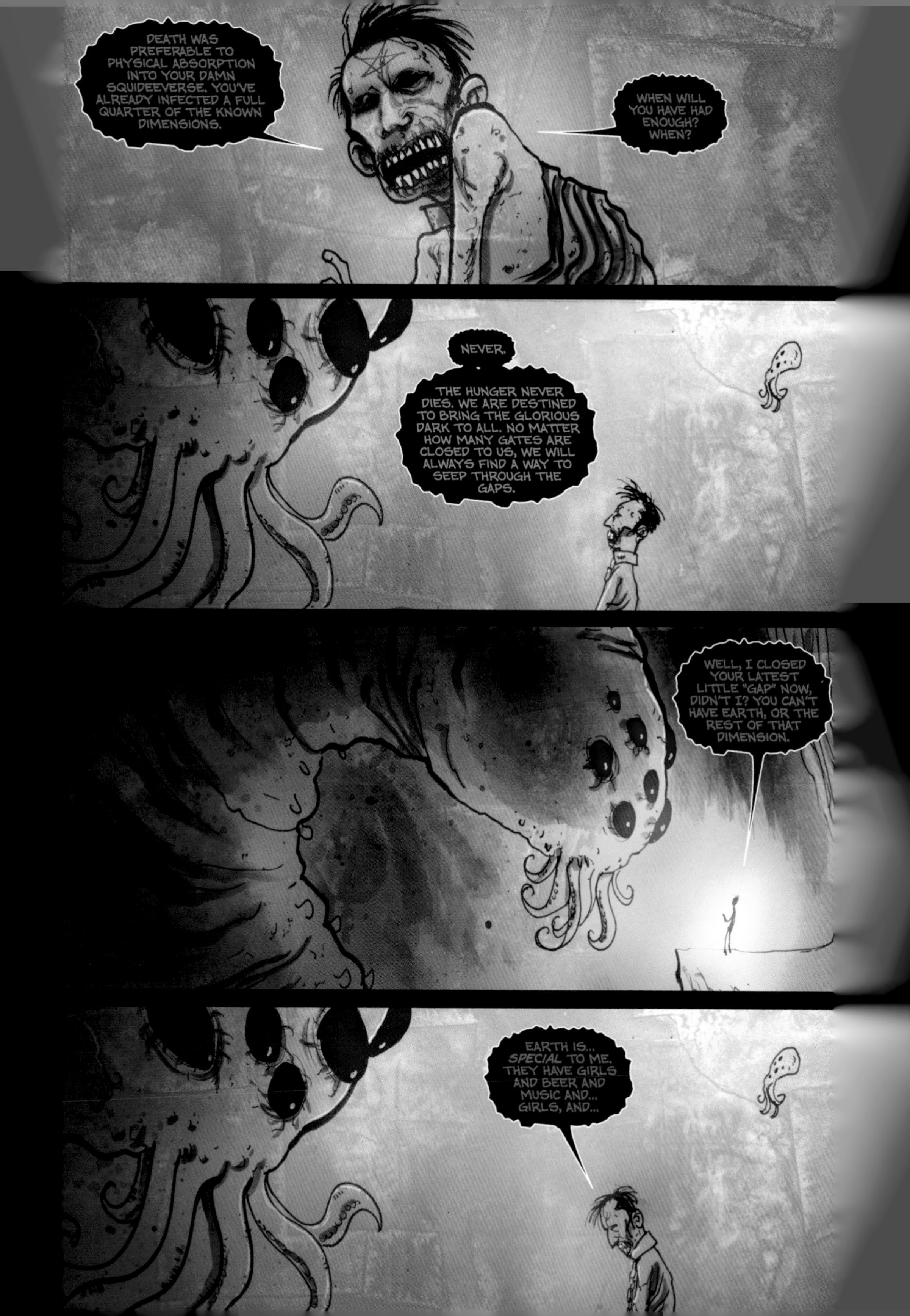

DEATH WAS PREFERABLE TO PHYSICAL ABSORPTION INTO YOUR DAMN SQUIDEEVERSE. YOU'VE ALREADY INFECTED A FULL QUARTER OF THE KNOWN DIMENSIONS.
WHEN WILL YOU HAVE HAD ENOUGH? WHEN?
NEVER.
THE HUNGER NEVER DIES. WE ARE DESTINED TO BRING THE GLORIOUS DARK TO ALL. NO MATTER HOW MANY GATES ARE CLOSED TO US, WE WILL ALWAYS FIND A WAY TO SEEP THROUGH THE GAPS.
WELL, I CLOSED YOUR LATEST LITTLE "GAP" NOW, DIDN'T I? YOU CAN'T HAVE EARTH, OR THE REST OF THAT DIMENSION.
EARTH IS... *SPECIAL* TO ME. THEY HAVE GIRLS AND BEER AND MUSIC AND... GIRLS, AND...

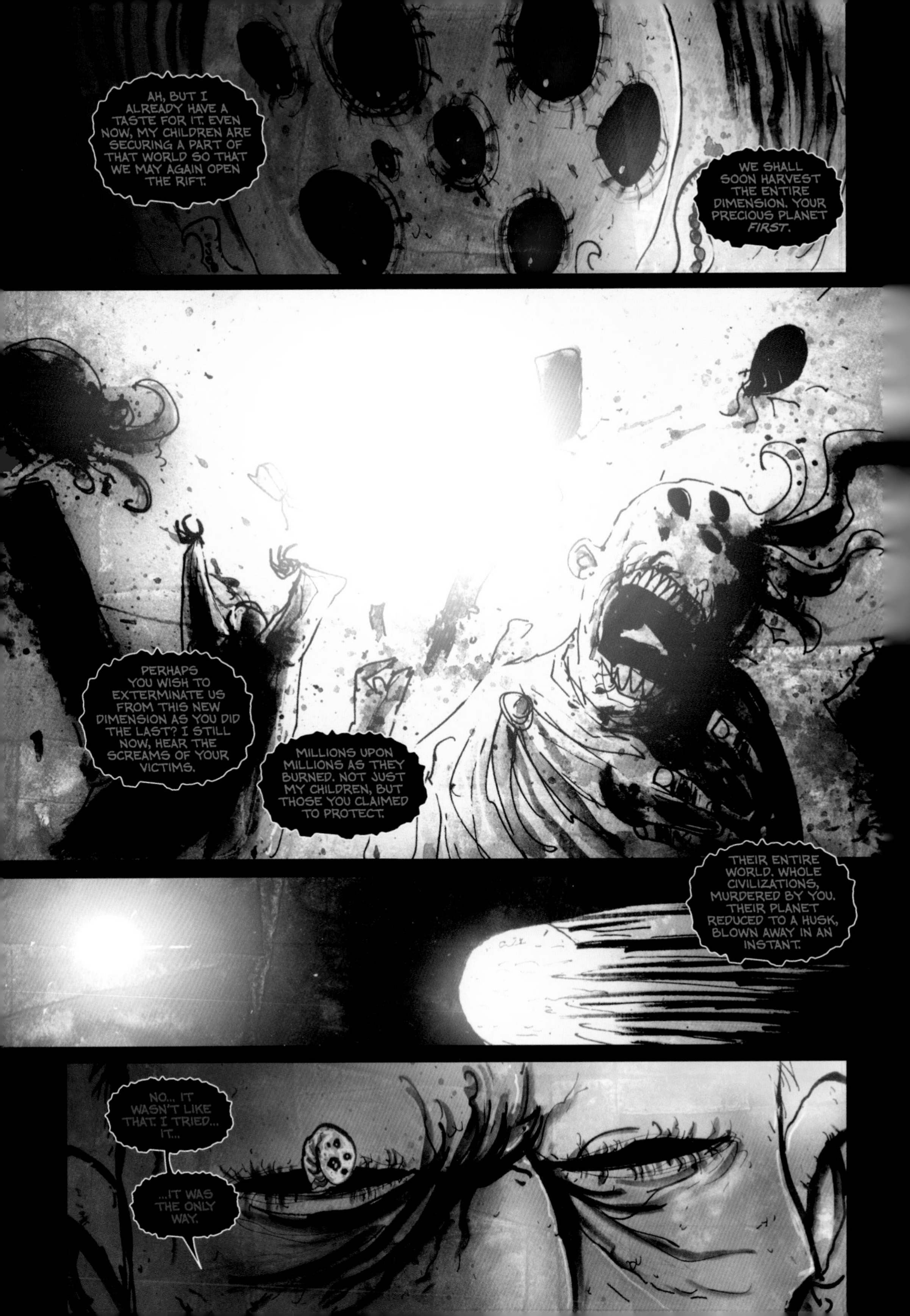
AH, BUT I ALREADY HAVE A TASTE FOR IT. EVEN NOW, MY CHILDREN ARE SECURING A PART OF THAT WORLD SO THAT WE MAY AGAIN OPEN THE RIFT.
WE SHALL SOON HARVEST THE ENTIRE DIMENSION. YOUR PRECIOUS PLANET *FIRST*.
PERHAPS YOU WISH TO EXTERMINATE US FROM THIS NEW DIMENSION AS YOU DID THE LAST? I STILL NOW, HEAR THE SCREAMS OF YOUR VICTIMS.
MILLIONS UPON MILLIONS AS THEY BURNED. NOT JUST MY CHILDREN, BUT THOSE YOU CLAIMED TO PROTECT.
THEIR ENTIRE WORLD. WHOLE CIVILIZATIONS, MURDERED BY YOU. THEIR PLANET REDUCED TO A HUSK, BLOWN AWAY IN AN INSTANT.
NO... IT WASN'T LIKE THAT. I TRIED... IT...
...IT WAS THE ONLY WAY.

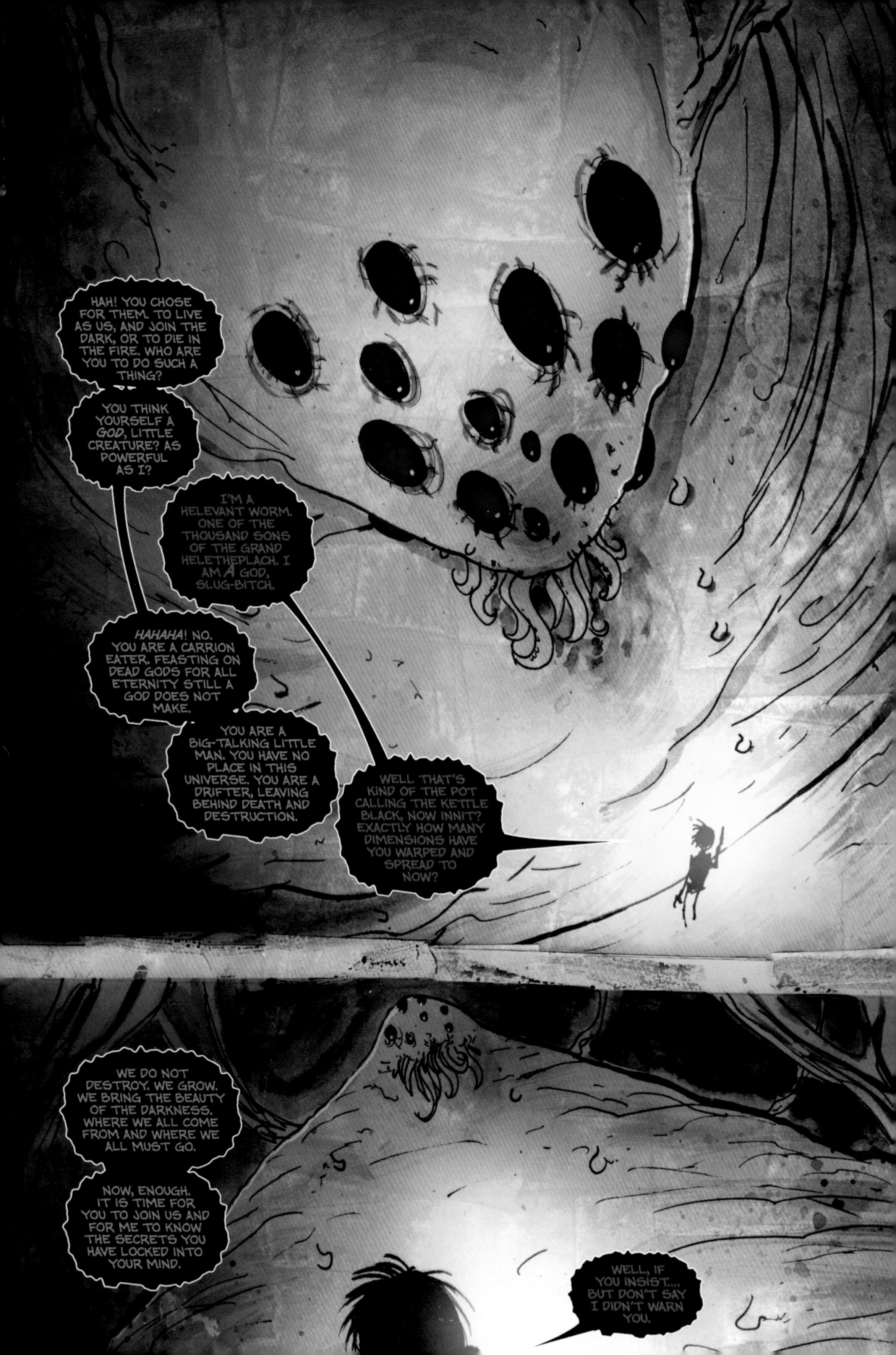
HAH! YOU CHOSE FOR THEM. TO LIVE AS US, AND JOIN THE DARK, OR TO DIE IN THE FIRE. WHO ARE YOU TO DO SUCH A THING?
YOU THINK YOURSELF A GOD, LITTLE CREATURE? AS POWERFUL AS I?
I'M A HELEVAN'T WORM. ONE OF THE THOUSAND SONS OF THE GRAND HELETHEPLACH. I AM A GOD, SLUG-BITCH.
HAHAHA! NO. YOU ARE A CARRION EATER. FEASTING ON DEAD GODS FOR ALL ETERNITY STILL A GOD DOES NOT MAKE.
YOU ARE A BIG-TALKING LITTLE MAN. YOU HAVE NO PLACE IN THIS UNIVERSE. YOU ARE A DRIFTER, LEAVING BEHIND DEATH AND DESTRUCTION.
WELL THAT'S KIND OF THE POT CALLING THE KETTLE BLACK, NOW INNIT? EXACTLY HOW MANY DIMENSIONS HAVE YOU WARPED AND SPREAD TO NOW?
WE DO NOT DESTROY. WE GROW. WE BRING THE BEAUTY OF THE DARKNESS, WHERE WE ALL COME FROM AND WHERE WE ALL MUST GO.
NOW, ENOUGH. IT IS TIME FOR YOU TO JOIN US AND FOR ME TO KNOW THE SECRETS YOU HAVE LOCKED INTO YOUR MIND.
WELL, IF YOU INSIST.... BUT DON'T SAY I DIDN'T WARN YOU.

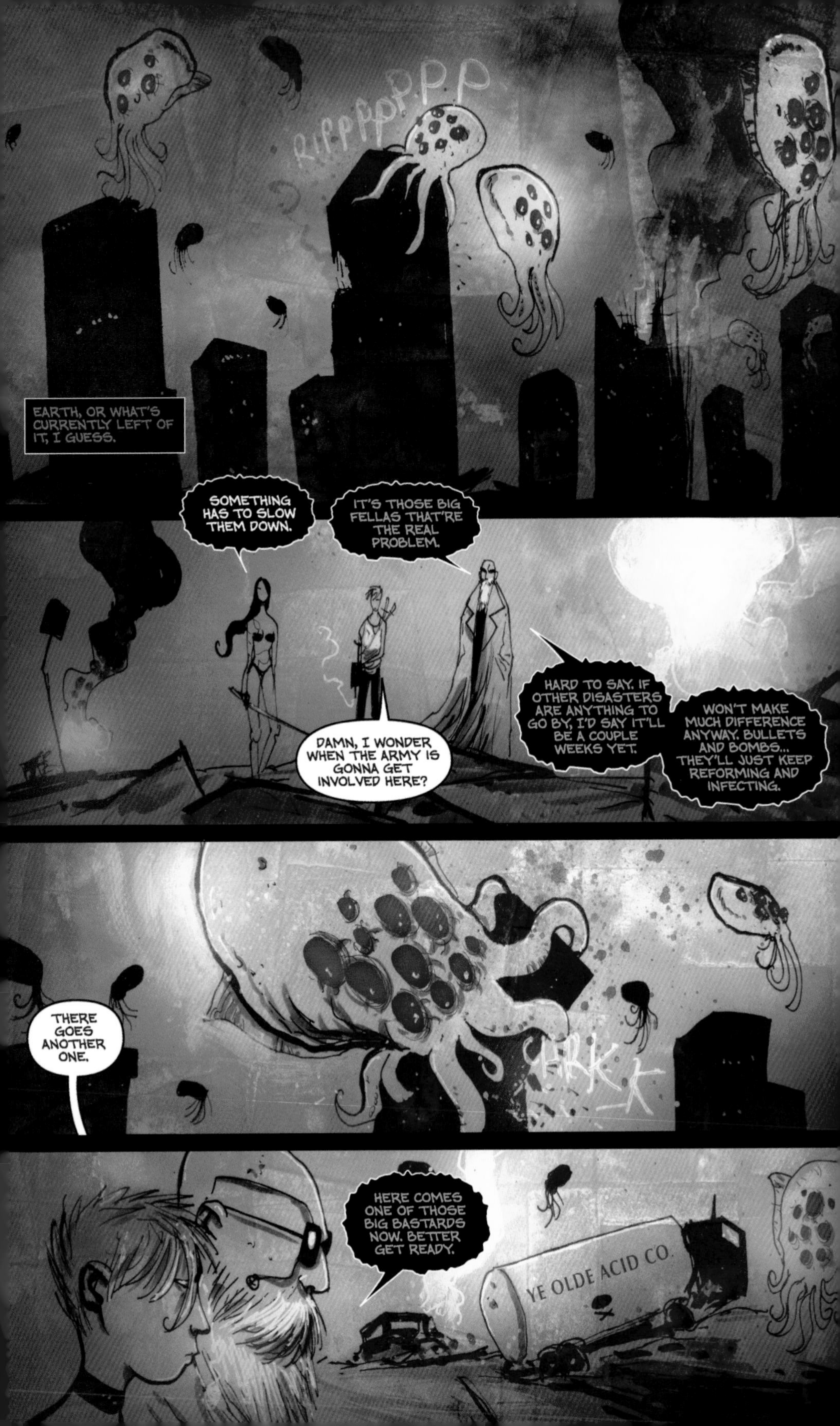
RIPPPPPPPPP
EARTH, OR WHAT'S CURRENTLY LEFT OF IT, I GUESS.
SOMETHING HAS TO SLOW THEM DOWN.
IT'S THOSE BIG FELLAS THAT'RE THE REAL PROBLEM.
DAMN, I WONDER WHEN THE ARMY IS GONNA GET INVOLVED HERE?
HARD TO SAY. IF OTHER DISASTERS ARE ANYTHING TO GO BY, I'D SAY IT'LL BE A COUPLE WEEKS YET.
WON'T MAKE MUCH DIFFERENCE ANYWAY. BULLETS AND BOMBS... THEY'LL JUST KEEP REFORMING AND INFECTING.
THERE GOES ANOTHER ONE.
HRK-K
HERE COMES ONE OF THOSE BIG BASTARDS NOW. BETTER GET READY.
YE OLDE ACID CO.

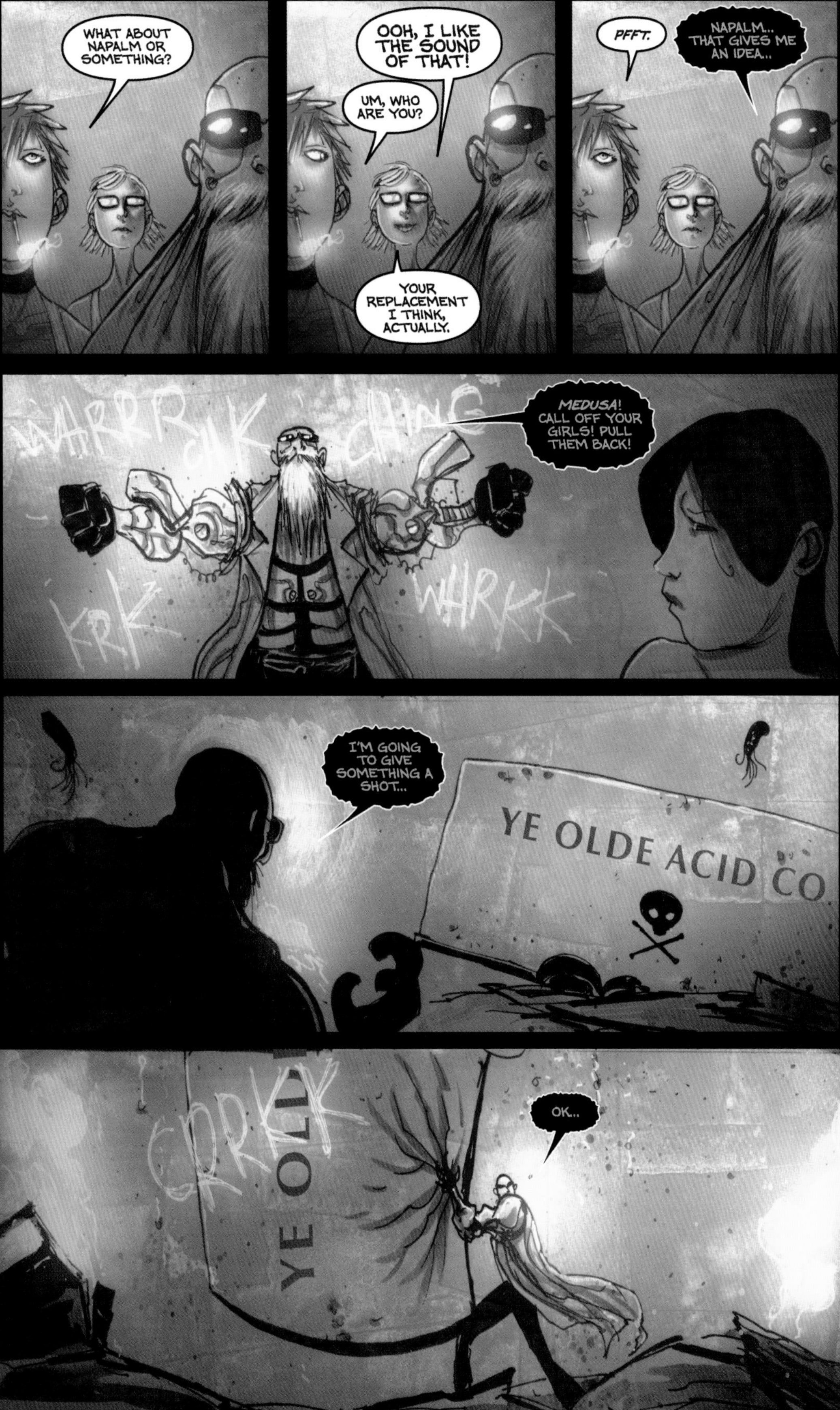
WHAT ABOUT NAPALM OR SOMETHING?
OOH, I LIKE THE SOUND OF THAT!
UM, WHO ARE YOU?
YOUR REPLACEMENT I THINK, ACTUALLY.
PFFT.
NAPALM... THAT GIVES ME AN IDEA...
WARRR
CHK
CHING
MEDUSA! CALL OFF YOUR GIRLS! PULL THEM BACK!
KRK
WHRKK
I'M GOING TO GIVE SOMETHING A SHOT...
YE OLDE ACID CO
CRRKK
YE OLD
OK...

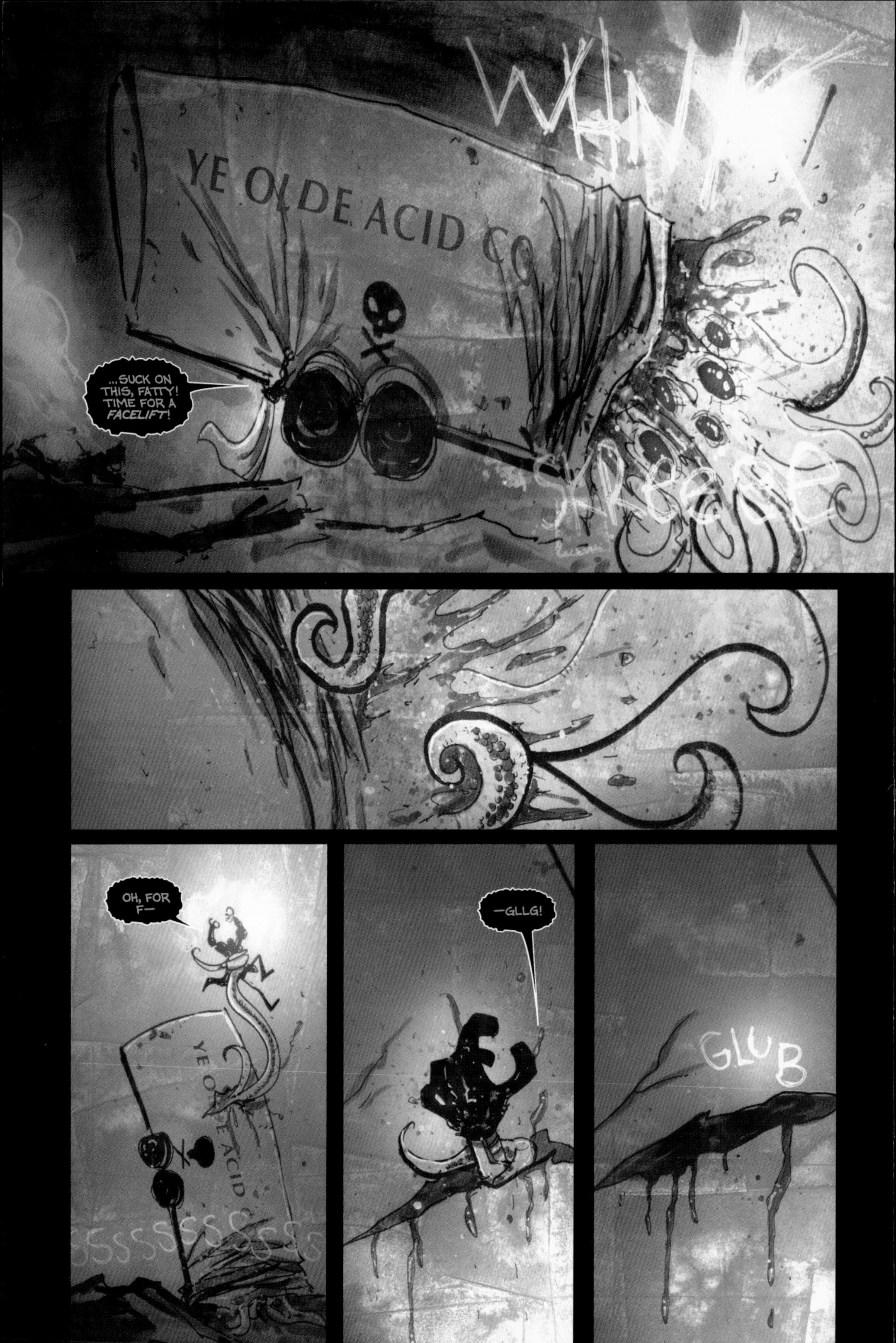
YE OLDE ACID CO
...SUCK ON THIS, FATTY! TIME FOR A *FACELIFT*!
OH, FOR F—
YE OLDE ACID
—GLLG!
GLUB

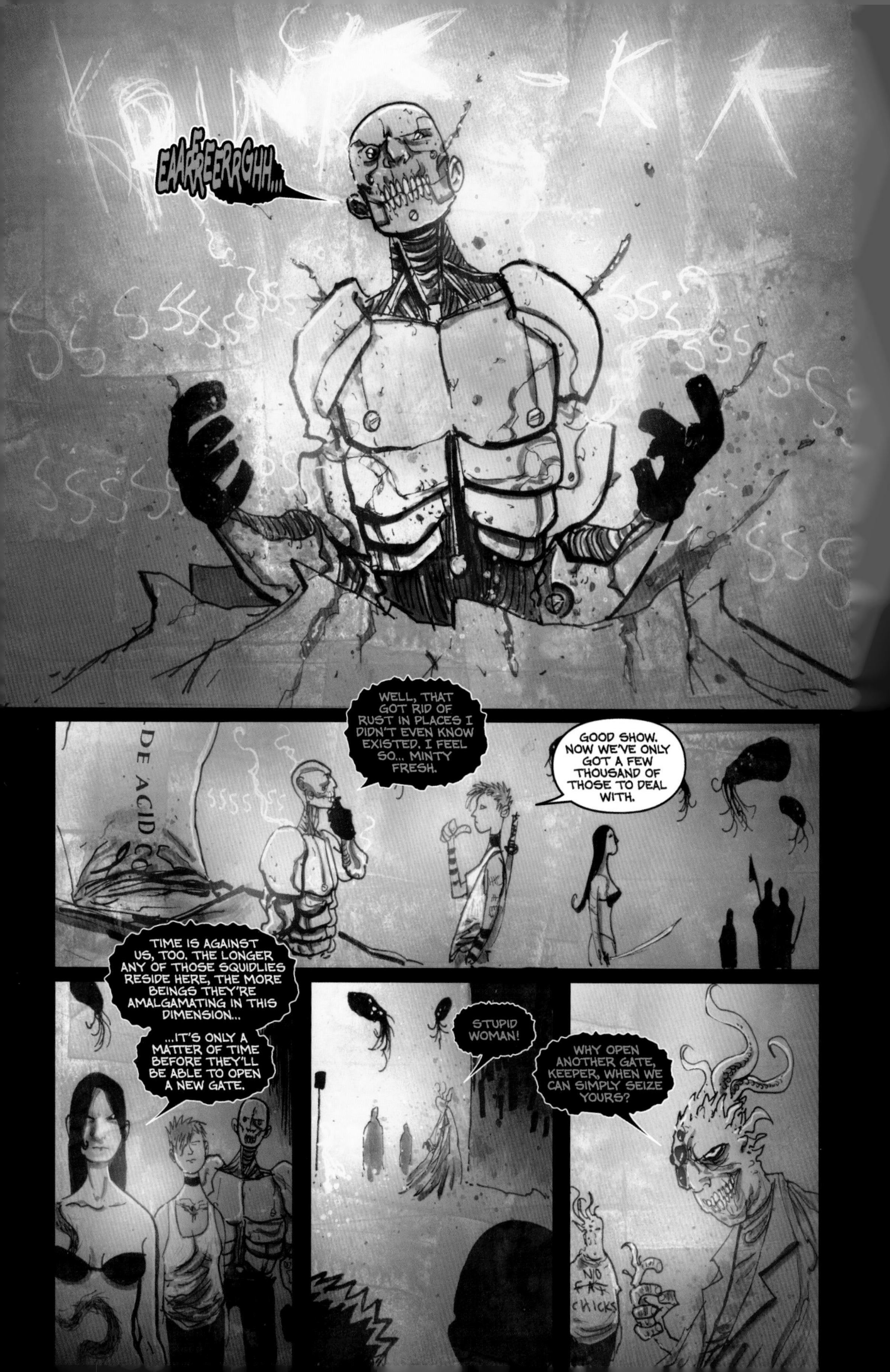
EAARREERRGHH...
WELL, THAT GOT RID OF RUST IN PLACES I DIDN'T EVEN KNOW EXISTED. I FEEL SO... MINTY FRESH.
GOOD SHOW. NOW WE'VE ONLY GOT A FEW THOUSAND OF THOSE TO DEAL WITH.
DE ACID CO
TIME IS AGAINST US, TOO. THE LONGER ANY OF THOSE SQUIDLIES RESIDE HERE, THE MORE BEINGS THEY'RE AMALGAMATING IN THIS DIMENSION...
...IT'S ONLY A MATTER OF TIME BEFORE THEY'LL BE ABLE TO OPEN A NEW GATE.
STUPID WOMAN!
WHY OPEN ANOTHER GATE, KEEPER, WHEN WE CAN SIMPLY SEIZE YOURS?

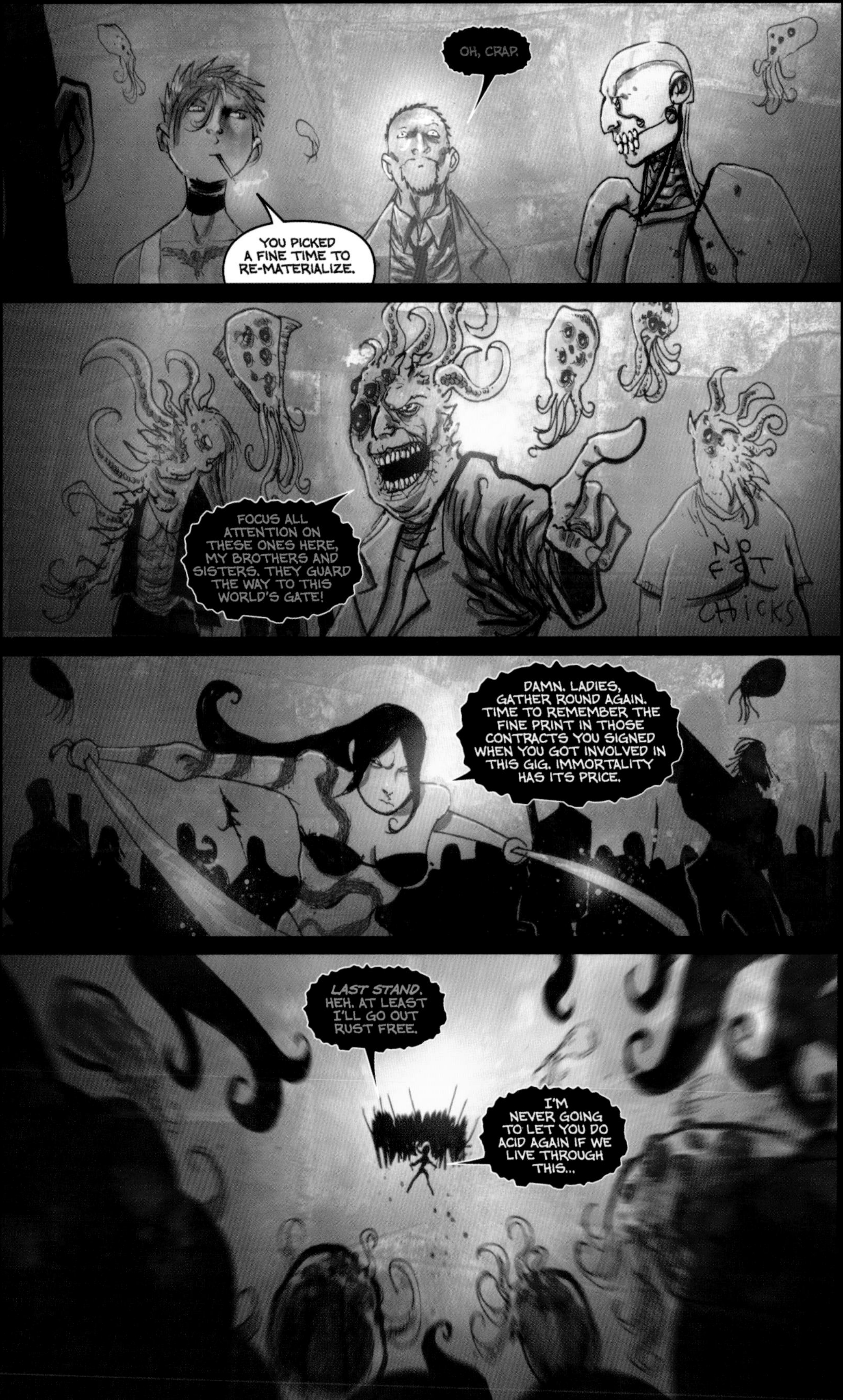
OH, CRAP.
YOU PICKED A FINE TIME TO RE-MATERIALIZE.
FOCUS ALL ATTENTION ON THESE ONES HERE, MY BROTHERS AND SISTERS. THEY GUARD THE WAY TO THIS WORLD'S GATE!
NO FAT CHICKS
DAMN. LADIES, GATHER ROUND AGAIN. TIME TO REMEMBER THE FINE PRINT IN THOSE CONTRACTS YOU SIGNED WHEN YOU GOT INVOLVED IN THIS GIG. IMMORTALITY HAS ITS PRICE.
LAST STAND. HEH. AT LEAST I'LL GO OUT RUST FREE.
I'M NEVER GOING TO LET YOU DO ACID AGAIN IF WE LIVE THROUGH THIS...

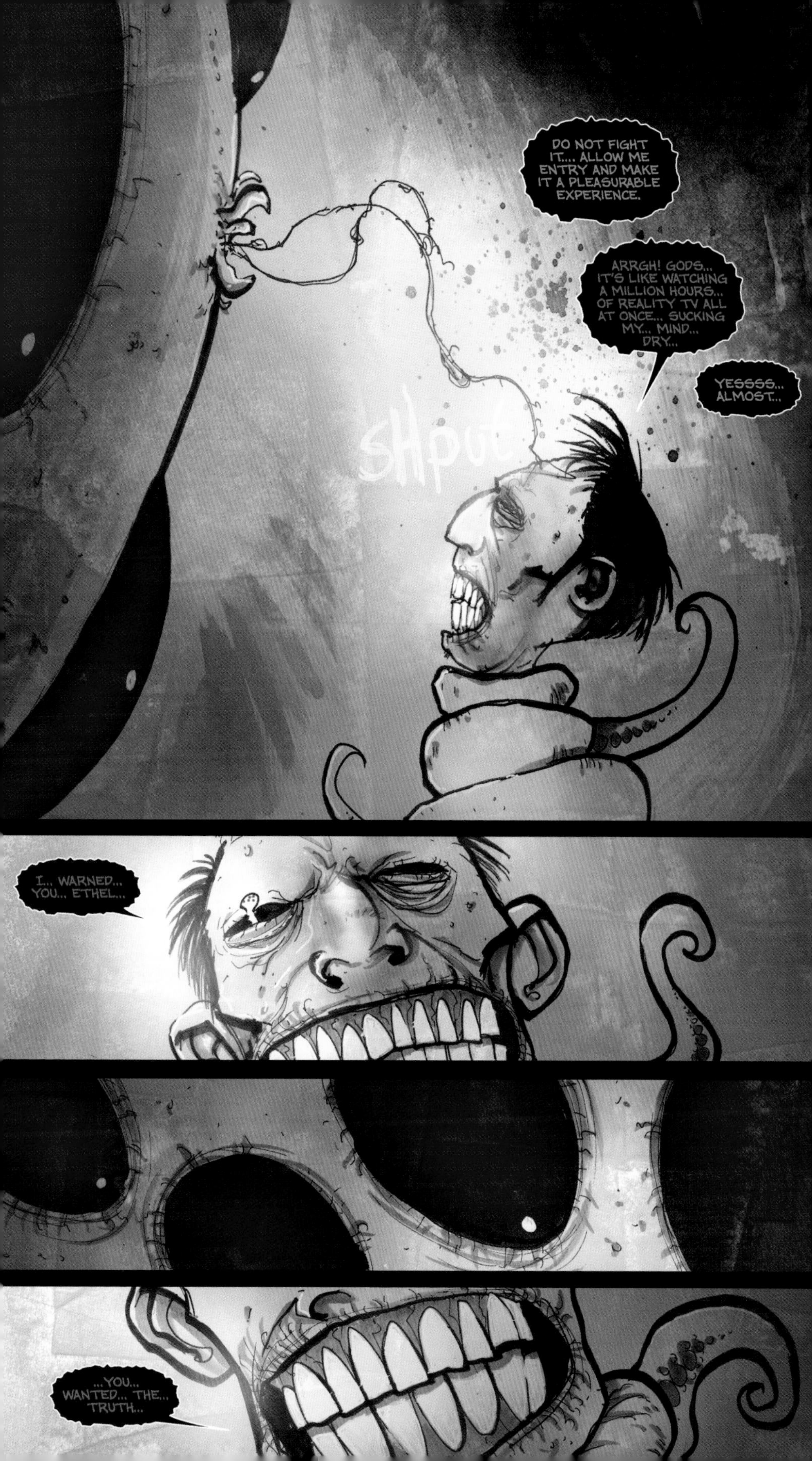
DO NOT FIGHT IT.... ALLOW ME ENTRY AND MAKE IT A PLEASURABLE EXPERIENCE.
ARRGH! GODS... IT'S LIKE WATCHING A MILLION HOURS... OF REALITY TV ALL AT ONCE... SUCKING MY... MIND... DRY...
YESSSS... ALMOST...
SHPUT
I... WARNED... YOU... ETHEL...
...YOU... WANTED... THE... TRUTH...

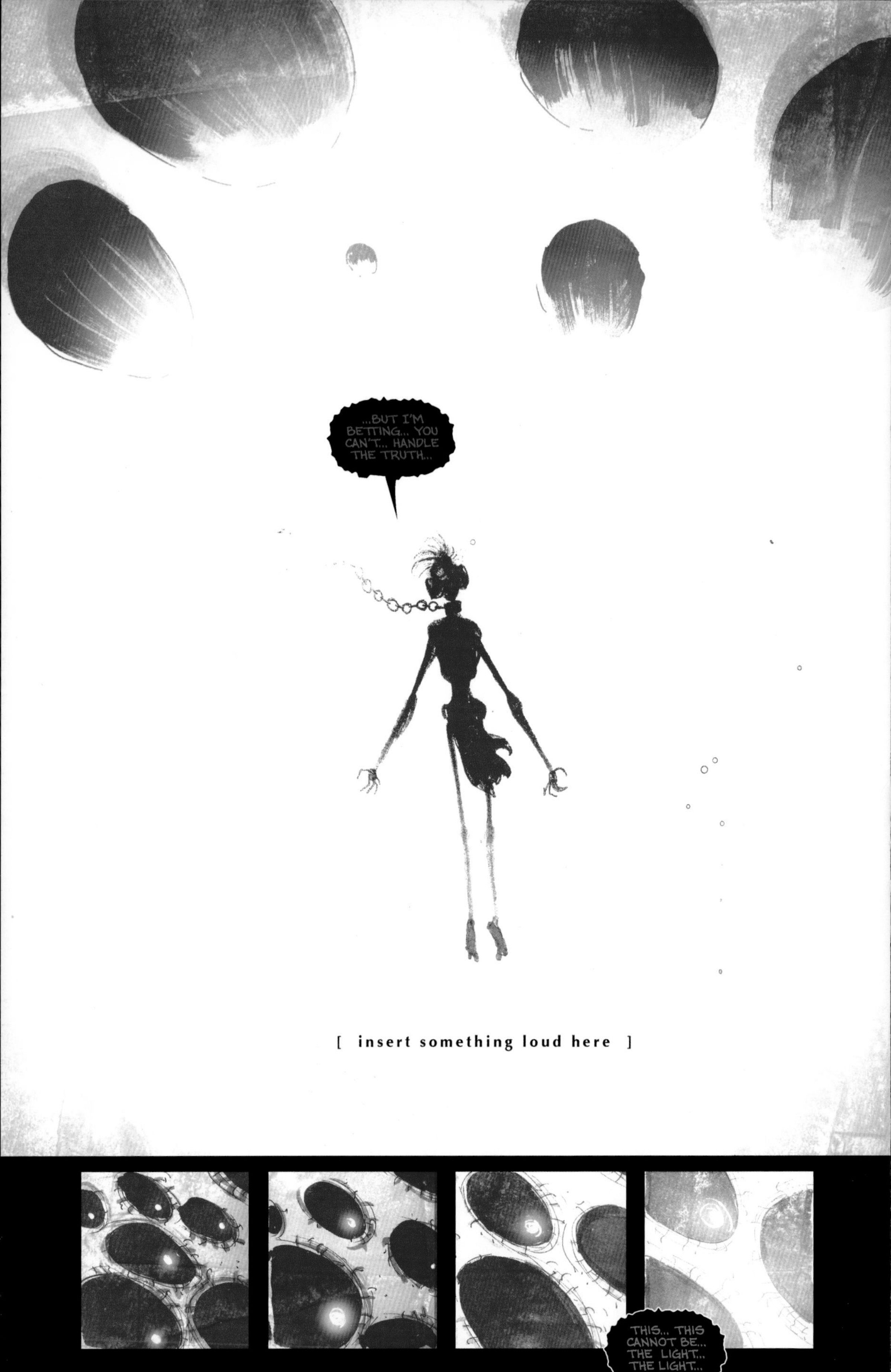
...BUT I'M BETTING... YOU CAN'T... HANDLE THE TRUTH...
[insert something loud here]
THIS... THIS CANNOT BE... THE LIGHT... THE LIGHT...

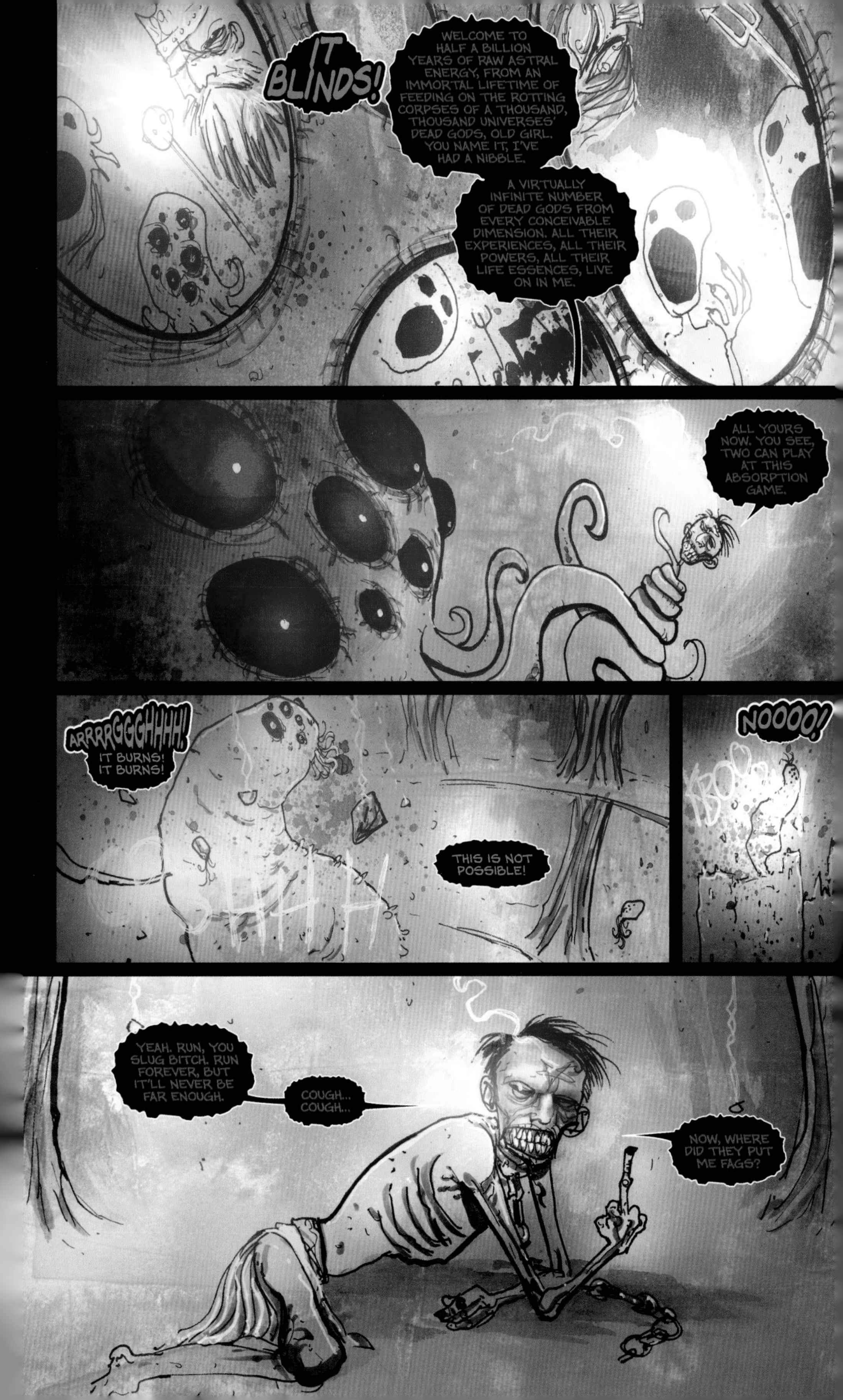
IT BLINDS!
WELCOME TO HALF A BILLION YEARS OF RAW ASTRAL ENERGY, FROM AN IMMORTAL LIFETIME OF FEEDING ON THE ROTTING CORPSES OF A THOUSAND, THOUSAND UNIVERSES' DEAD GODS, OLD GIRL. YOU NAME IT, I'VE HAD A NIBBLE.
A VIRTUALLY INFINITE NUMBER OF DEAD GODS FROM EVERY CONCEIVABLE DIMENSION. ALL THEIR EXPERIENCES, ALL THEIR POWERS, ALL THEIR LIFE ESSENCES, LIVE ON IN ME.
ALL YOURS NOW. YOU SEE, TWO CAN PLAY AT THIS ABSORPTION GAME.
ARRRRGGGHHHH! IT BURNS! IT BURNS!
SHHHH
THIS IS NOT POSSIBLE!
NOOOO!
YEAH. RUN, YOU SLUG BITCH. RUN FOREVER, BUT IT'LL NEVER BE FAR ENOUGH.
COUGH... COUGH...
NOW, WHERE DID THEY PUT ME FAGS?

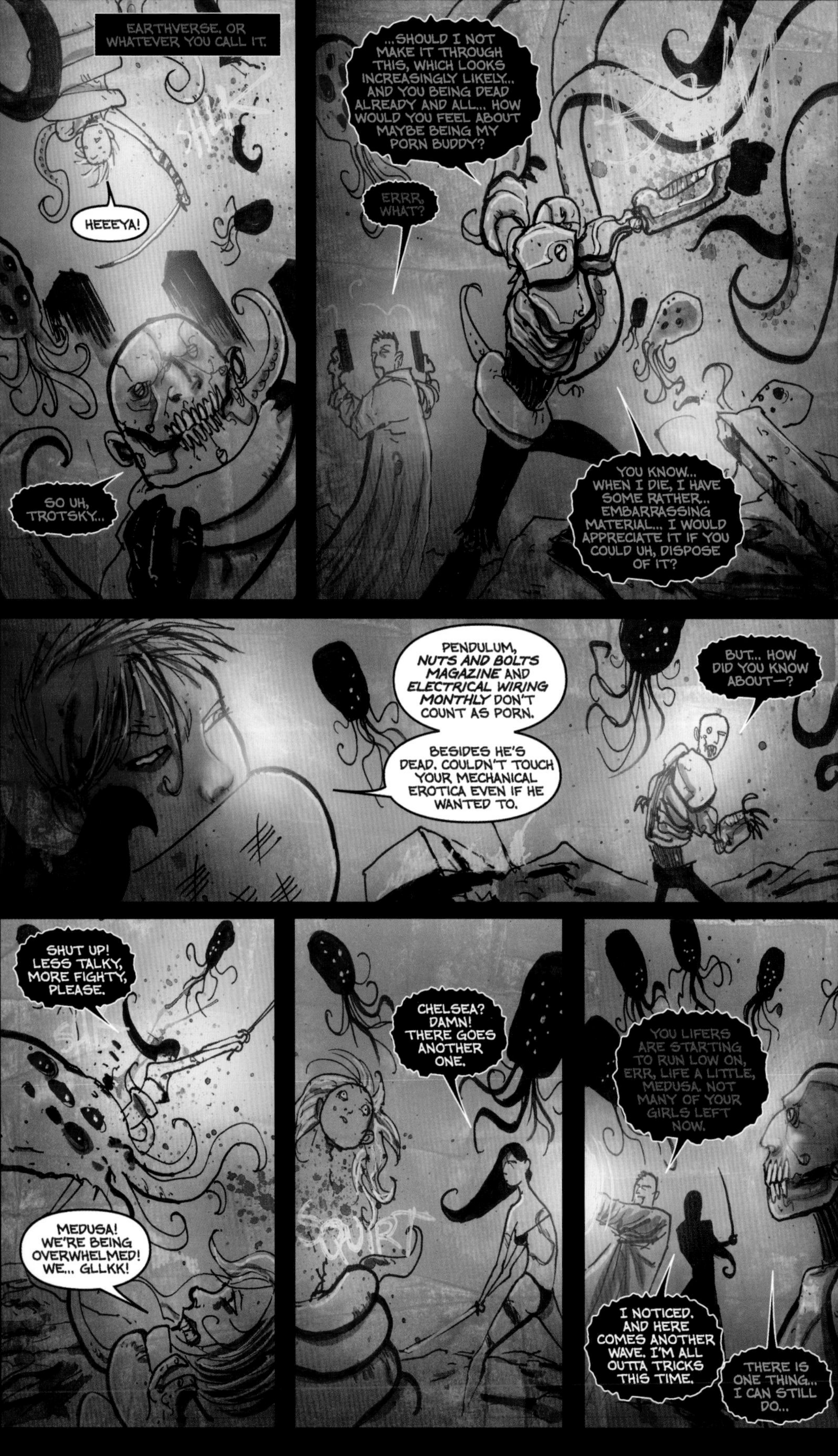
EARTHVERSE. OR WHATEVER YOU CALL IT.
HEEEYA!
SO UH, TROTSKY...
...SHOULD I NOT MAKE IT THROUGH THIS, WHICH LOOKS INCREASINGLY LIKELY... AND YOU BEING DEAD ALREADY AND ALL... HOW WOULD YOU FEEL ABOUT MAYBE BEING MY PORN BUDDY?
ERRR, WHAT?
YOU KNOW... WHEN I DIE, I HAVE SOME RATHER... EMBARRASSING MATERIAL... I WOULD APPRECIATE IT IF YOU COULD UH, DISPOSE OF IT?
PENDULUM, *NUTS AND BOLTS MAGAZINE* AND *ELECTRICAL WIRING MONTHLY* DON'T COUNT AS PORN.
BESIDES HE'S DEAD. COULDN'T TOUCH YOUR MECHANICAL EROTICA EVEN IF HE WANTED TO.
BUT... HOW DID YOU KNOW ABOUT—?
SHUT UP! LESS TALKY, MORE FIGHTY, PLEASE.
MEDUSA! WE'RE BEING OVERWHELMED! WE... GLLKK!
CHELSEA? DAMN! THERE GOES ANOTHER ONE.
SQUIRT
YOU LIFERS ARE STARTING TO RUN LOW ON, ERR, LIFE A LITTLE, MEDUSA. NOT MANY OF YOUR GIRLS LEFT NOW.
I NOTICED. AND HERE COMES ANOTHER WAVE. I'M ALL OUTTA TRICKS THIS TIME.
THERE IS ONE THING... I CAN STILL DO...

WZZZZ
MY PARTICLE ACCRETION BATTERY. IF I SHORT IT, I MIGHT JUST... BE ABLE TO...
...BUY YOU GUYS A LITTLE MORE TIME...
OVER HERE, YOU SQUID BASTARDS! OVER HE—
boom.

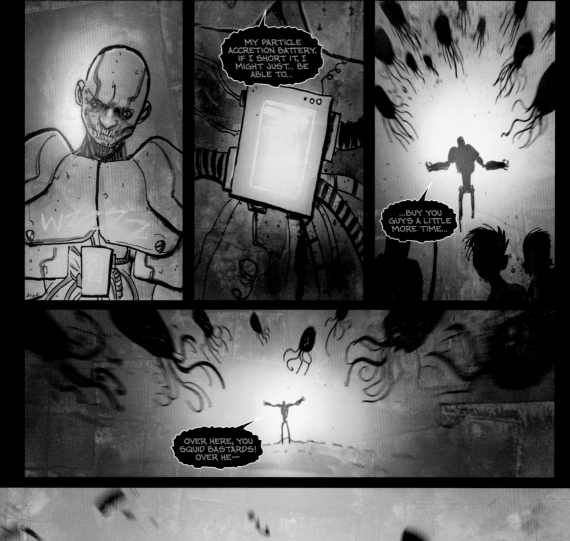

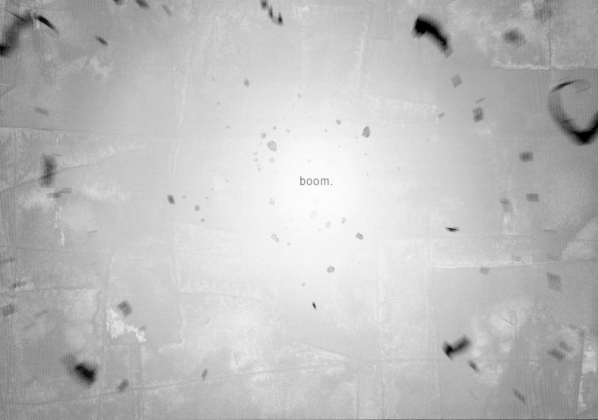

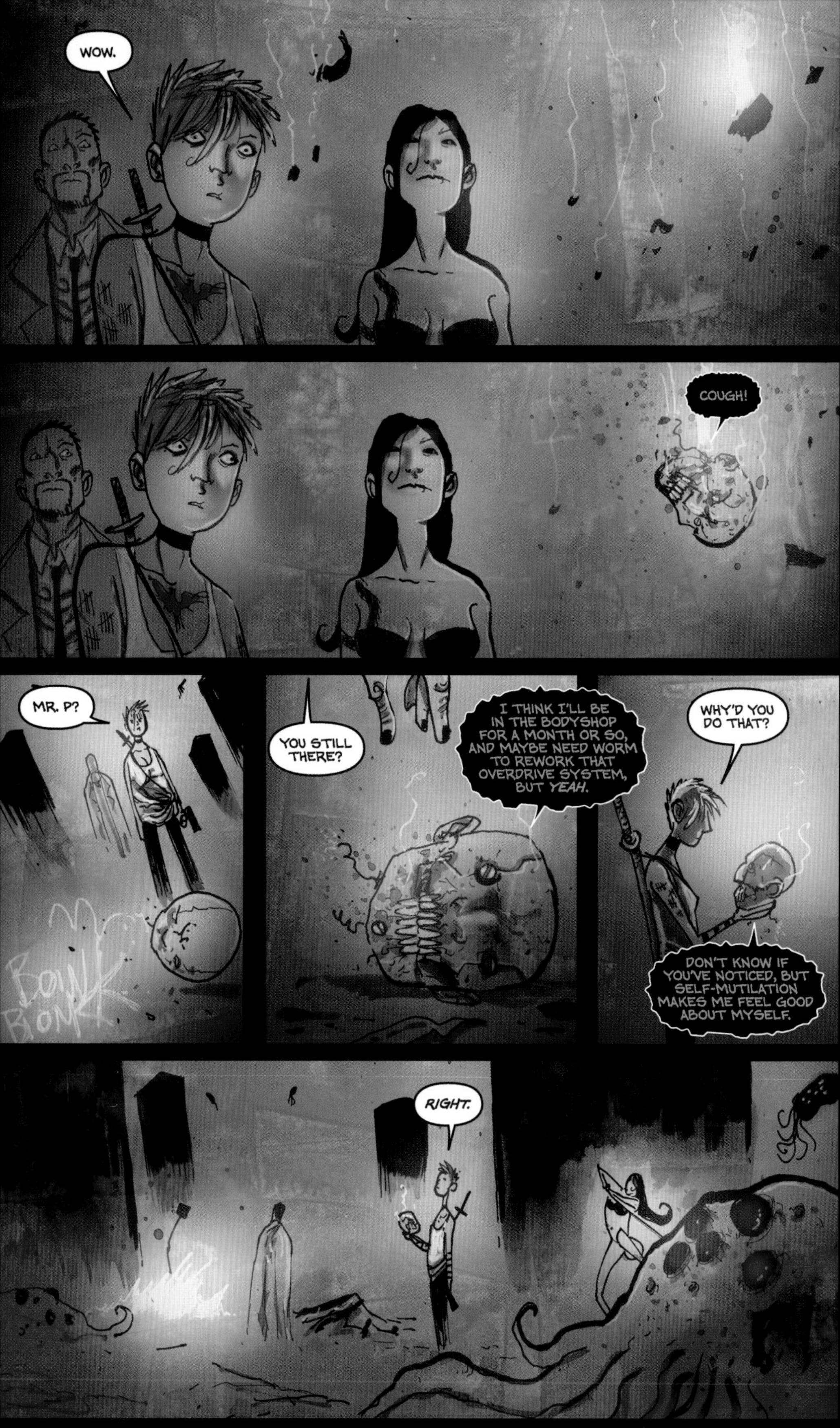
WOW.
COUGH!
MR. P?
BOINK
BONK
YOU STILL THERE?
I THINK I'LL BE IN THE BODYSHOP FOR A MONTH OR SO, AND MAYBE NEED WORM TO REWORK THAT OVERDRIVE SYSTEM, BUT YEAH.
WHY'D YOU DO THAT?
DON'T KNOW IF YOU'VE NOTICED, BUT SELF-MUTILATION MAKES ME FEEL GOOD ABOUT MYSELF.
RIGHT.

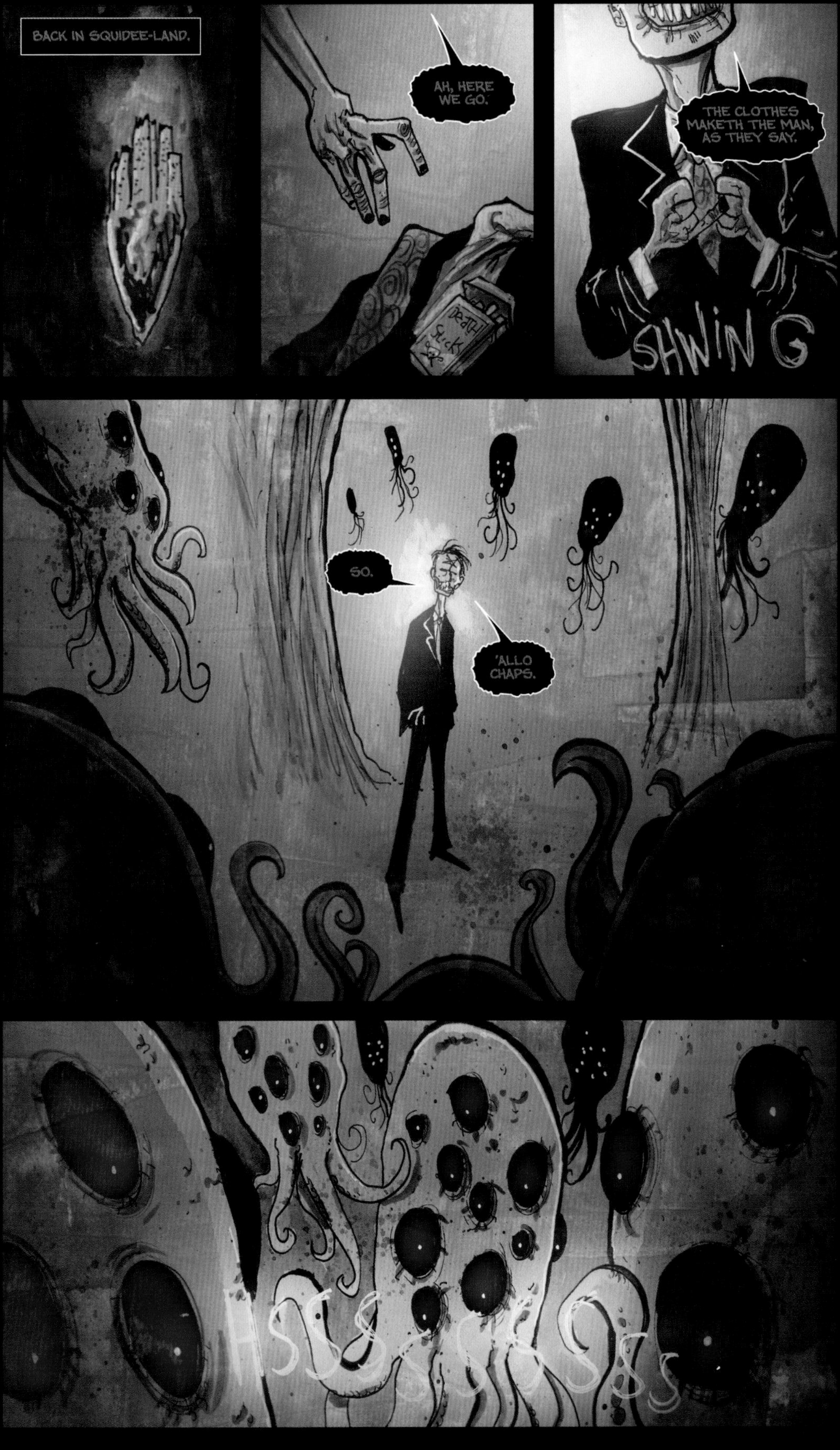
BACK IN SQUIDEE-LAND.
AH, HERE WE GO.
DEATH STICK
THE CLOTHES MAKETH THE MAN, AS THEY SAY.
SHWING
SO.
'ALLO CHAPS.
HSSSSSSSSSS

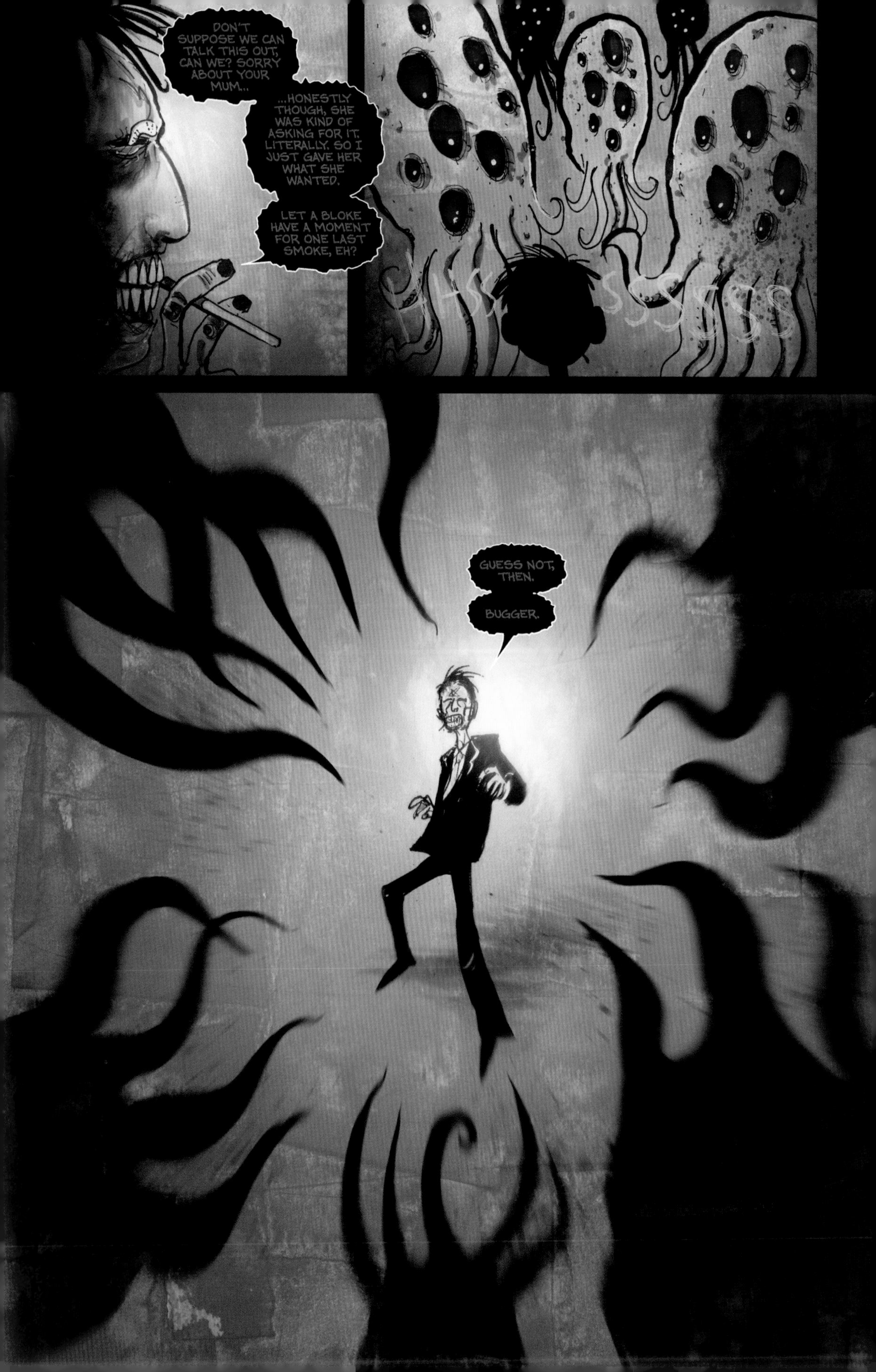
DON'T SUPPOSE WE CAN TALK THIS OUT, CAN WE? SORRY ABOUT YOUR MUM...
...HONESTLY THOUGH, SHE WAS KIND OF ASKING FOR IT. LITERALLY. SO I JUST GAVE HER WHAT SHE WANTED.
LET A BLOKE HAVE A MOMENT FOR ONE LAST SMOKE, EH?
GUESS NOT, THEN.
BUGGER.

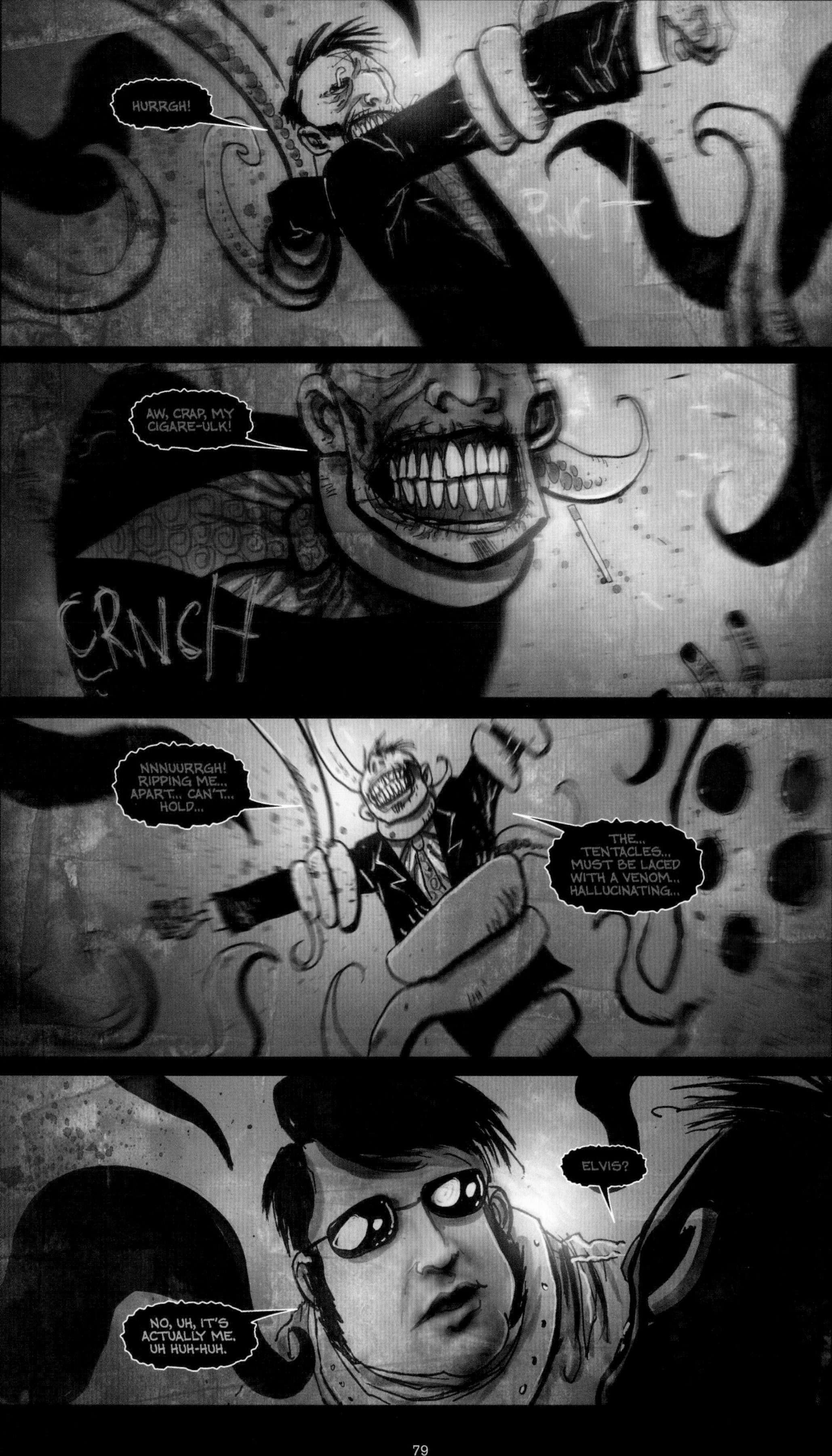
HURRGH!
AW, CRAP, MY CIGARE-ULK!
CRNCH
NNNUURRGH! RIPPING ME... APART... CAN'T... HOLD...
THE... TENTACLES... MUST BE LACED WITH A VENOM... HALLUCINATING...
ELVIS?
NO, UH, IT'S ACTUALLY ME. UH HUH-HUH.

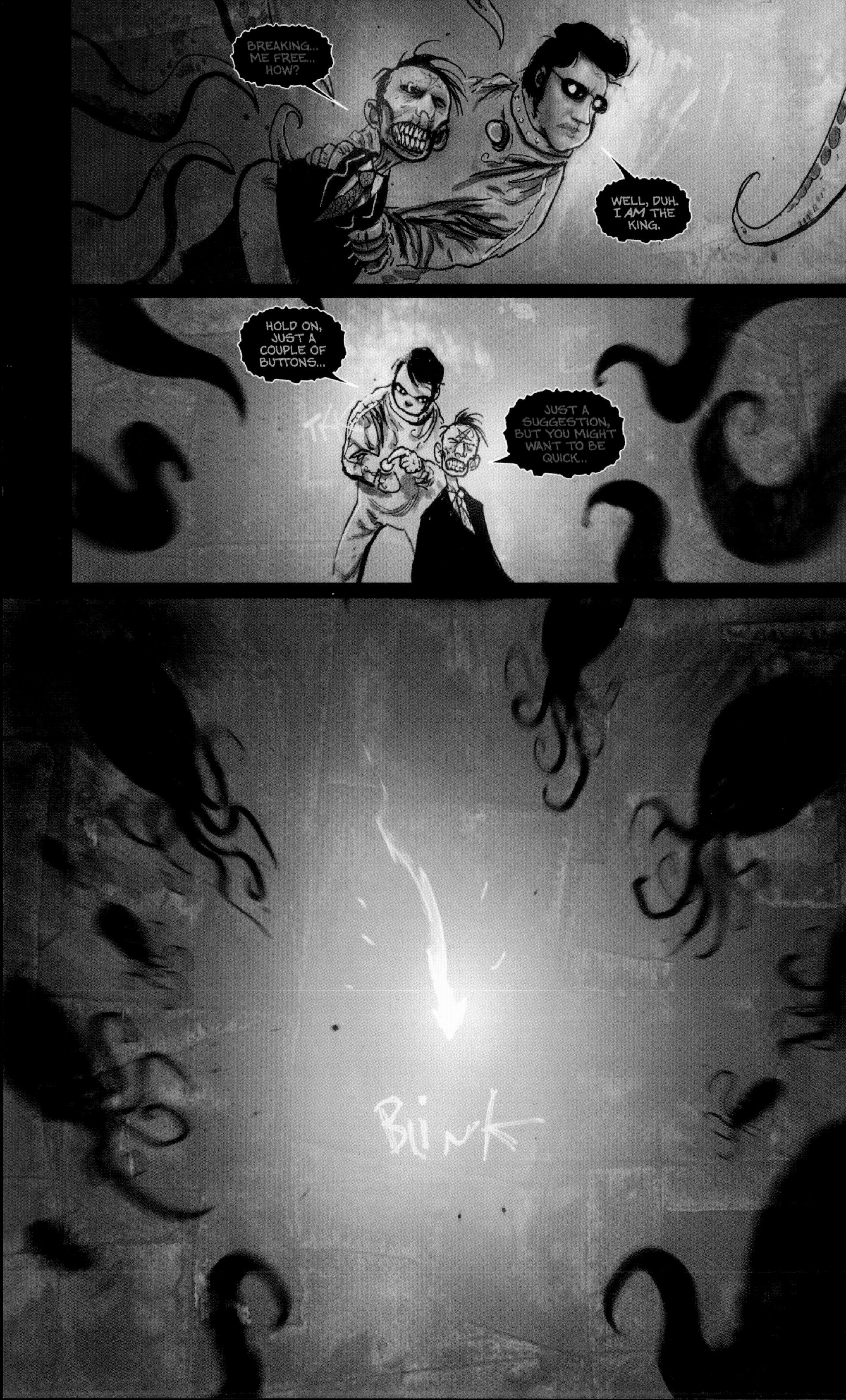
BREAKING... ME FREE... HOW?
WELL, DUH. I AM THE KING.
HOLD ON, JUST A COUPLE OF BUTTONS...
JUST A SUGGESTION, BUT YOU MIGHT WAN'T TO BE QUICK...
BLINK

Chapter 4

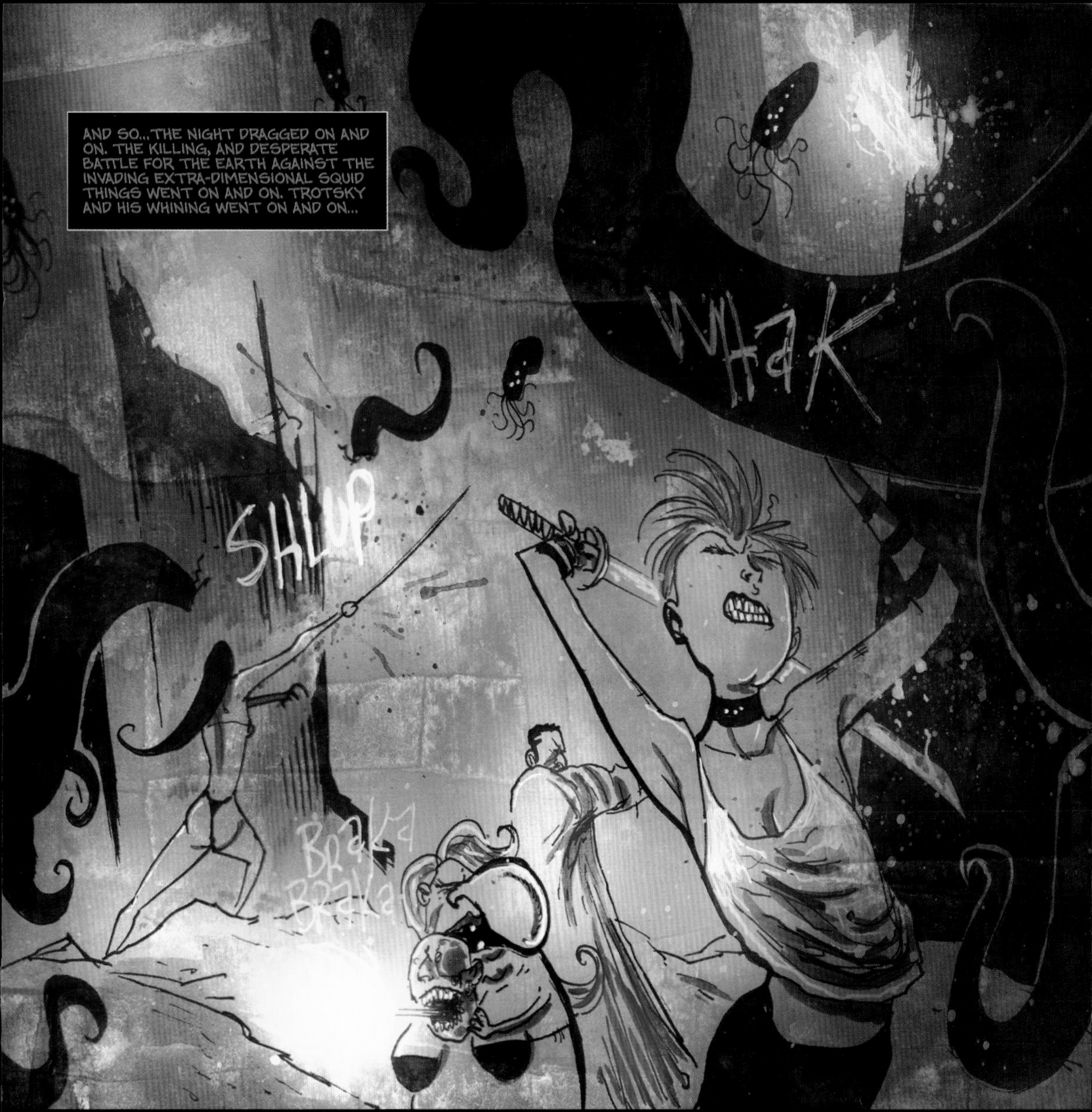
AND SO...THE NIGHT DRAGGED ON AND ON. THE KILLING, AND DESPERATE BATTLE FOR THE EARTH AGAINST THE INVADING EXTRA-DIMENSIONAL SQUID THINGS WENT ON AND ON. TROTSKY AND HIS WHINING WENT ON AND ON...
WHAK
SHLUP
BRAKA
BRAKA

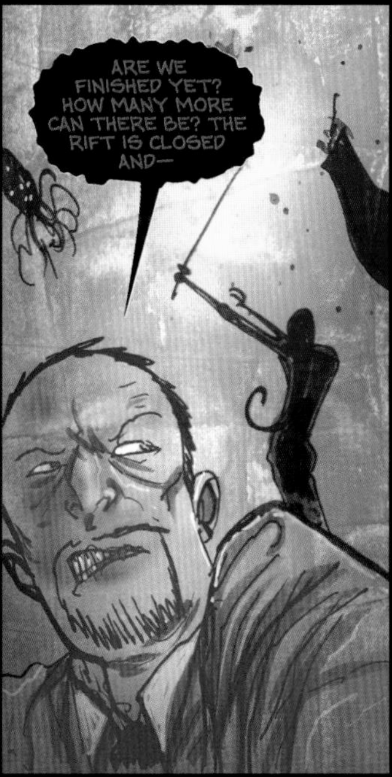
ARE WE FINISHED YET? HOW MANY MORE CAN THERE BE? THE RIFT IS CLOSED AND—

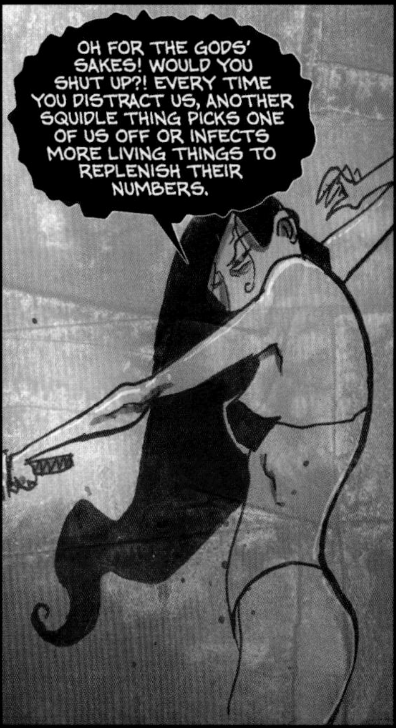
OH FOR THE GODS' SAKES! WOULD YOU SHUT UP?! EVERY TIME YOU DISTRACT US, ANOTHER SQUIDLE THING PICKS ONE OF US OFF OR INFECTS MORE LIVING THINGS TO REPLENISH THEIR NUMBERS.

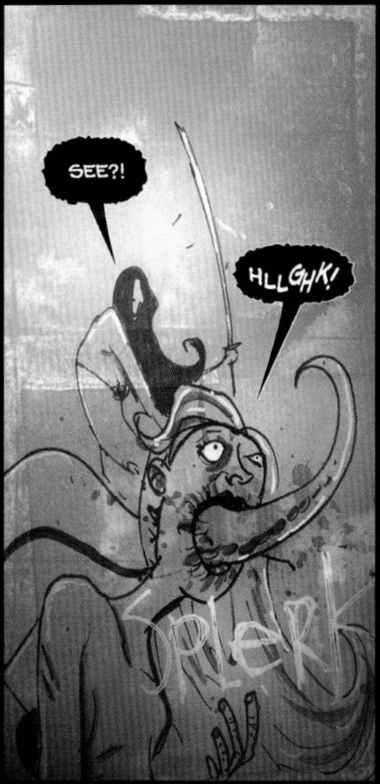
SEE?!
HLLGHK!
SPLERK

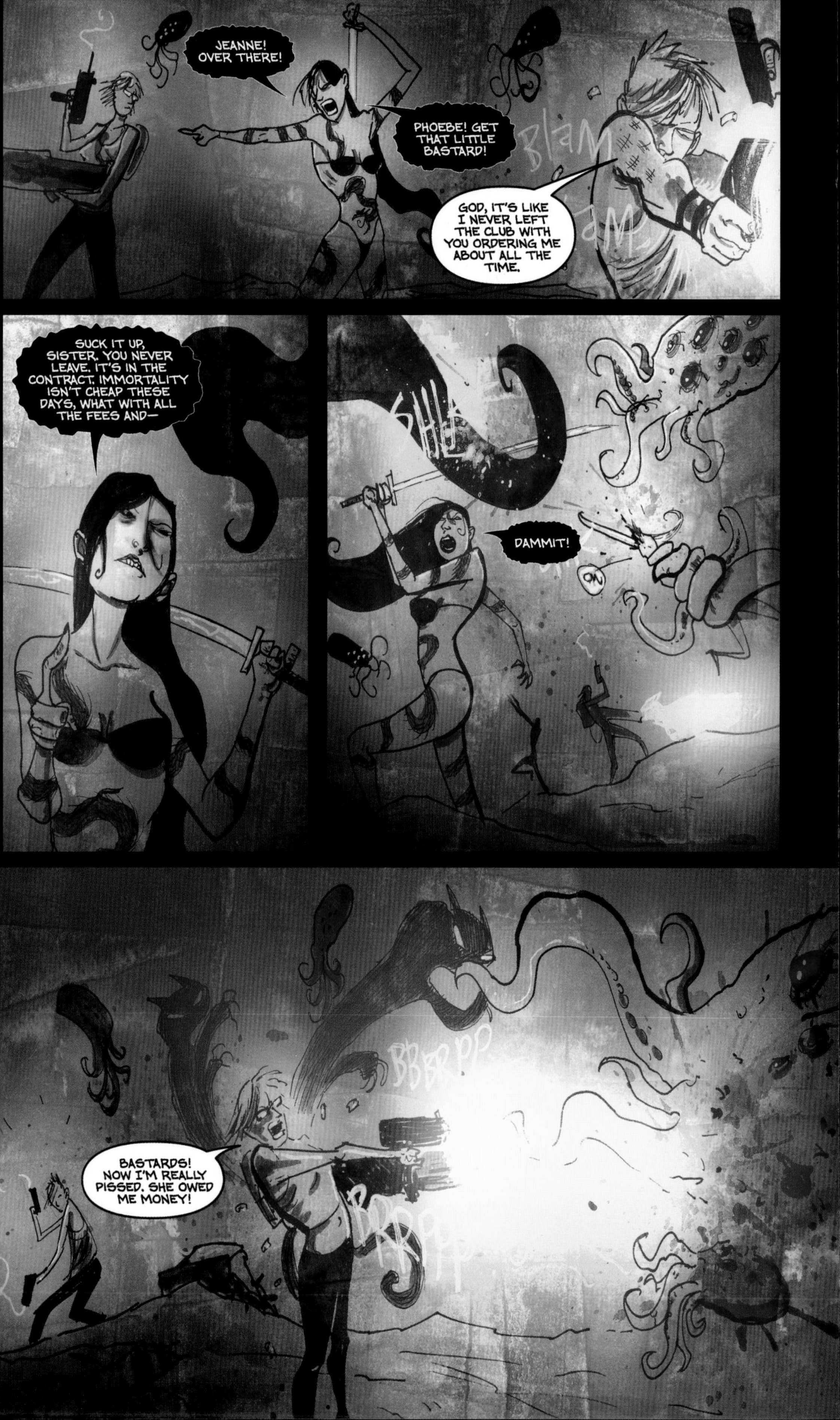
JEANNE! OVER THERE!
PHOEBE! GET THAT LITTLE BASTARD!
BLAM
BLAM
GOD, IT'S LIKE I NEVER LEFT THE CLUB WITH YOU ORDERING ME ABOUT ALL THE TIME.
SUCK IT UP, SISTER. YOU NEVER LEAVE. IT'S IN THE CONTRACT. IMMORTALITY ISN'T CHEAP THESE DAYS, WHAT WITH ALL THE FEES AND—
DAMMIT!
BBBRPP
BASTARDS! NOW I'M REALLY PISSED. SHE OWED ME MONEY!

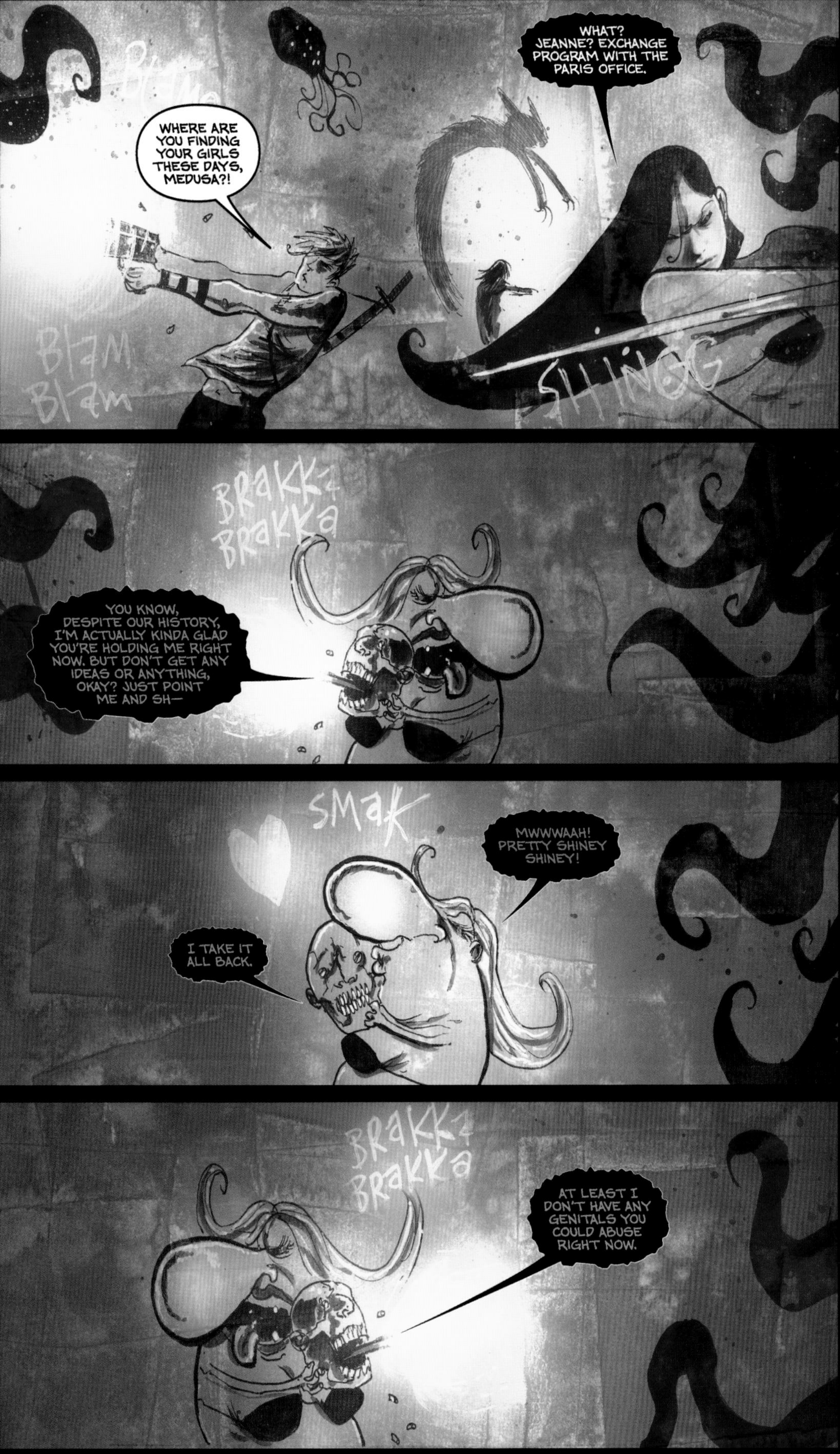

Blam
WHERE ARE YOU FINDING YOUR GIRLS THESE DAYS, MEDUSA?!
WHAT? JEANNE? EXCHANGE PROGRAM WITH THE PARIS OFFICE.
Blam Blam
SHINGG
BRAKKA BRAKKA
YOU KNOW, DESPITE OUR HISTORY, I'M ACTUALLY KINDA GLAD YOU'RE HOLDING ME RIGHT NOW. BUT DON'T GET ANY IDEAS OR ANYTHING, OKAY? JUST POINT ME AND SH—
SMAK
MWWWAAH! PRETTY SHINEY SHINEY!
I TAKE IT ALL BACK.
BRAKKA BRAKKA
AT LEAST I DON'T HAVE ANY GENITALS YOU COULD ABUSE RIGHT NOW.

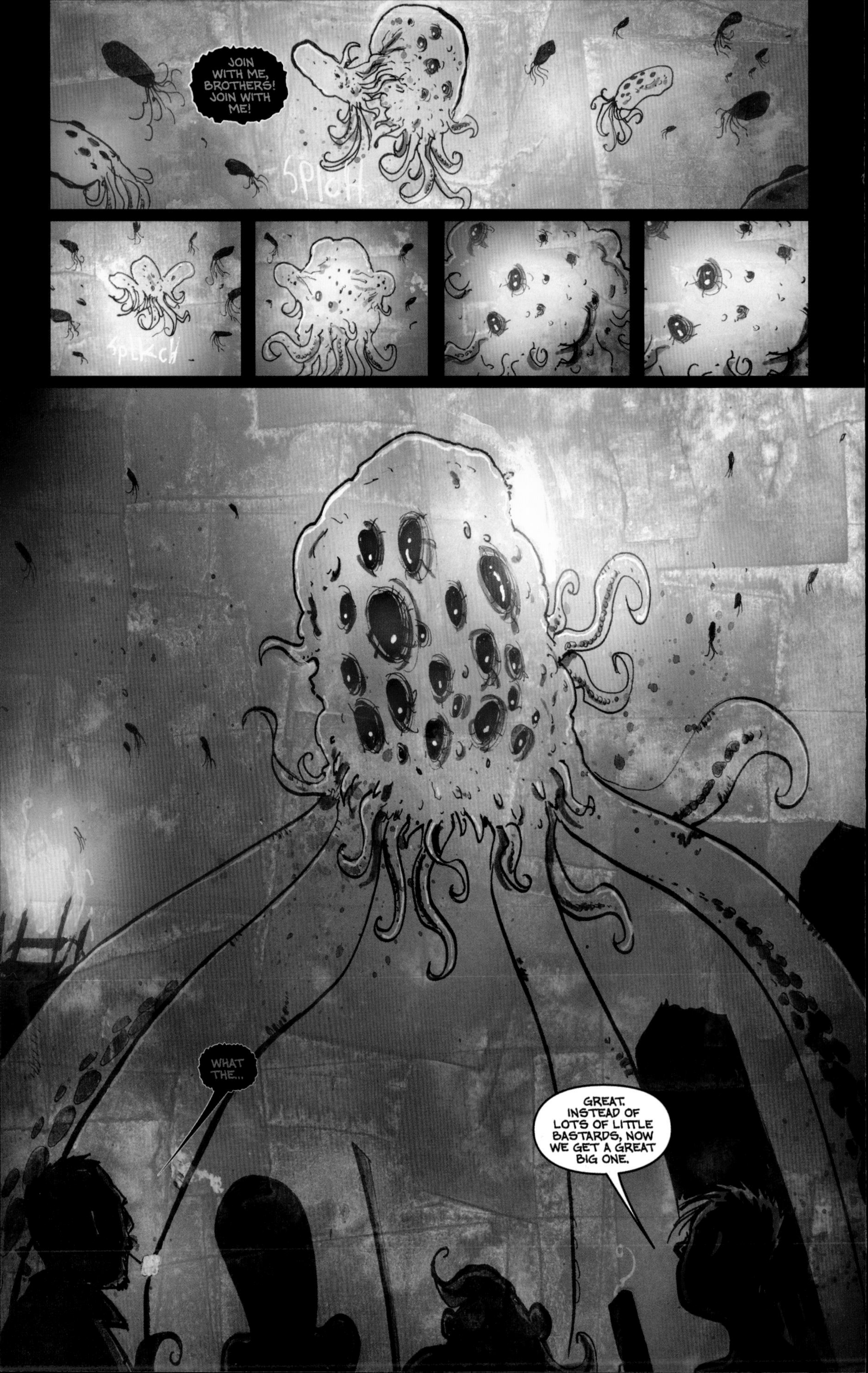
JOIN WITH ME, BROTHERS! JOIN WITH ME!
SPLCH
SPLKCH
WHAT THE...
GREAT. INSTEAD OF LOTS OF LITTLE BASTARDS, NOW WE GET A GREAT BIG ONE.

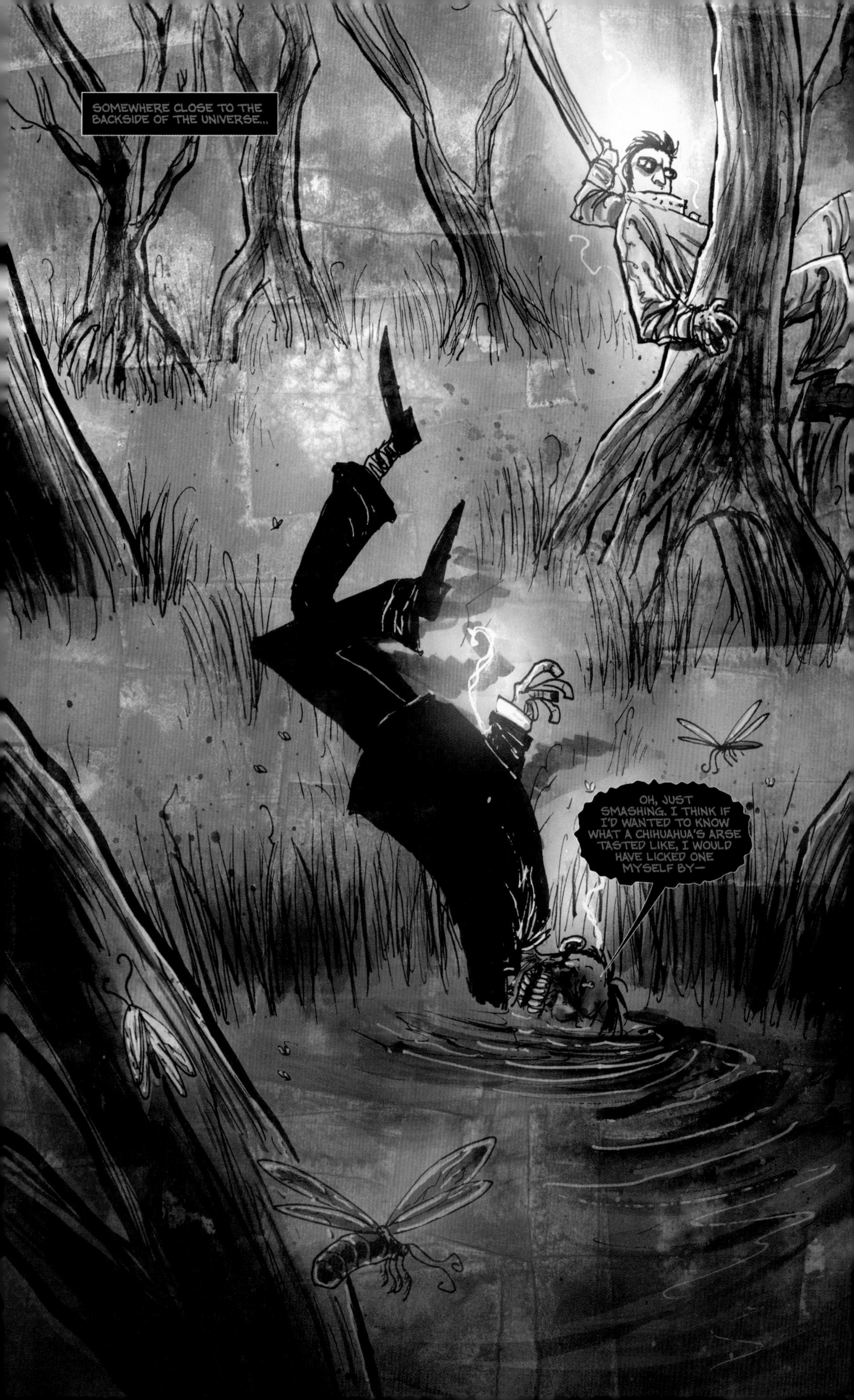
SOMEWHERE CLOSE TO THE BACKSIDE OF THE UNIVERSE...
OH, JUST SMASHING. I THINK IF I'D WANTED TO KNOW WHAT A CHIHUAHUA'S ARSE TASTED LIKE, I WOULD HAVE LICKED ONE MYSELF BY—

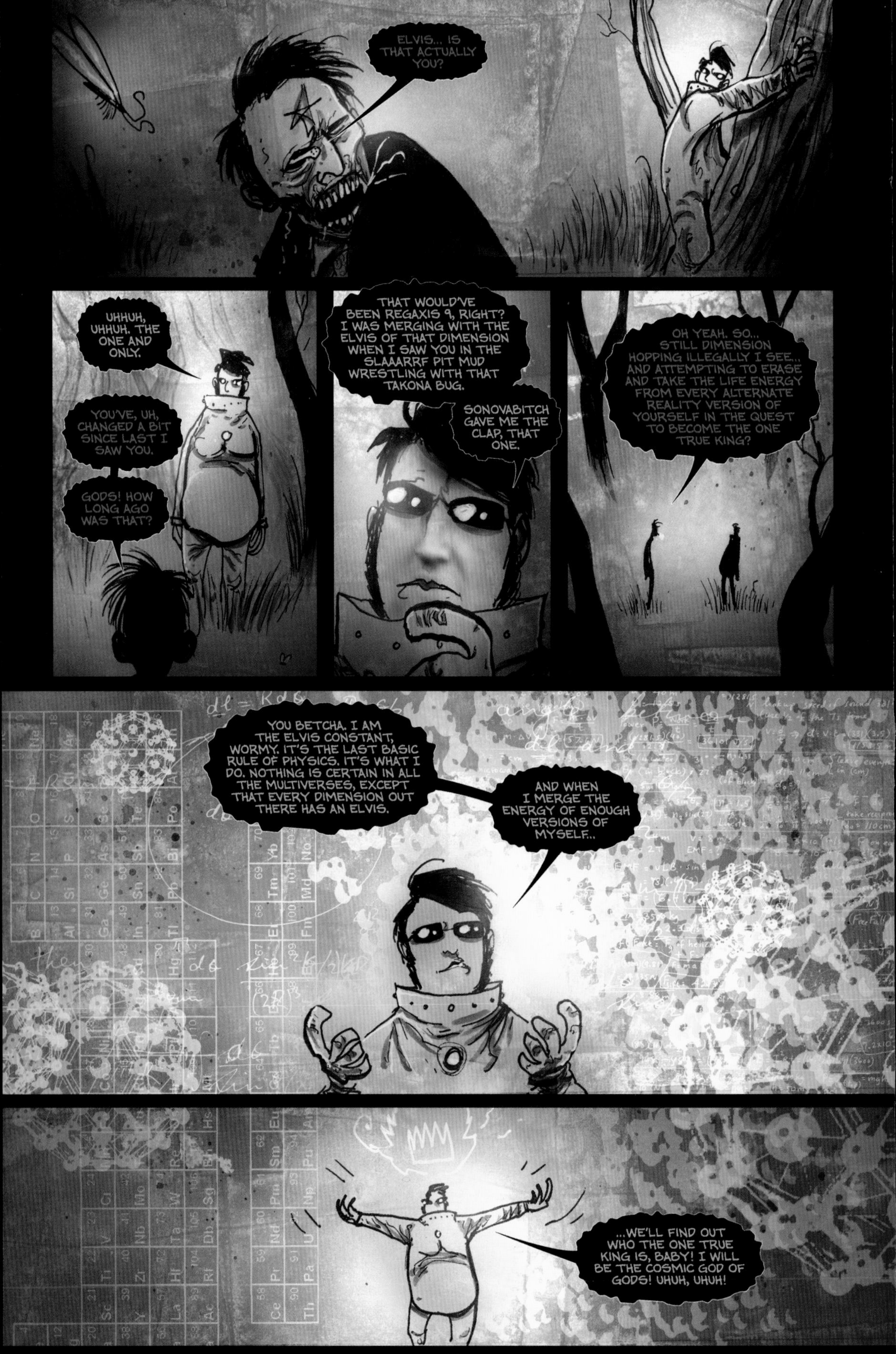
ELVIS... IS THAT ACTUALLY YOU?
UHHUH, UHHUH. THE ONE AND ONLY.
YOU'VE, UH, CHANGED A BIT SINCE LAST I SAW YOU.
GODS! HOW LONG AGO WAS THAT?
THAT WOULD'VE BEEN REGAXIS 9, RIGHT? I WAS MERGING WITH THE ELVIS OF THAT DIMENSION WHEN I SAW YOU IN THE SLAAARRF PIT MUD WRESTLING WITH THAT TAKONA BUG.
SONOVABITCH GAVE ME THE CLAP, THAT ONE.
OH YEAH. SO... STILL DIMENSION HOPPING ILLEGALLY I SEE... AND ATTEMPTING TO ERASE AND TAKE THE LIFE ENERGY FROM EVERY ALTERNATE REALITY VERSION OF YOURSELF IN THE QUEST TO BECOME THE ONE TRUE KING?
YOU BETCHA. I AM THE ELVIS CONSTANT, WORMY. IT'S THE LAST BASIC RULE OF PHYSICS. IT'S WHAT I DO. NOTHING IS CERTAIN IN ALL THE MULTIVERSES, EXCEPT THAT EVERY DIMENSION OUT THERE HAS AN ELVIS.
AND WHEN I MERGE THE ENERGY OF ENOUGH VERSIONS OF MYSELF...
...WE'LL FIND OUT WHO THE ONE TRUE KING IS, BABY! I WILL BE THE COSMIC GOD OF GODS! UHUH, UHUH!

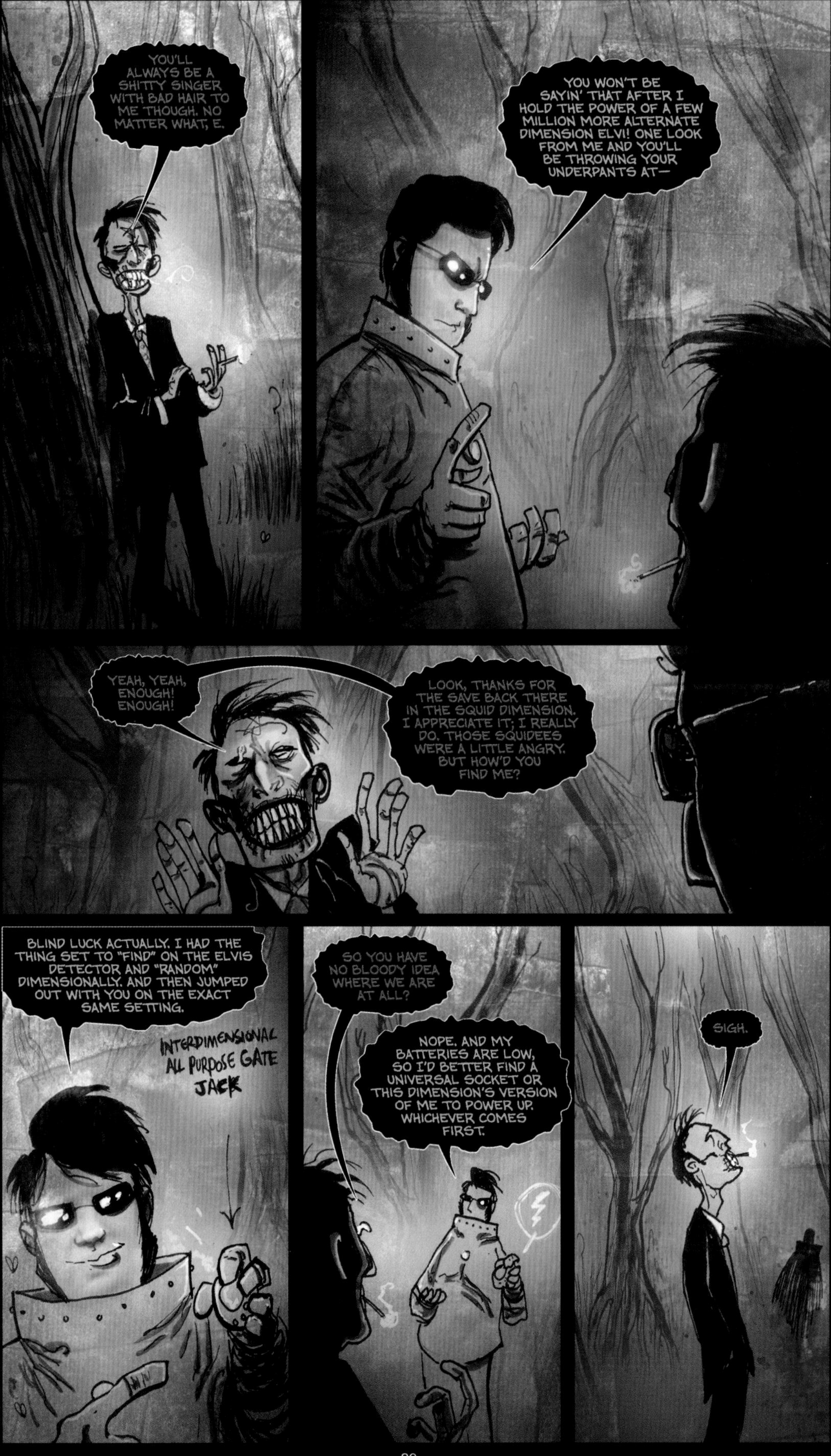
YOU'LL ALWAYS BE A SHITTY SINGER WITH BAD HAIR TO ME THOUGH. NO MATTER WHAT, E.
YOU WON'T BE SAYIN' THAT AFTER I HOLD THE POWER OF A FEW MILLION MORE ALTERNATE DIMENSION ELVI! ONE LOOK FROM ME AND YOU'LL BE THROWING YOUR UNDERPANTS AT—
YEAH, YEAH, ENOUGH! ENOUGH!
LOOK, THANKS FOR THE SAVE BACK THERE IN THE SQUID DIMENSION. I APPRECIATE IT; I REALLY DO. THOSE SQUIDEES WERE A LITTLE ANGRY. BUT HOW'D YOU FIND ME?
BLIND LUCK ACTUALLY. I HAD THE THING SET TO "FIND" ON THE ELVIS DETECTOR AND "RANDOM" DIMENSIONALLY. AND THEN JUMPED OUT WITH YOU ON THE EXACT SAME SETTING.
INTERDIMENSIONAL ALL PURPOSE GATE JACK
SO YOU HAVE NO BLOODY IDEA WHERE WE ARE AT ALL?
NOPE. AND MY BATTERIES ARE LOW, SO I'D BETTER FIND A UNIVERSAL SOCKET OR THIS DIMENSION'S VERSION OF ME TO POWER UP. WHICHEVER COMES FIRST.
SIGH.

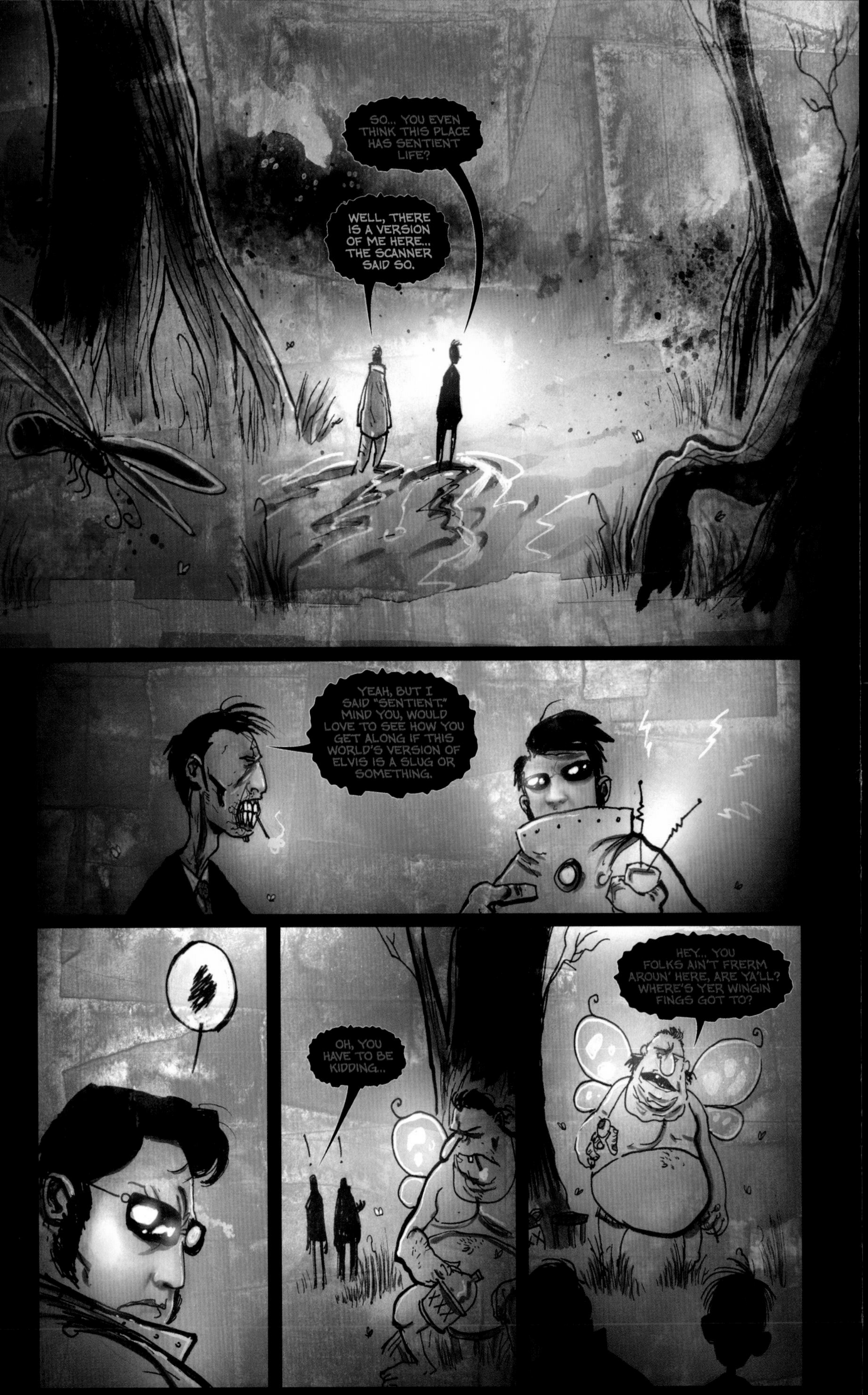
SO... YOU EVEN THINK THIS PLACE HAS SENTIENT LIFE?
WELL, THERE IS A VERSION OF ME HERE... THE SCANNER SAID SO.
YEAH, BUT I SAID "SENTIENT." MIND YOU, WOULD LOVE TO SEE HOW YOU GET ALONG IF THIS WORLD'S VERSION OF ELVIS IS A SLUG OR SOMETHING.
OH, YOU HAVE TO BE KIDDING...
HEY... YOU FOLKS AIN'T FRERM AROUN' HERE, ARE YA'LL? WHERE'S YER WINGIN FINGS GOT TO?

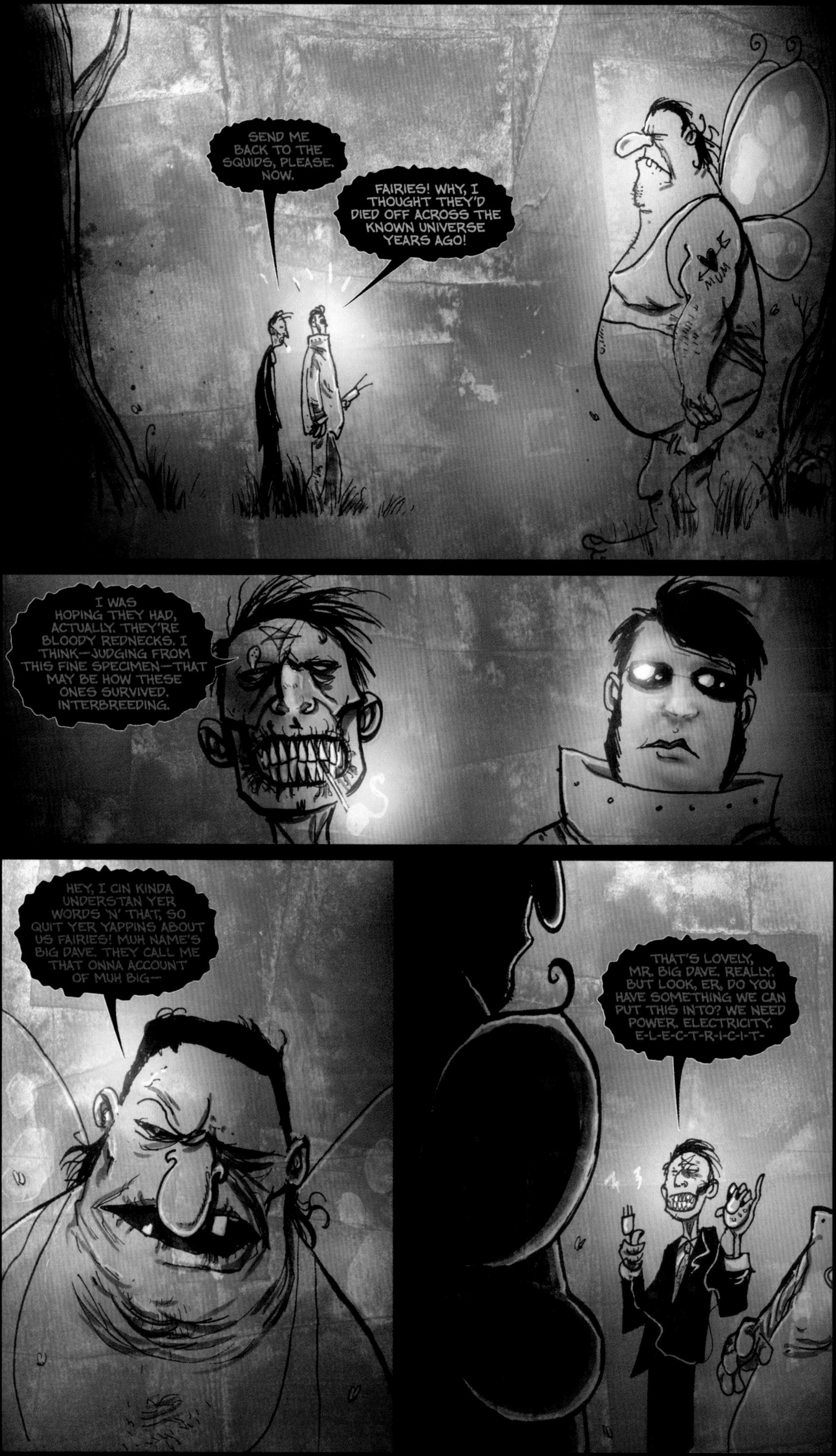
SEND ME BACK TO THE SQUIDS, PLEASE. NOW.
FAIRIES! WHY, I THOUGHT THEY'D DIED OFF ACROSS THE KNOWN UNIVERSE YEARS AGO!
MUM
I WAS HOPING THEY HAD, ACTUALLY. THEY'RE BLOODY REDNECKS. I THINK—JUDGING FROM THIS FINE SPECIMEN—THAT MAY BE HOW THESE ONES SURVIVED. INTERBREEDING.
HEY, I CIN KINDA UNDERSTAN YER WORDS 'N' THAT, SO QUIT YER YAPPINS ABOUT US FAIRIES! MUH NAME'S BIG DAVE. THEY CALL ME THAT ONNA ACCOUNT OF MUH BIG—
THAT'S LOVELY, MR. BIG DAVE. REALLY. BUT LOOK, ER, DO YOU HAVE SOMETHING WE CAN PUT THIS INTO? WE NEED POWER. ELECTRICITY. E-L-E-C-T-R-I-C-I-T-

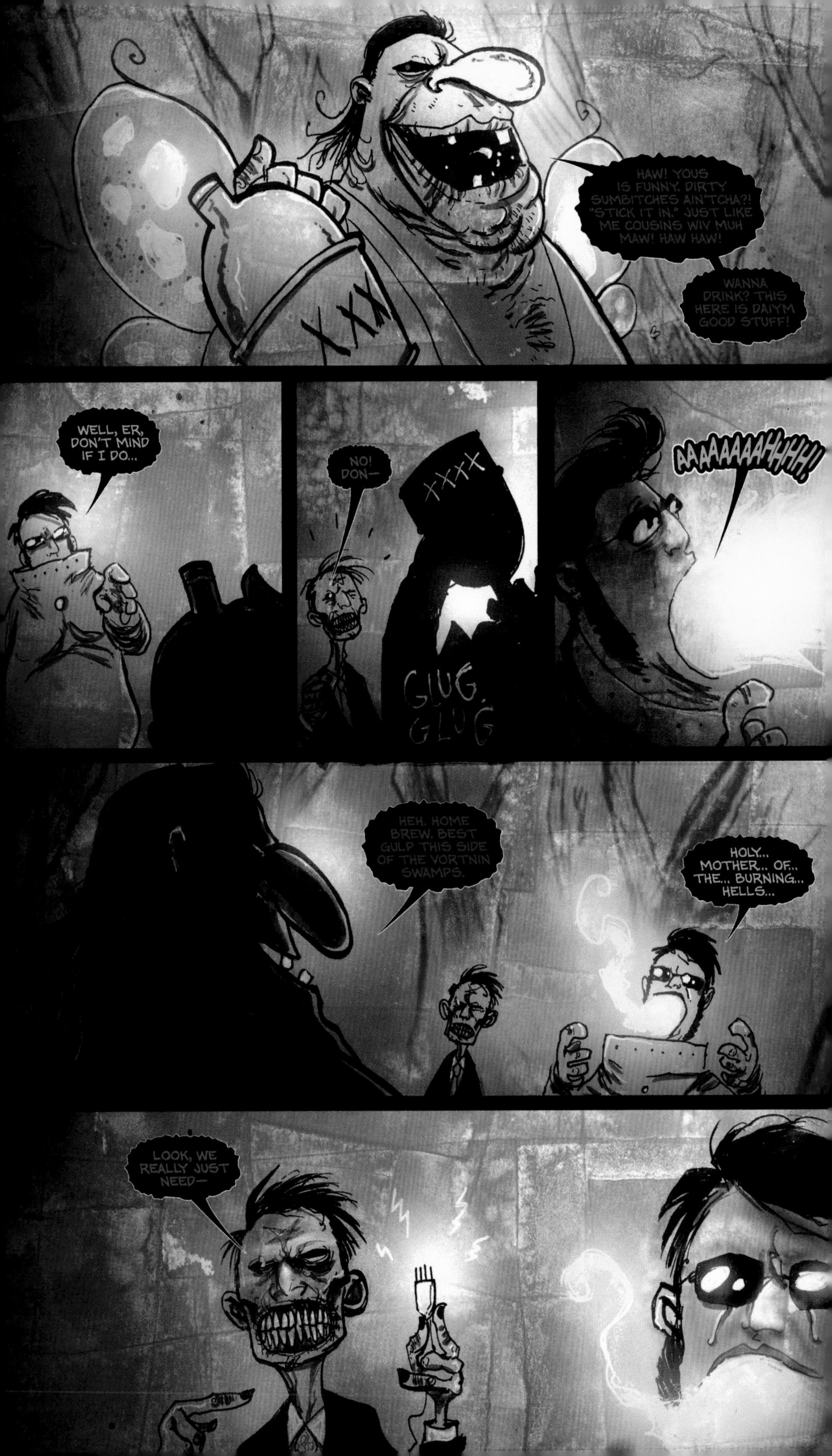
HAW! YOUS IS FUNNY. DIRTY SUMBITCHES AIN'TCHA?! "STICK IT IN," JUST LIKE ME COUSINS WIV MUH MAW! HAW HAW!
WANNA DRINK? THIS HERE IS DAIYM GOOD STUFF!
WELL, ER, DON'T MIND IF I DO...
NO! DON—
XXXX
GLUG GLUG
AAAAAAAAHHHH!
HEH. HOME BREW. BEST GULP THIS SIDE OF THE VORTNIN SWAMPS.
HOLY... MOTHER... OF... THE... BURNING... HELLS...
LOOK, WE REALLY JUST NEED—

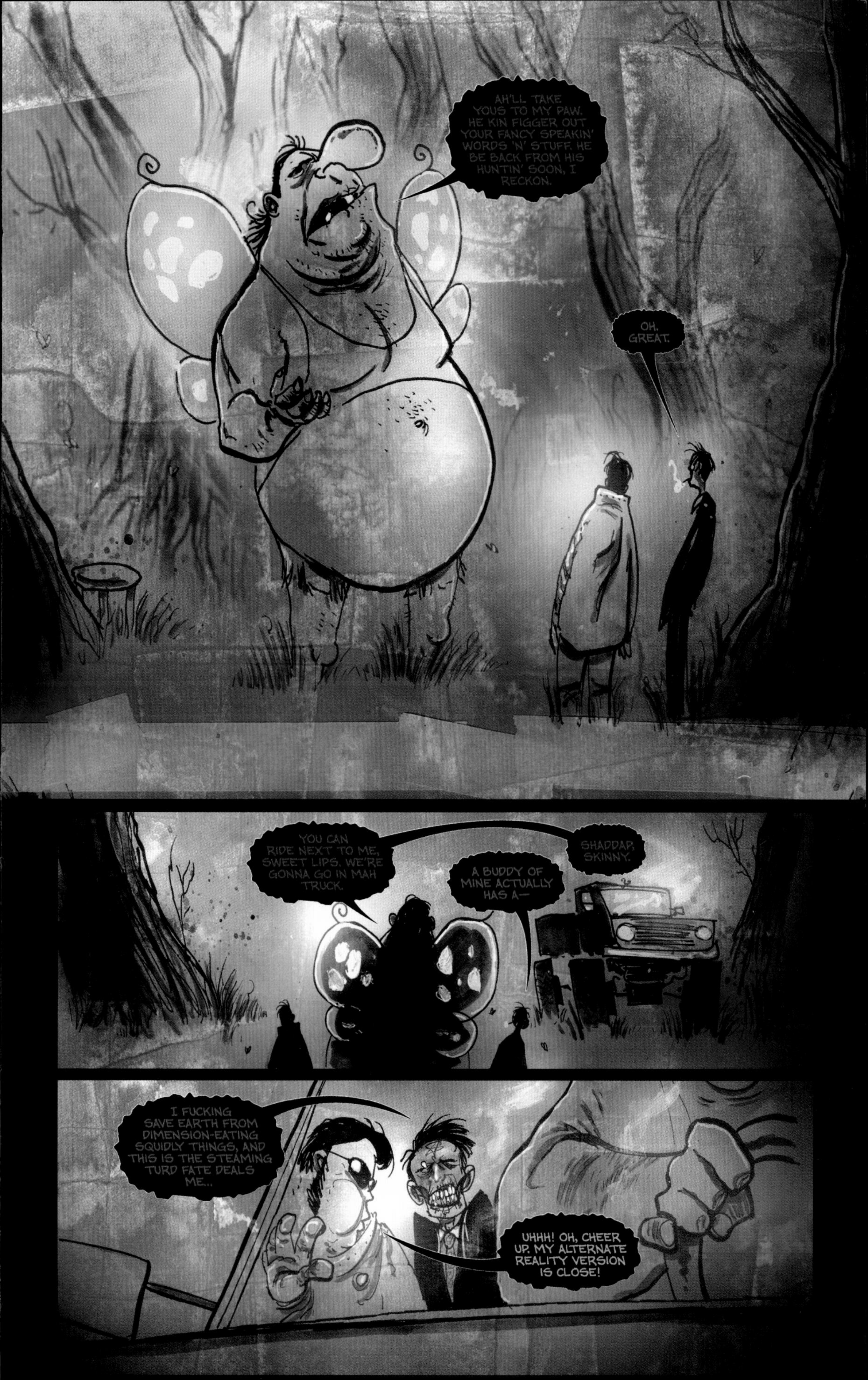
AH'LL TAKE YOUS TO MY PAW. HE KIN FIGGER OUT YOUR FANCY SPEAKIN' WORDS 'N' STUFF. HE BE BACK FROM HIS HUNTIN' SOON, I RECKON.
OH. GREAT.
YOU CAN RIDE NEXT TO ME, SWEET LIPS. WE'RE GONNA GO IN MAH TRUCK.
A BUDDY OF MINE ACTUALLY HAS A—
SHADDAP, SKINNY.
I FUCKING SAVE EARTH FROM DIMENSION-EATING SQUIDLY THINGS, AND THIS IS THE STEAMING TURD FATE DEALS ME...
UHHH! OH, CHEER UP. MY ALTERNATE REALITY VERSION IS CLOSE!

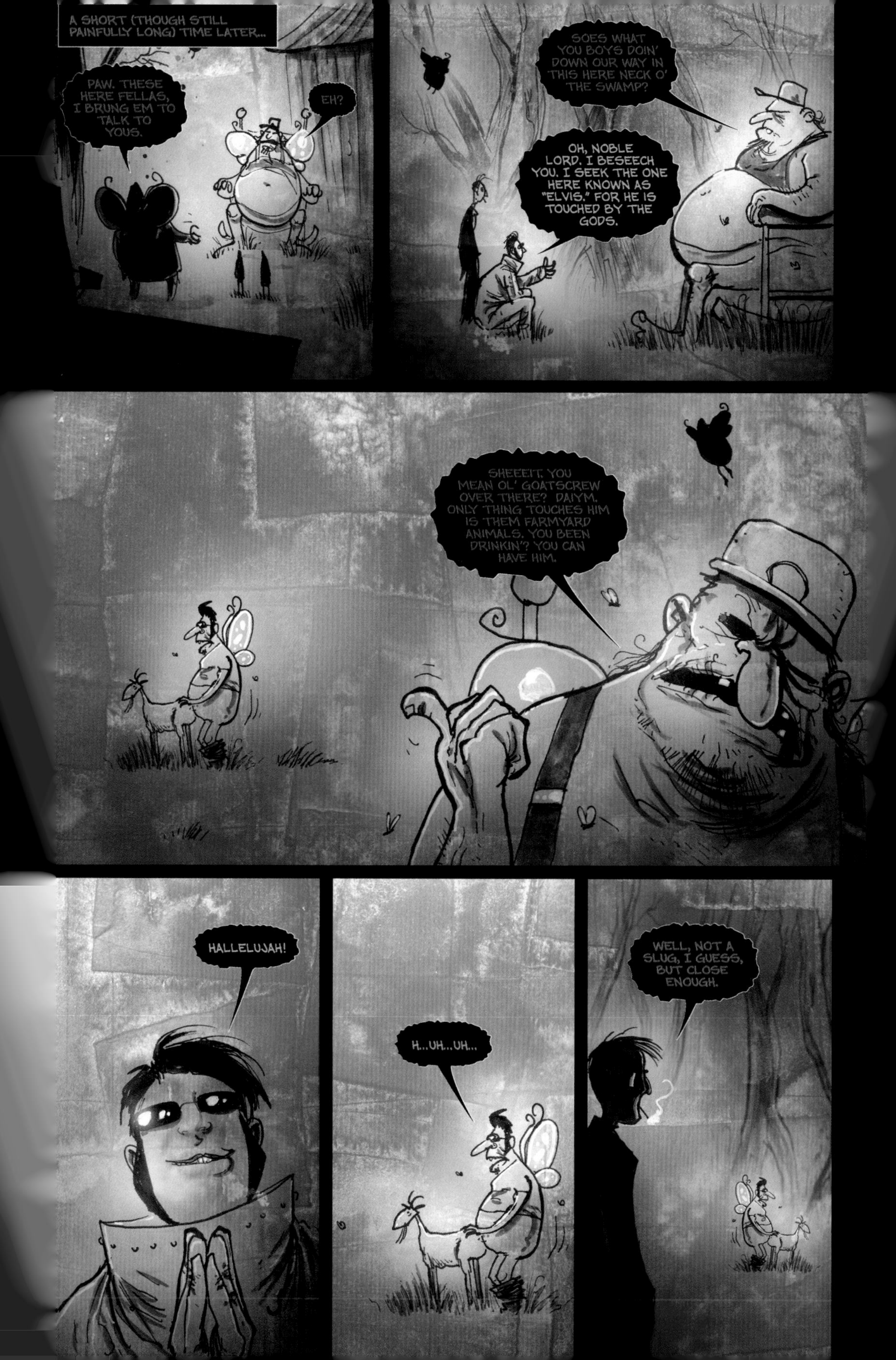
A SHORT (THOUGH STILL PAINFULLY LONG) TIME LATER...
PAW. THESE HERE FELLAS, I BRUNG EM TO TALK TO YOUS.
EH?
SOES WHAT YOU BOYS DOIN' DOWN OUR WAY IN THIS HERE NECK O' THE SWAMP?
OH, NOBLE LORD. I BESEECH YOU. I SEEK THE ONE HERE KNOWN AS "ELVIS." FOR HE IS TOUCHED BY THE GODS.
SHEEEIT. YOU MEAN OL' GOATSCREW OVER THERE? DAIYM. ONLY THING TOUCHES HIM IS THEM FARMYARD ANIMALS. YOU BEEN DRINKIN'? YOU CAN HAVE HIM.
HALLELUJAH!
H...UH...UH...
WELL, NOT A SLUG, I GUESS, BUT CLOSE ENOUGH.

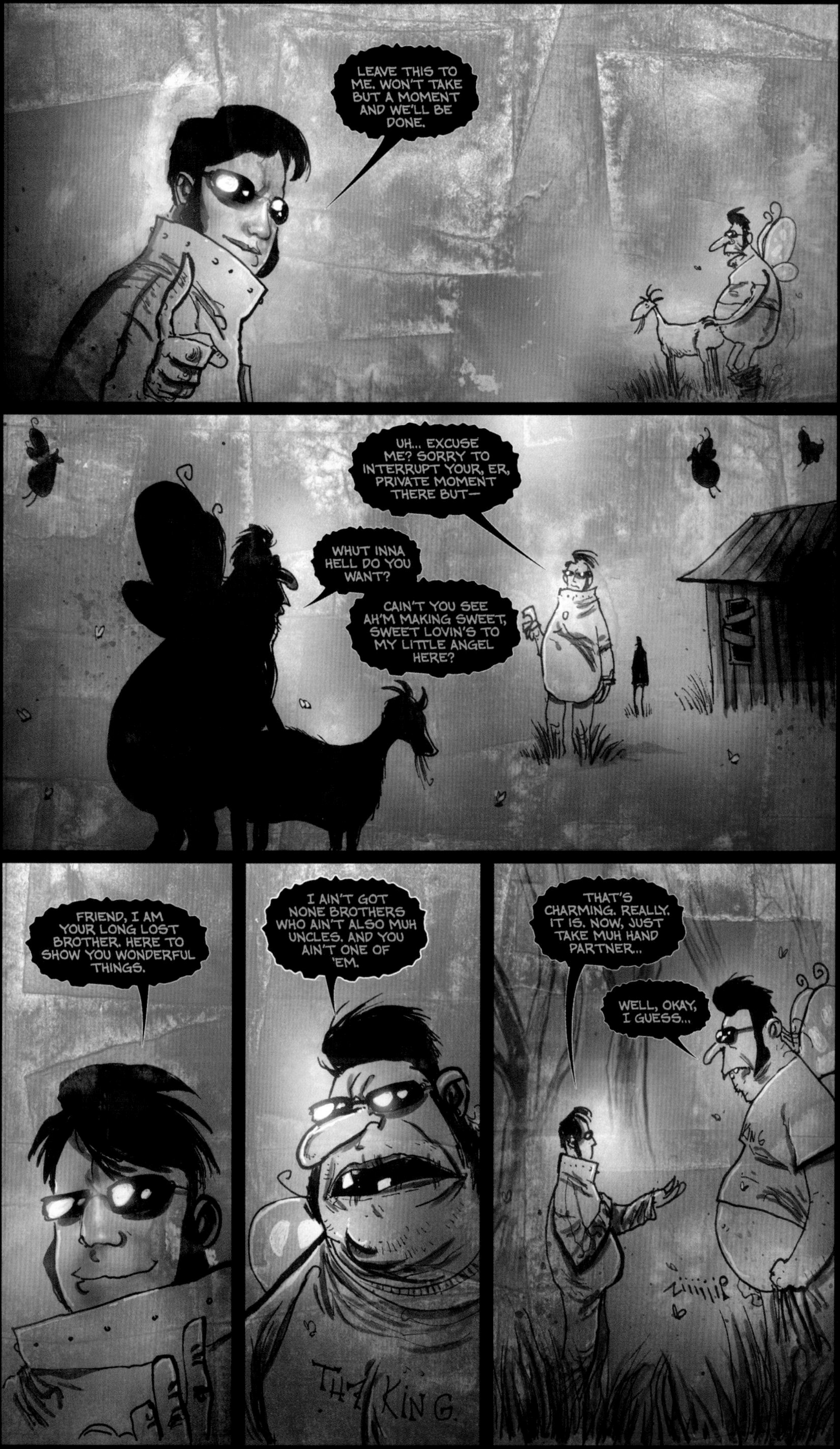
LEAVE THIS TO ME. WON'T TAKE BUT A MOMENT AND WE'LL BE DONE.
UH... EXCUSE ME? SORRY TO INTERRUPT YOUR, ER, PRIVATE MOMENT THERE BUT—
WHUT INNA HELL DO YOU WANT?
CAIN'T YOU SEE AH'M MAKING SWEET, SWEET LOVIN'S TO MY LITTLE ANGEL HERE?
FRIEND, I AM YOUR LONG LOST BROTHER. HERE TO SHOW YOU WONDERFUL THINGS.
I AIN'T GOT NONE BROTHERS WHO AIN'T ALSO MUH UNCLES. AND YOU AIN'T ONE OF 'EM.
THE KING
THAT'S CHARMING. REALLY. IT IS. NOW, JUST TAKE MUH HAND PARTNER...
WELL, OKAY, I GUESS...
KING
ZIIIIIP

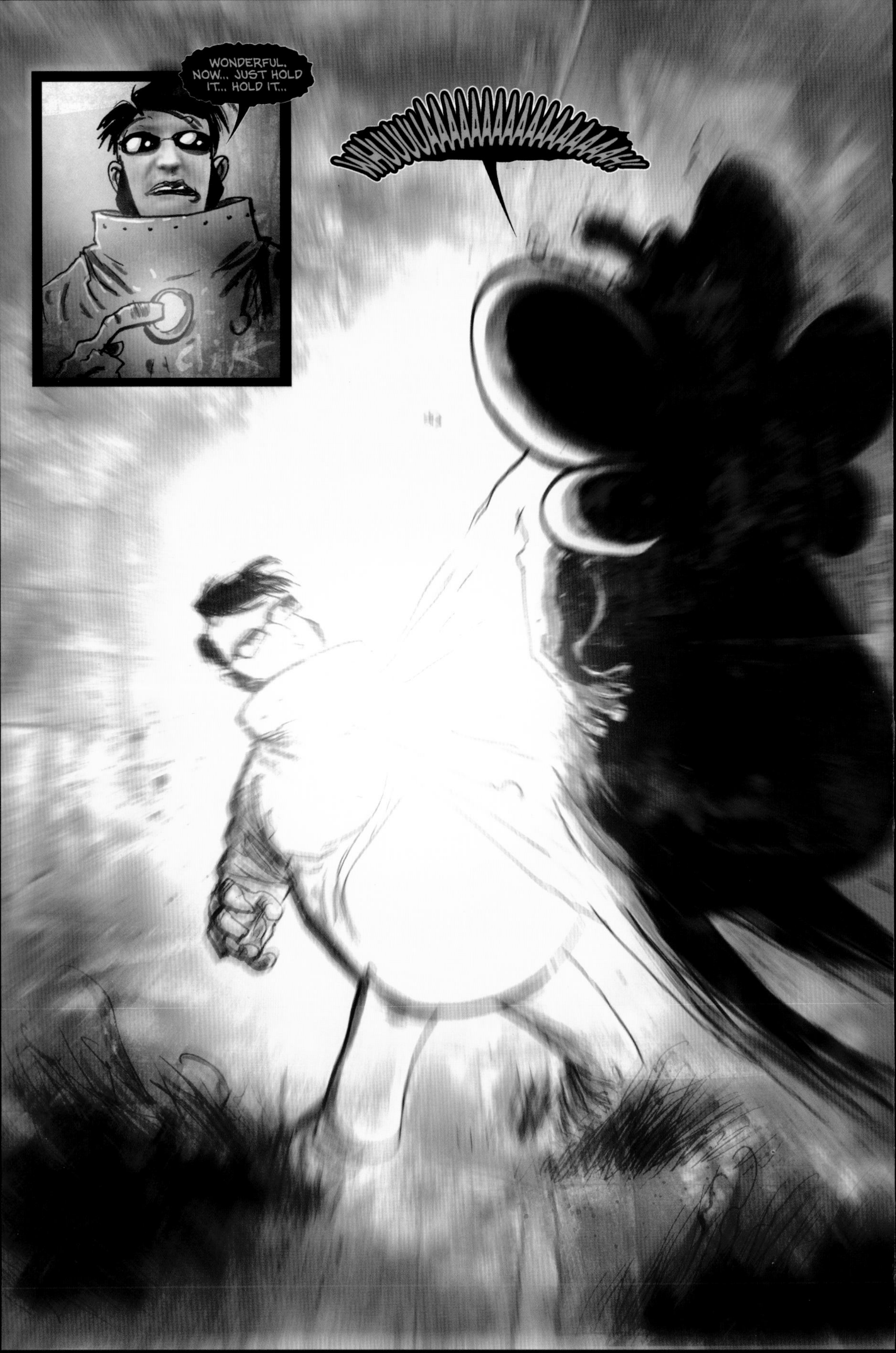
WONDERFUL. NOW... JUST HOLD IT... HOLD IT...
WHUUUAAAAAAAAAAAAAAAH!

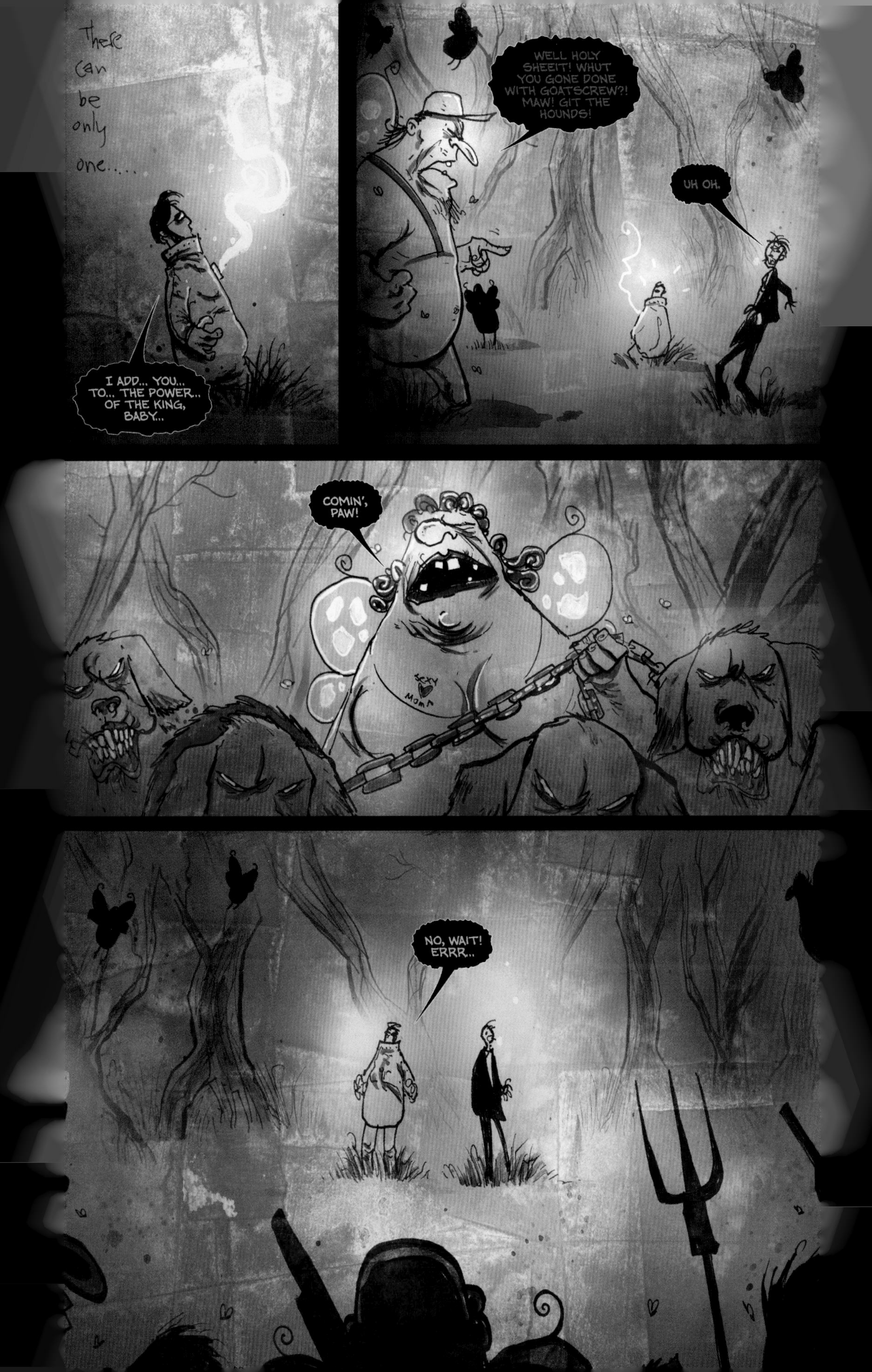

There can be only one.....
I ADD... YOU... TO... THE POWER... OF THE KING, BABY...
WELL HOLY SHEEIT! WHUT YOU GONE DONE WITH GOATSCREW?! MAW! GIT THE HOUNDS!
UH OH.
COMIN', PAW!
SEXY MOM
NO, WAIT! ERRR...

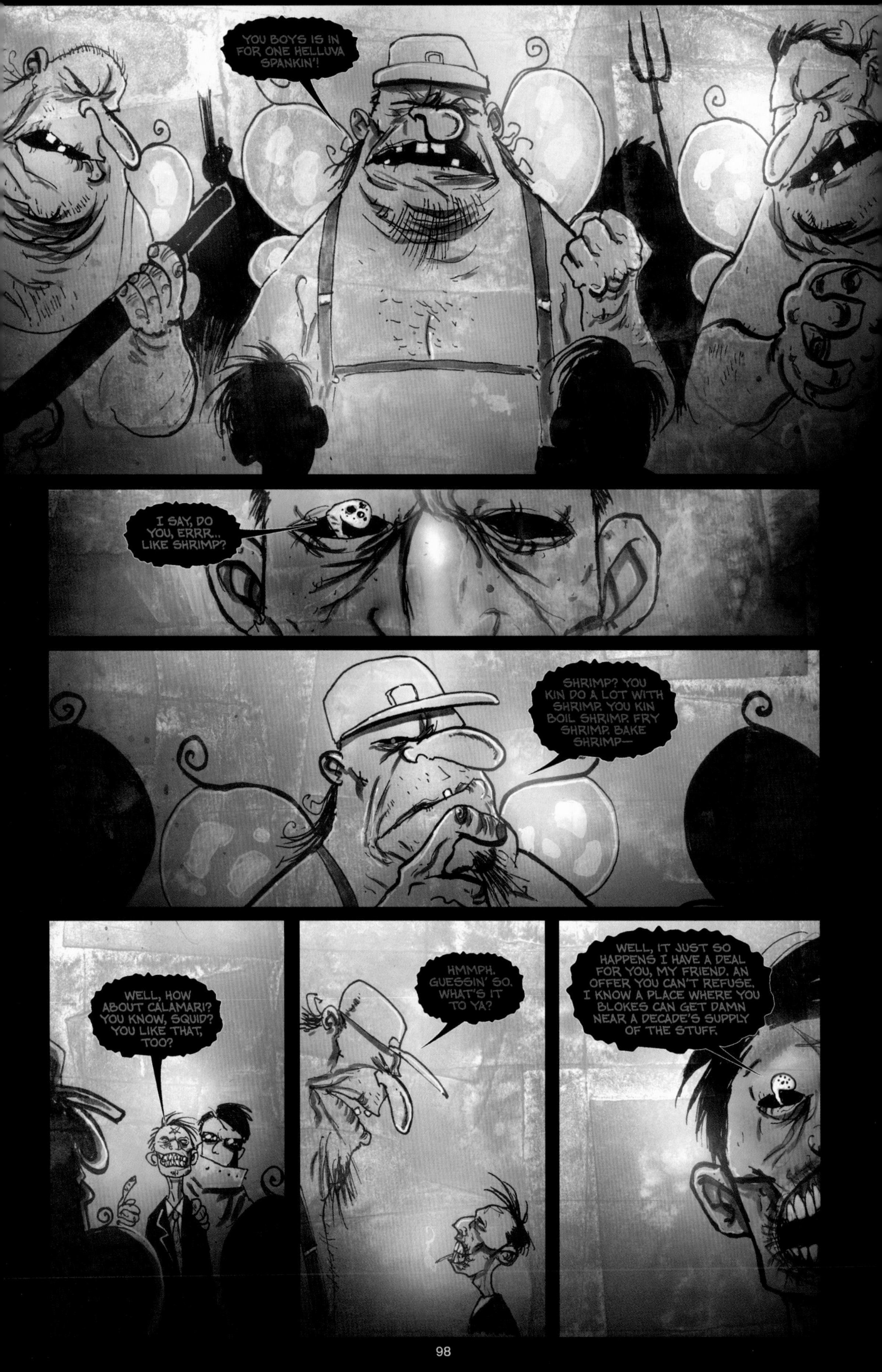
YOU BOYS IS IN FOR ONE HELLUVA SPANKIN'!
I SAY, DO YOU, ERRR... LIKE SHRIMP?
SHRIMP? YOU KIN DO A LOT WITH SHRIMP. YOU KIN BOIL SHRIMP. FRY SHRIMP. BAKE SHRIMP—
WELL, HOW ABOUT CALAMARI? YOU KNOW, SQUID? YOU LIKE THAT, TOO?
HMMPH. GUESSIN' SO. WHAT'S IT TO YA?
WELL, IT JUST SO HAPPENS I HAVE A DEAL FOR YOU, MY FRIEND. AN OFFER YOU CAN'T REFUSE. I KNOW A PLACE WHERE YOU BLOKES CAN GET DAMN NEAR A DECADE'S SUPPLY OF THE STUFF.

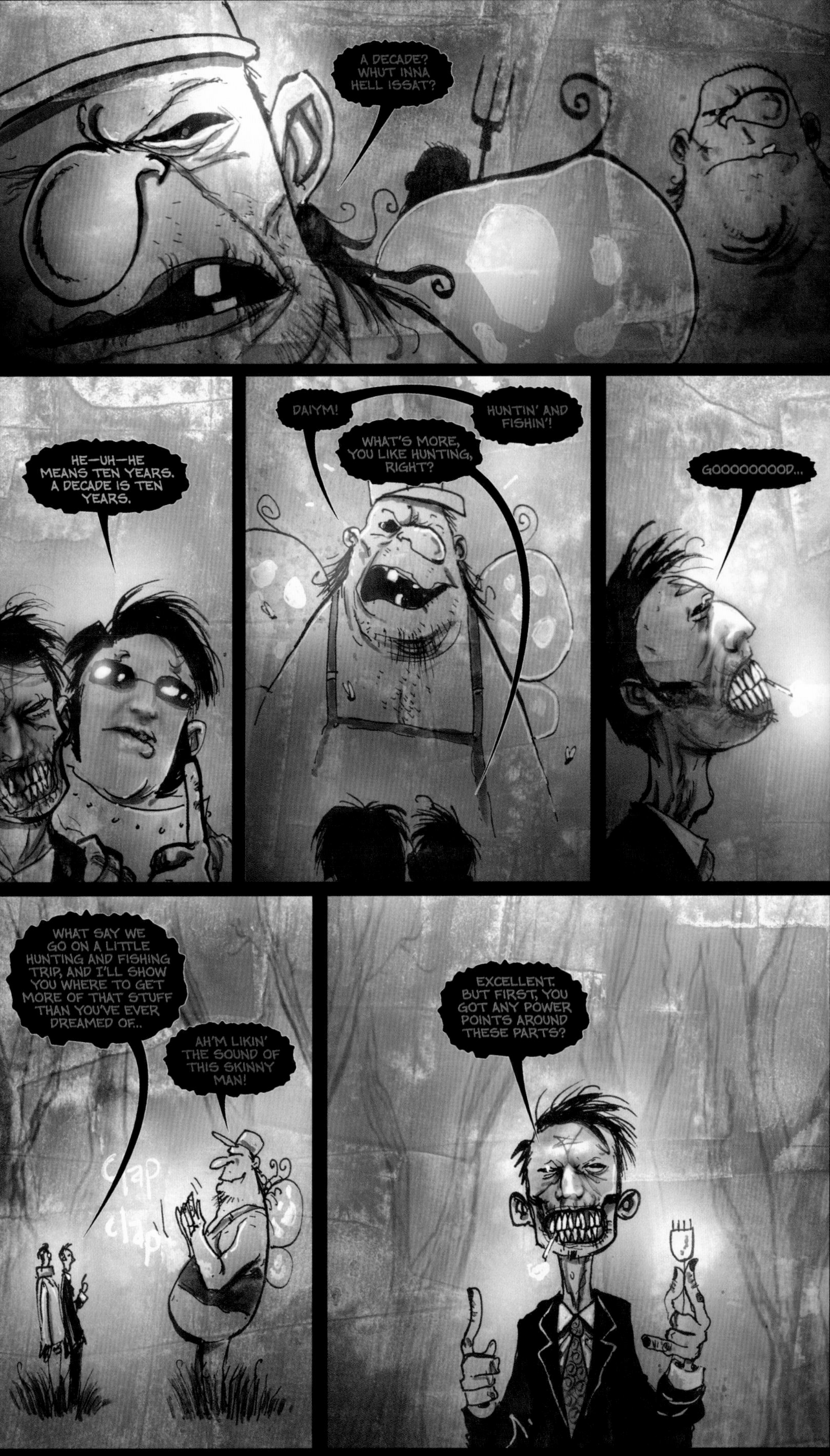
A DECADE? WHUT INNA HELL ISSAT?
HE—UH—HE MEANS TEN YEARS. A DECADE IS TEN YEARS.
DAIYM!
WHAT'S MORE, YOU LIKE HUNTING, RIGHT?
HUNTIN' AND FISHIN'!
GOOOOOOOOD...
WHAT SAY WE GO ON A LITTLE HUNTING AND FISHING TRIP, AND I'LL SHOW YOU WHERE TO GET MORE OF THAT STUFF THAN YOU'VE EVER DREAMED OF...
AH'M LIKIN' THE SOUND OF THIS SKINNY MAN!
clap clap!
EXCELLENT. BUT FIRST, YOU GOT ANY POWER POINTS AROUND THESE PARTS?

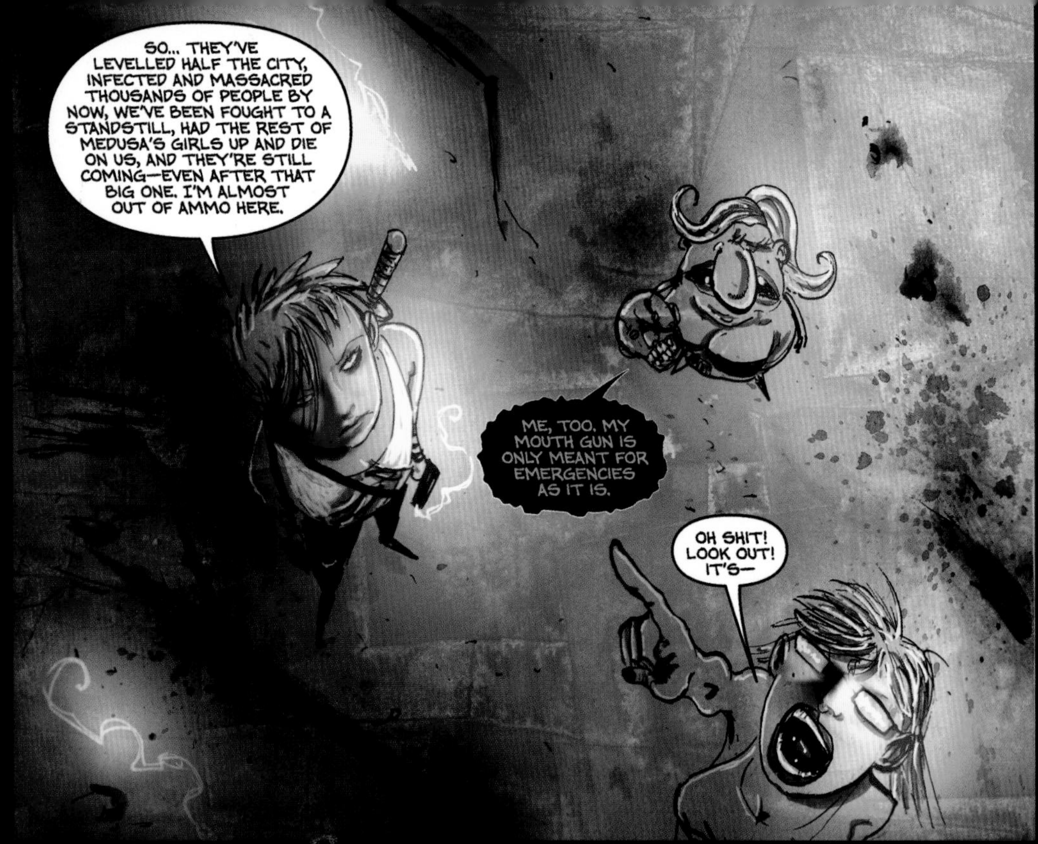
SO... THEY'VE LEVELLED HALF THE CITY, INFECTED AND MASSACRED THOUSANDS OF PEOPLE BY NOW, WE'VE BEEN FOUGHT TO A STANDSTILL, HAD THE REST OF MEDUSA'S GIRLS UP AND DIE ON US, AND THEY'RE STILL COMING—EVEN AFTER THAT BIG ONE. I'M ALMOST OUT OF AMMO HERE.
ME, TOO. MY MOUTH GUN IS ONLY MEANT FOR EMERGENCIES AS IT IS.
OH SHIT! LOOK OUT! IT'S—

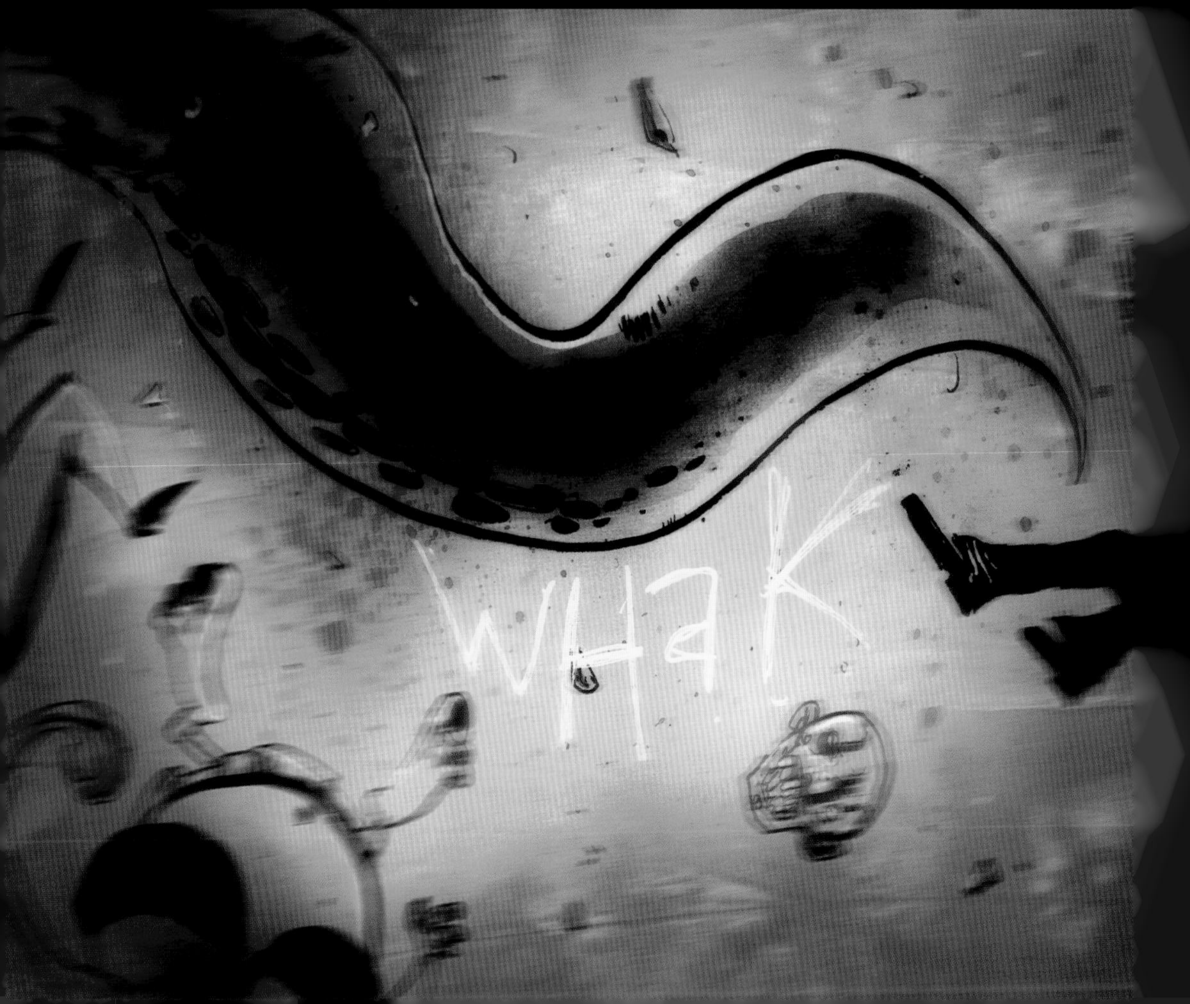
WHAK

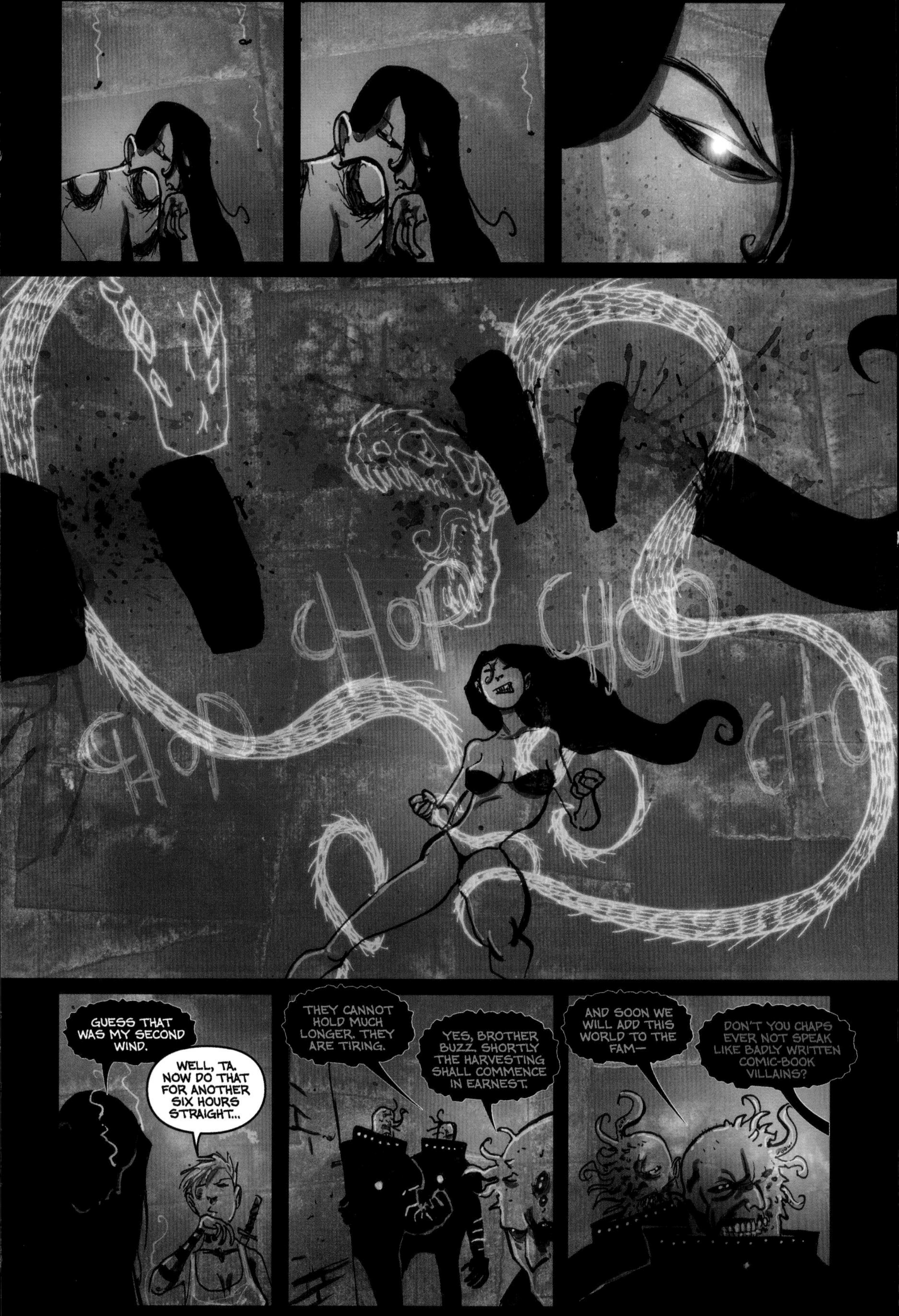
CHOP
CHOP
CHOP
CHOP
GUESS THAT WAS MY SECOND WIND.
WELL, TA. NOW DO THAT FOR ANOTHER SIX HOURS STRAIGHT...
THEY CANNOT HOLD MUCH LONGER. THEY ARE TIRING.
YES, BROTHER BUZZ. SHORTLY THE HARVESTING SHALL COMMENCE IN EARNEST.
AND SOON WE WILL ADD THIS WORLD TO THE FAM—
DON'T YOU CHAPS EVER NOT SPEAK LIKE BADLY WRITTEN COMIC-BOOK VILLAINS?

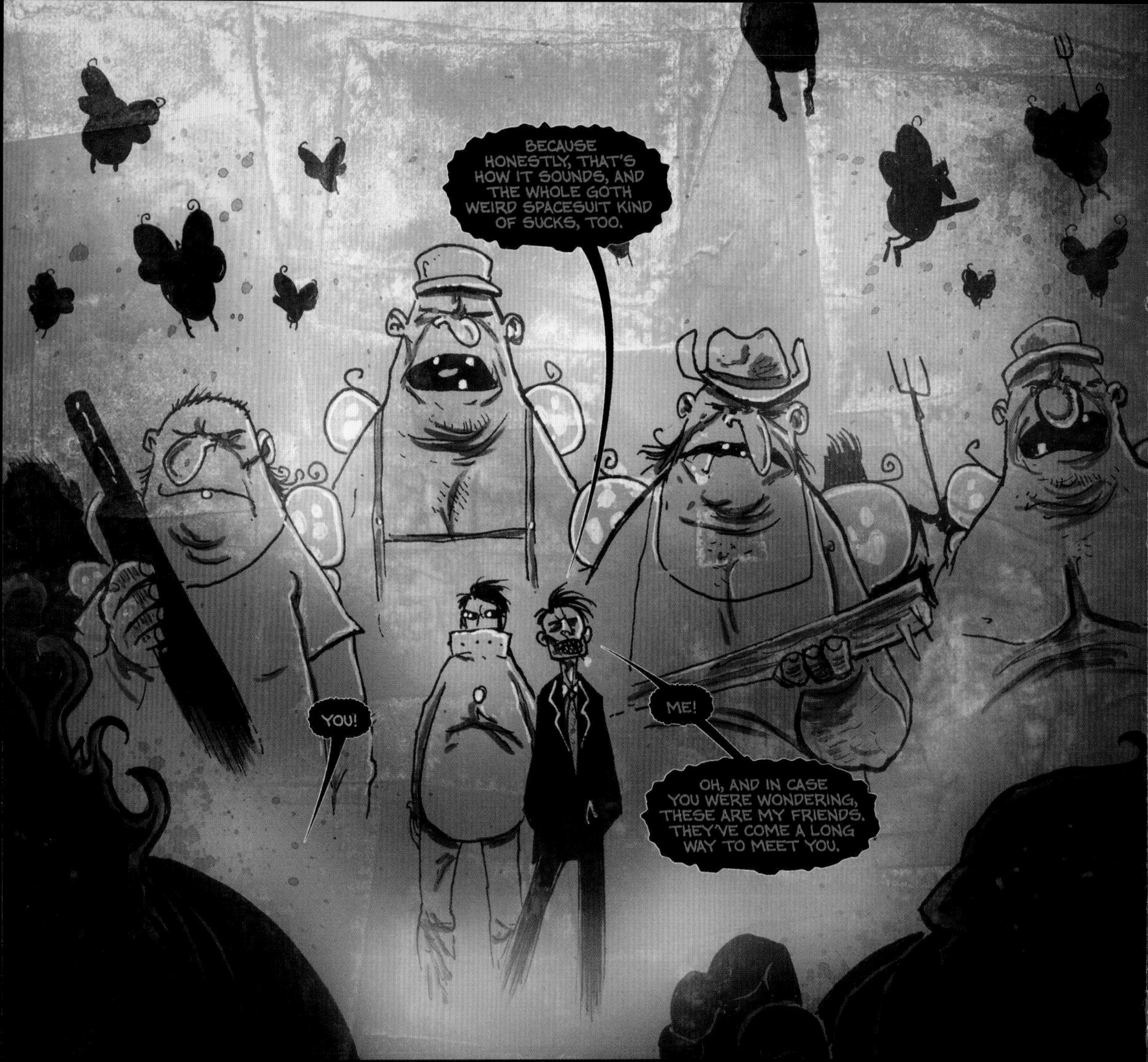
BECAUSE HONESTLY, THAT'S HOW IT SOUNDS, AND THE WHOLE GOTH WEIRD SPACESUIT KIND OF SUCKS, TOO.
YOU!
ME!
OH, AND IN CASE YOU WERE WONDERING, THESE ARE MY FRIENDS. THEY'VE COME A LONG WAY TO MEET YOU.

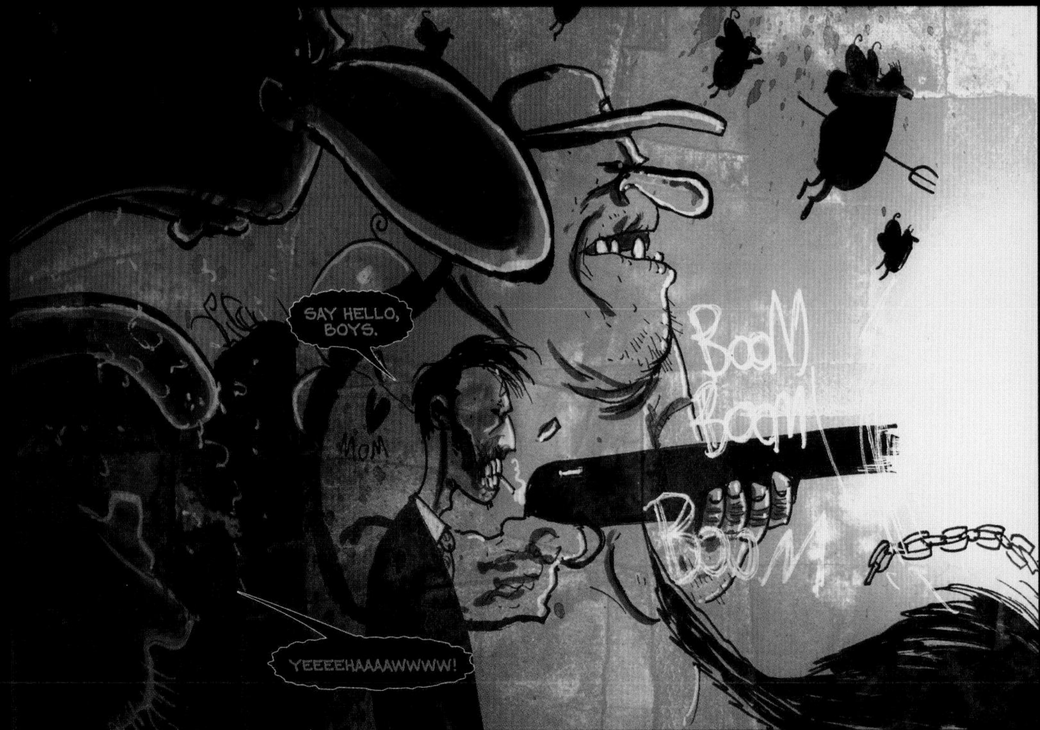
SAY HELLO, BOYS.
MOM
BOOM
BOOM
BOOM
YEEEEHAAAAWWWW!

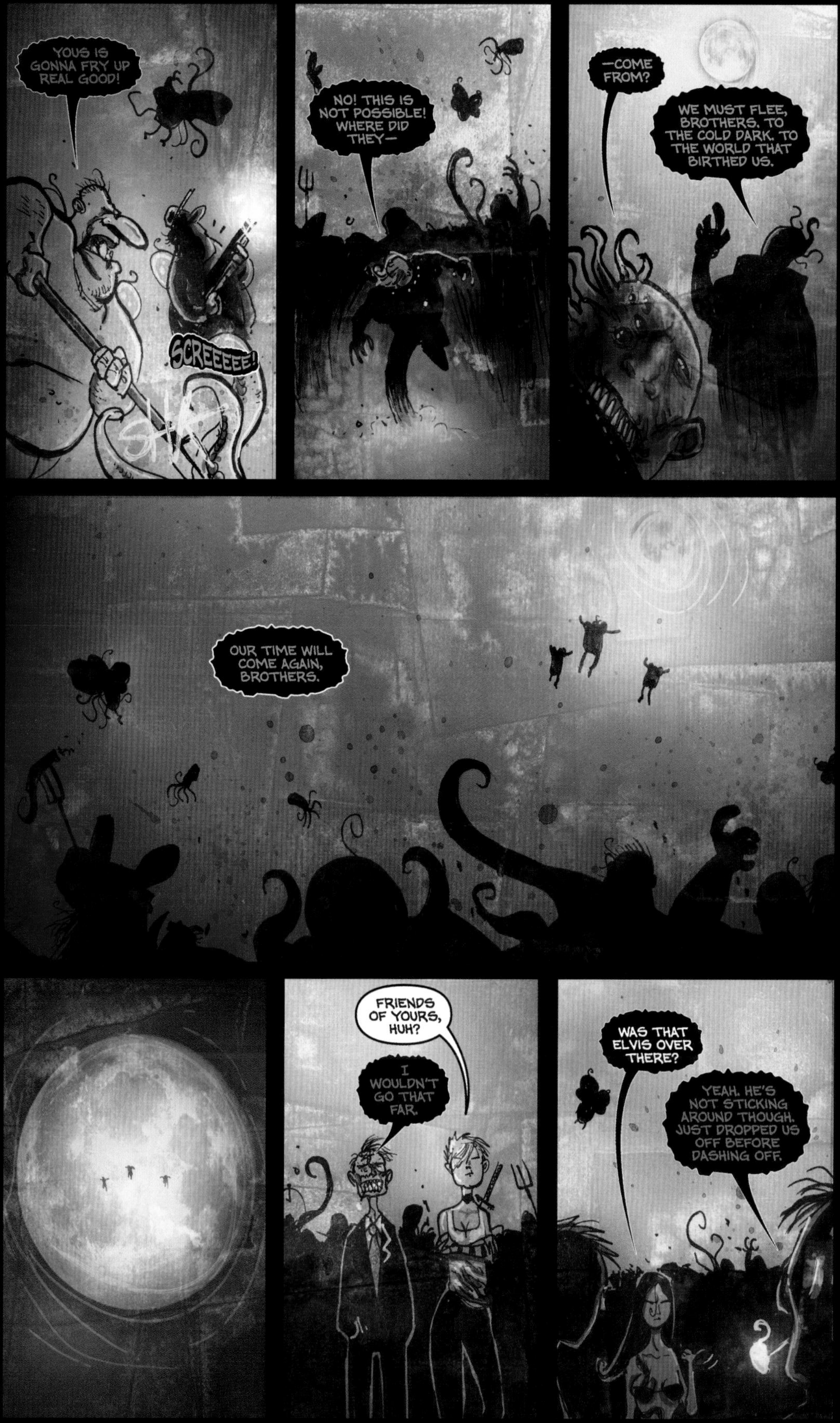
YOUS IS GONNA FRY UP REAL GOOD!
SCREEEEE!
NO! THIS IS NOT POSSIBLE! WHERE DID THEY—
—COME FROM?
WE MUST FLEE, BROTHERS, TO THE COLD DARK, TO THE WORLD THAT BIRTHED US.
OUR TIME WILL COME AGAIN, BROTHERS.
FRIENDS OF YOURS, HUH?
I WOULDN'T GO THAT FAR.
WAS THAT ELVIS OVER THERE?
YEAH. HE'S NOT STICKING AROUND THOUGH. JUST DROPPED US OFF BEFORE DASHING OFF.

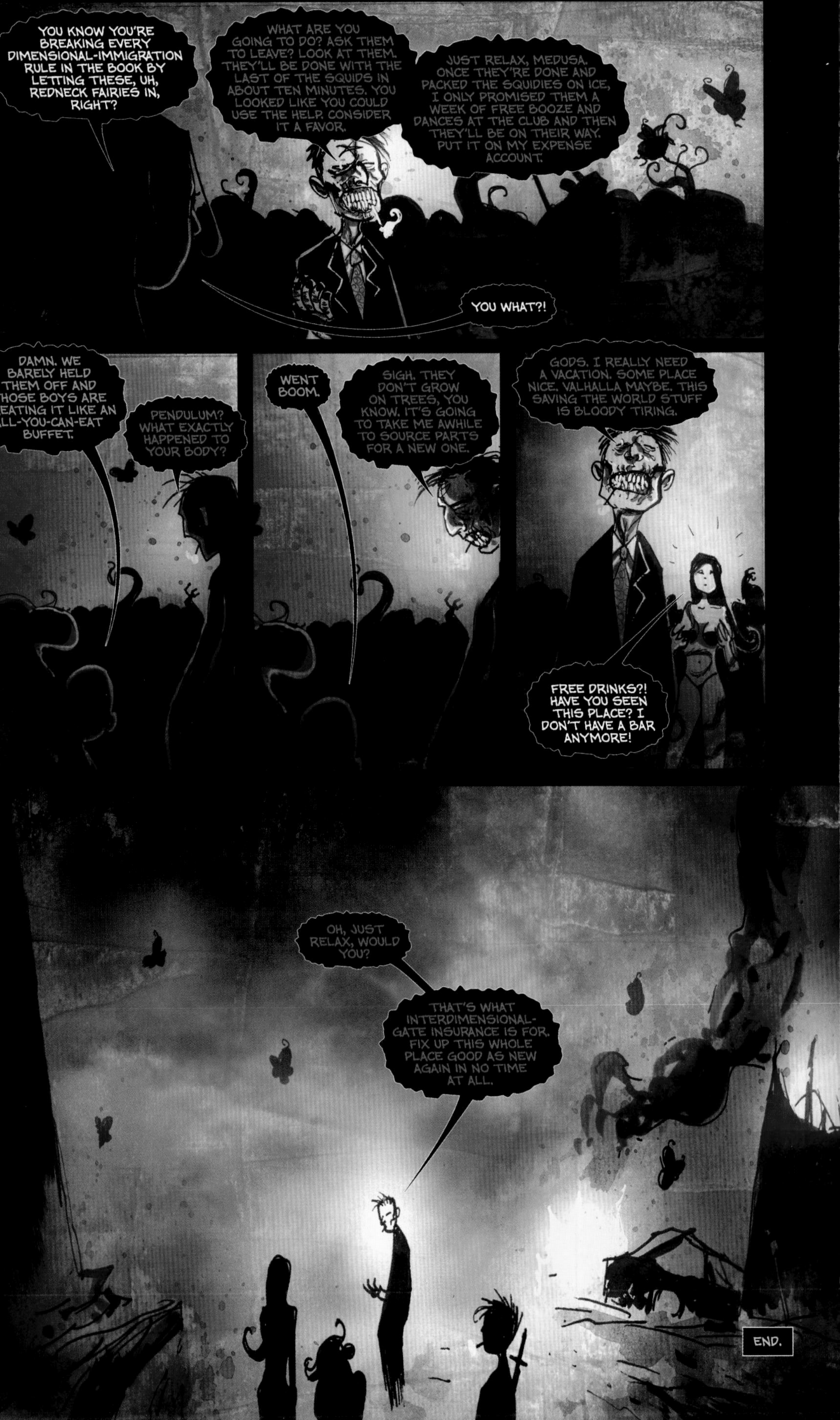
YOU KNOW YOU'RE BREAKING EVERY DIMENSIONAL-IMMIGRATION RULE IN THE BOOK BY LETTING THESE, UH, REDNECK FAIRIES IN, RIGHT?
WHAT ARE YOU GOING TO DO? ASK THEM TO LEAVE? LOOK AT THEM. THEY'LL BE DONE WITH THE LAST OF THE SQUIDS IN ABOUT TEN MINUTES. YOU LOOKED LIKE YOU COULD USE THE HELP. CONSIDER IT A FAVOR.
JUST RELAX, MEDUSA. ONCE THEY'RE DONE AND PACKED THE SQUIDIES ON ICE, I ONLY PROMISED THEM A WEEK OF FREE BOOZE AND DANCES AT THE CLUB AND THEN THEY'LL BE ON THEIR WAY. PUT IT ON MY EXPENSE ACCOUNT.
YOU WHAT?!
DAMN. WE BARELY HELD THEM OFF AND THOSE BOYS ARE EATING IT LIKE AN ALL-YOU-CAN-EAT BUFFET.
PENDULUM? WHAT EXACTLY HAPPENED TO YOUR BODY?
WENT BOOM.
SIGH. THEY DON'T GROW ON TREES, YOU KNOW. IT'S GOING TO TAKE ME AWHILE TO SOURCE PARTS FOR A NEW ONE.
GODS. I REALLY NEED A VACATION. SOME PLACE NICE. VALHALLA MAYBE. THIS SAVING THE WORLD STUFF IS BLOODY TIRING.
FREE DRINKS?! HAVE YOU SEEN THIS PLACE? I DON'T HAVE A BAR ANYMORE!
OH, JUST RELAX, WOULD YOU?
THAT'S WHAT INTERDIMENSIONAL-GATE INSURANCE IS FOR. FIX UP THIS WHOLE PLACE GOOD AS NEW AGAIN IN NO TIME AT ALL.
END.

Art Gallery & Previous Covers

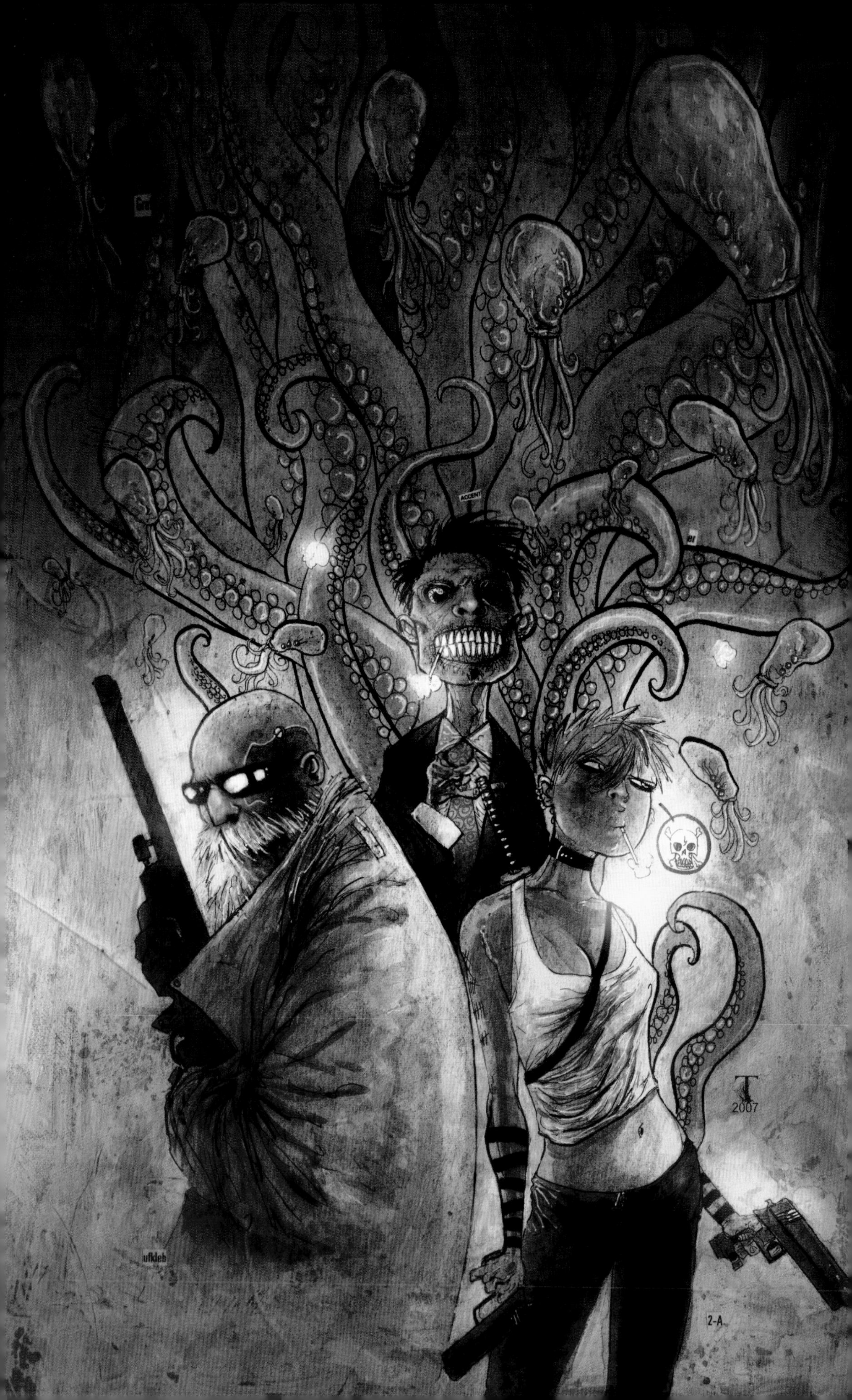
ACCENT
2007
ufkleb
2-A

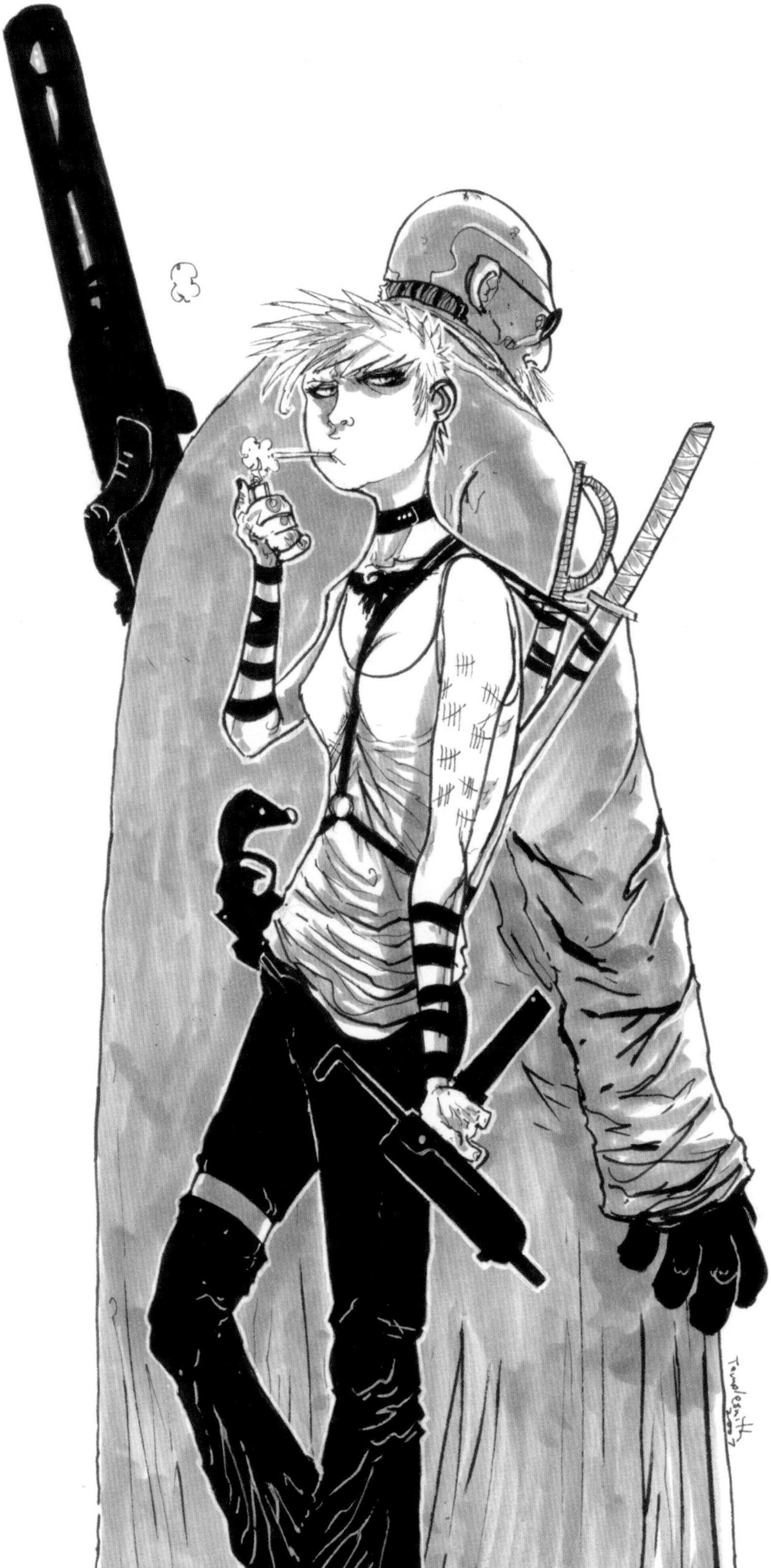

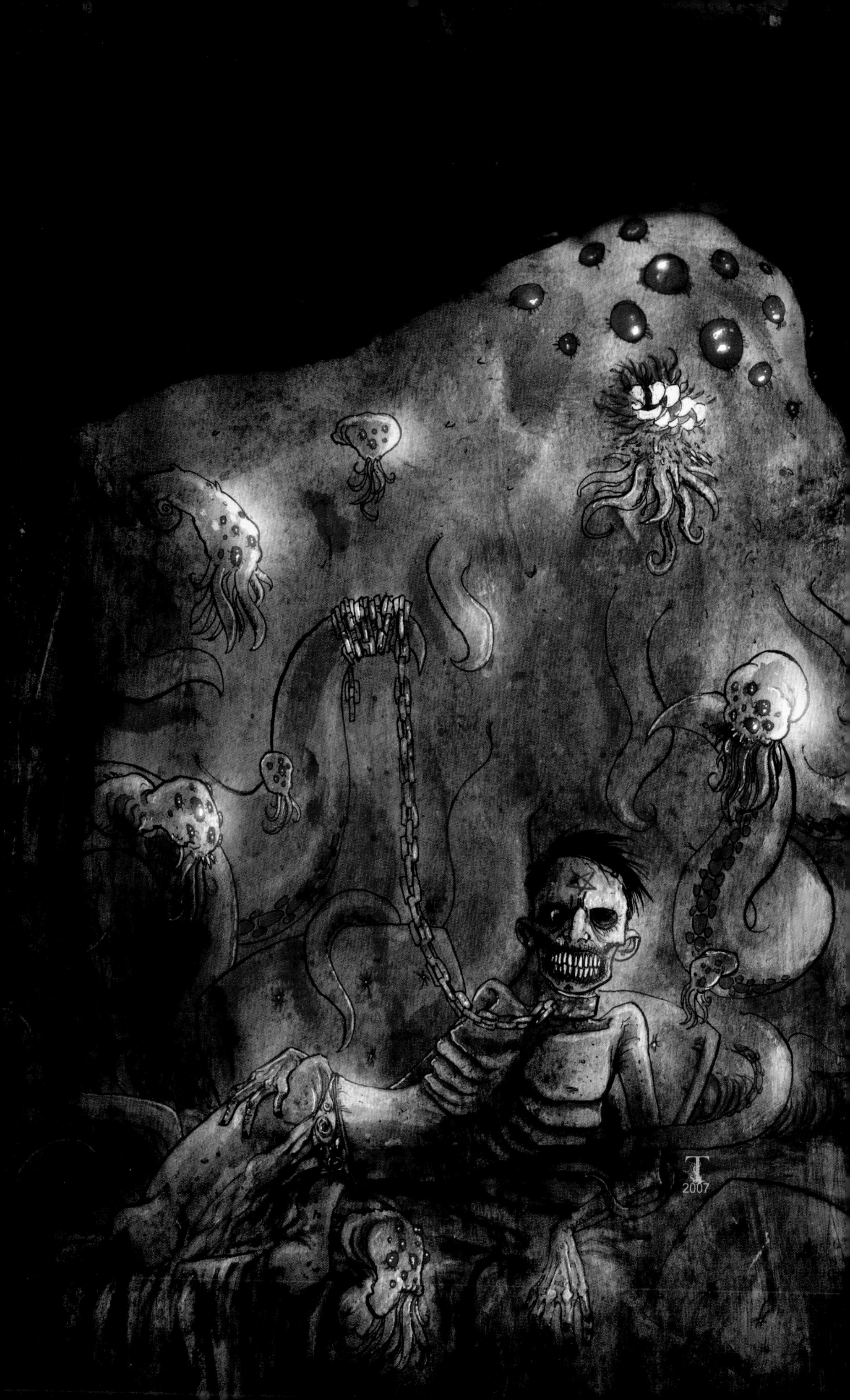
T
2007

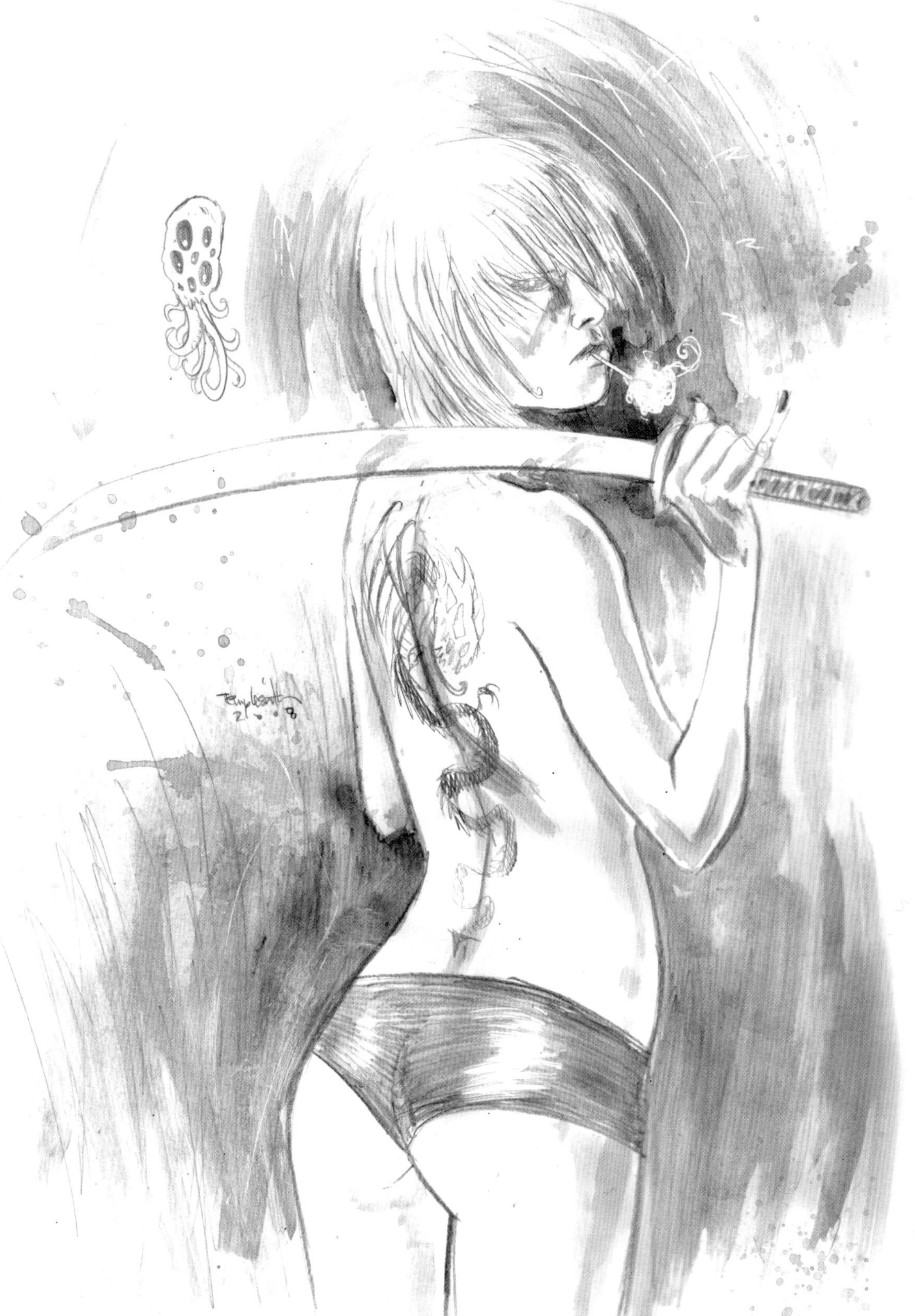

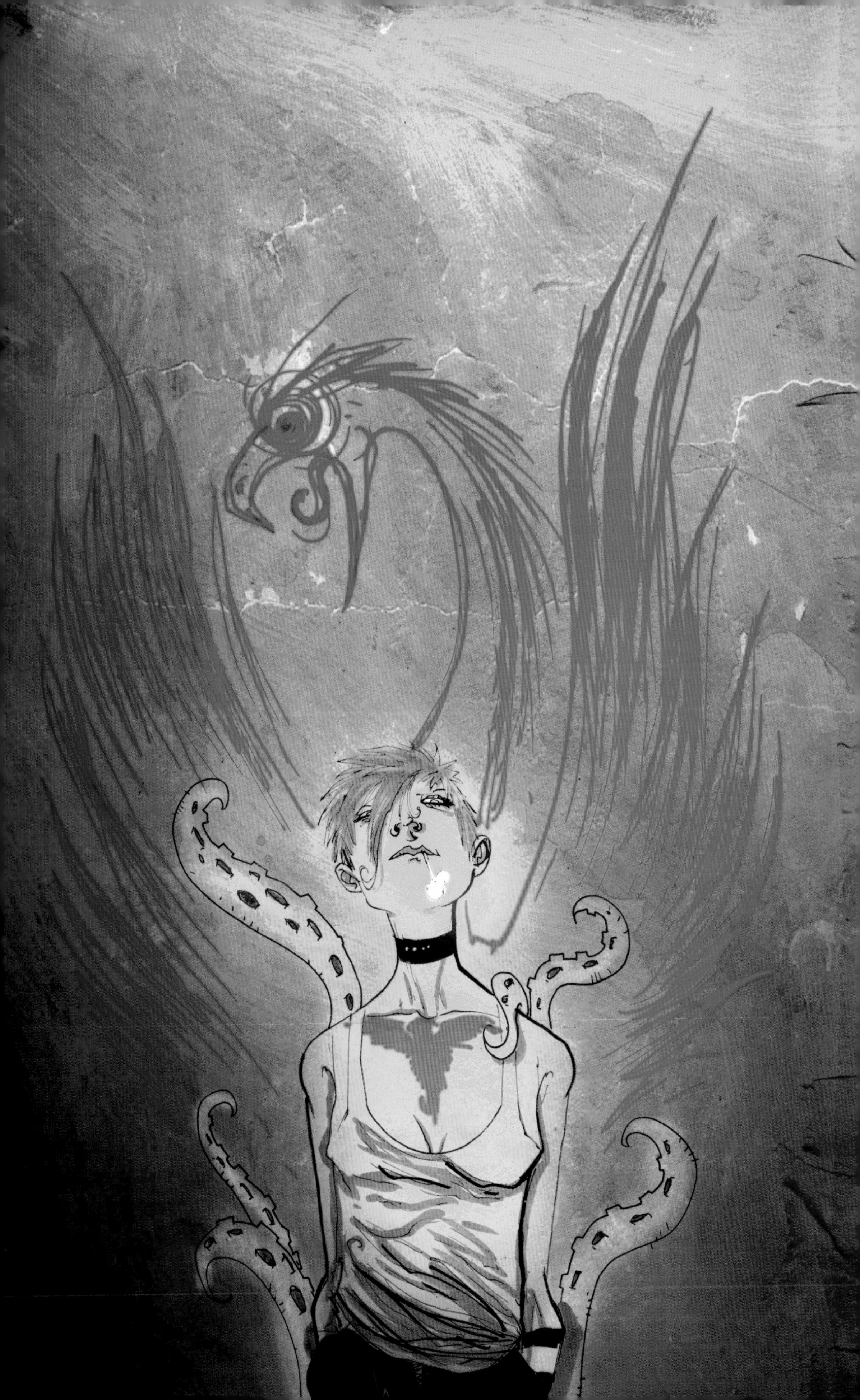

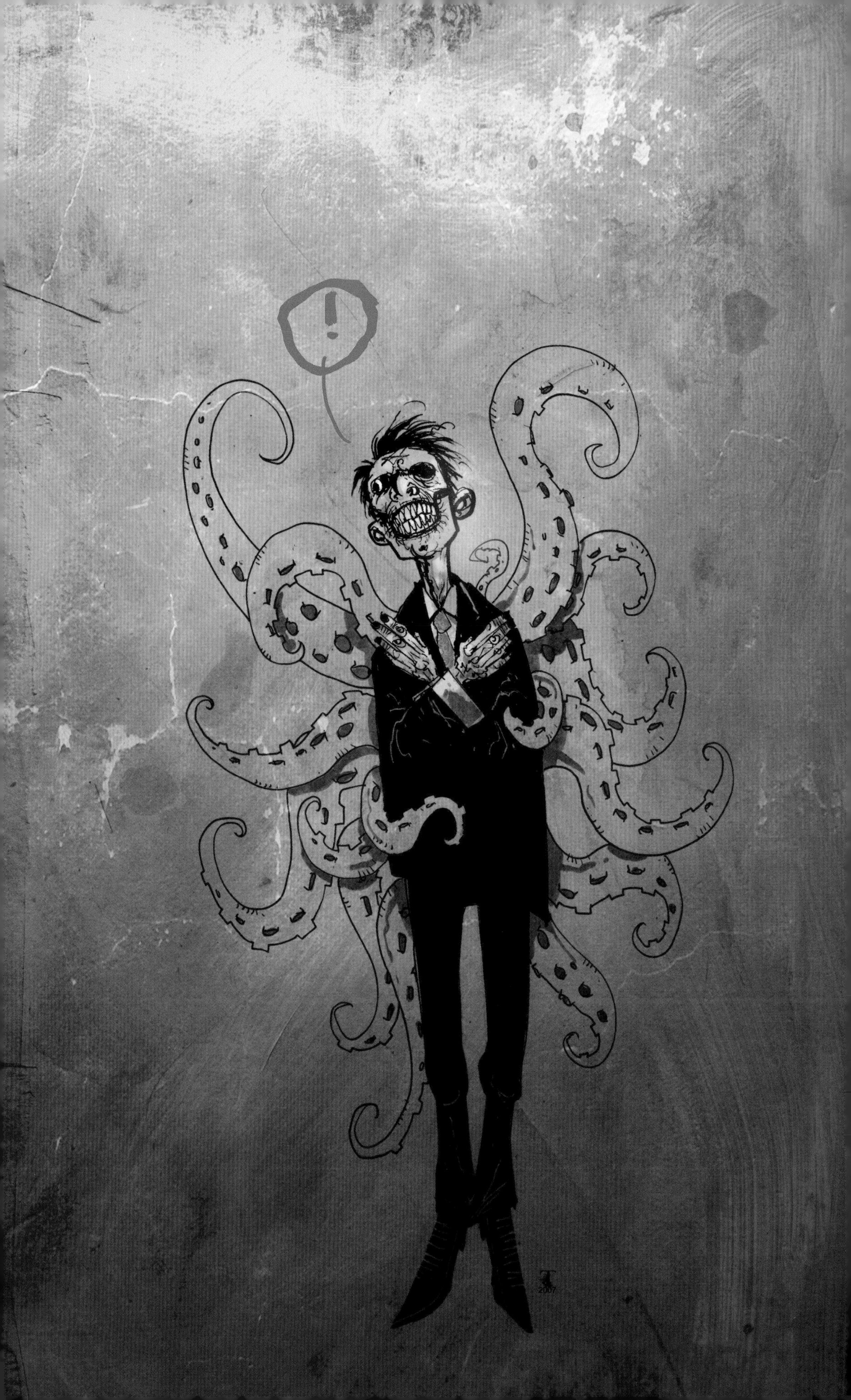
!
2007

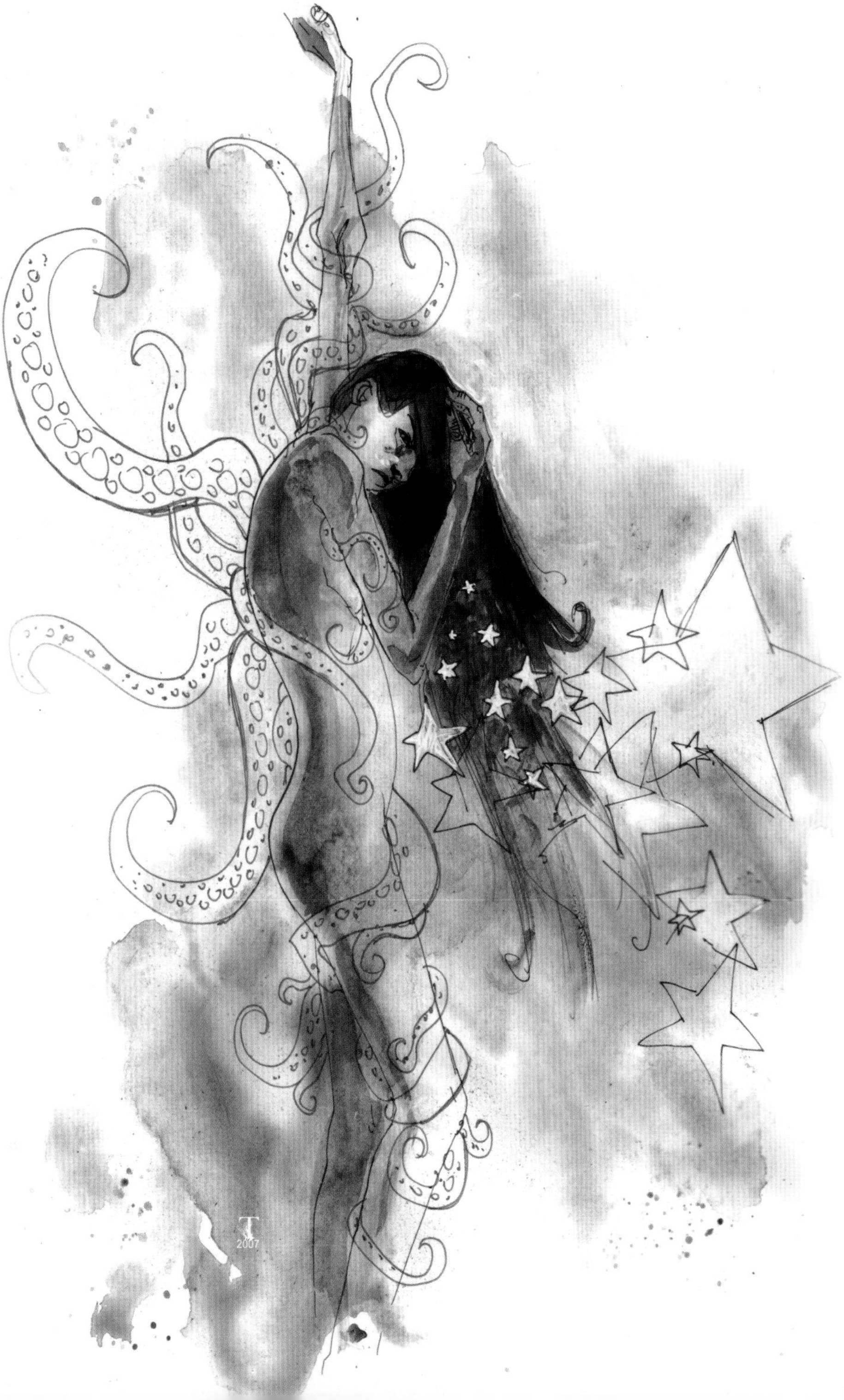

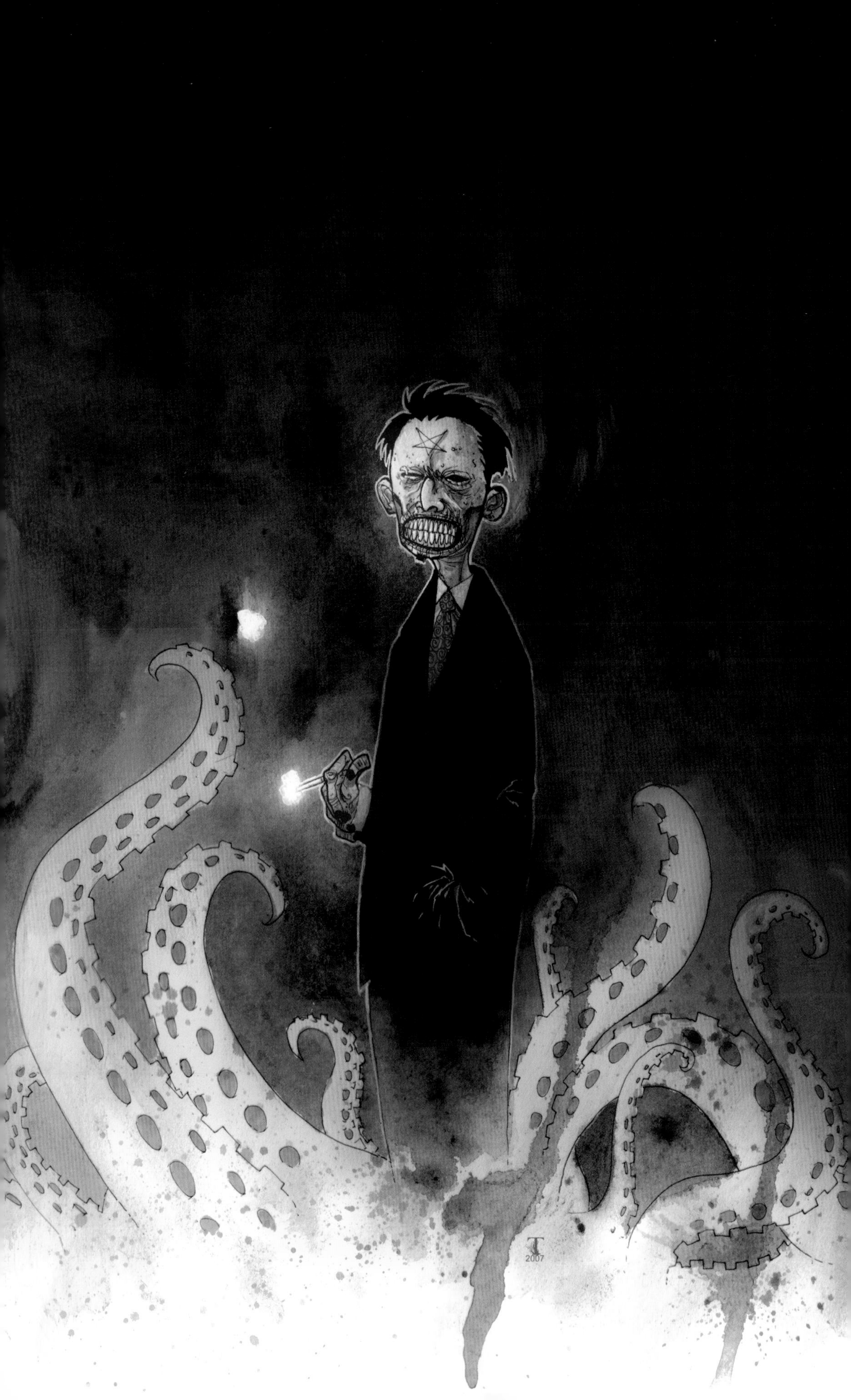
2007

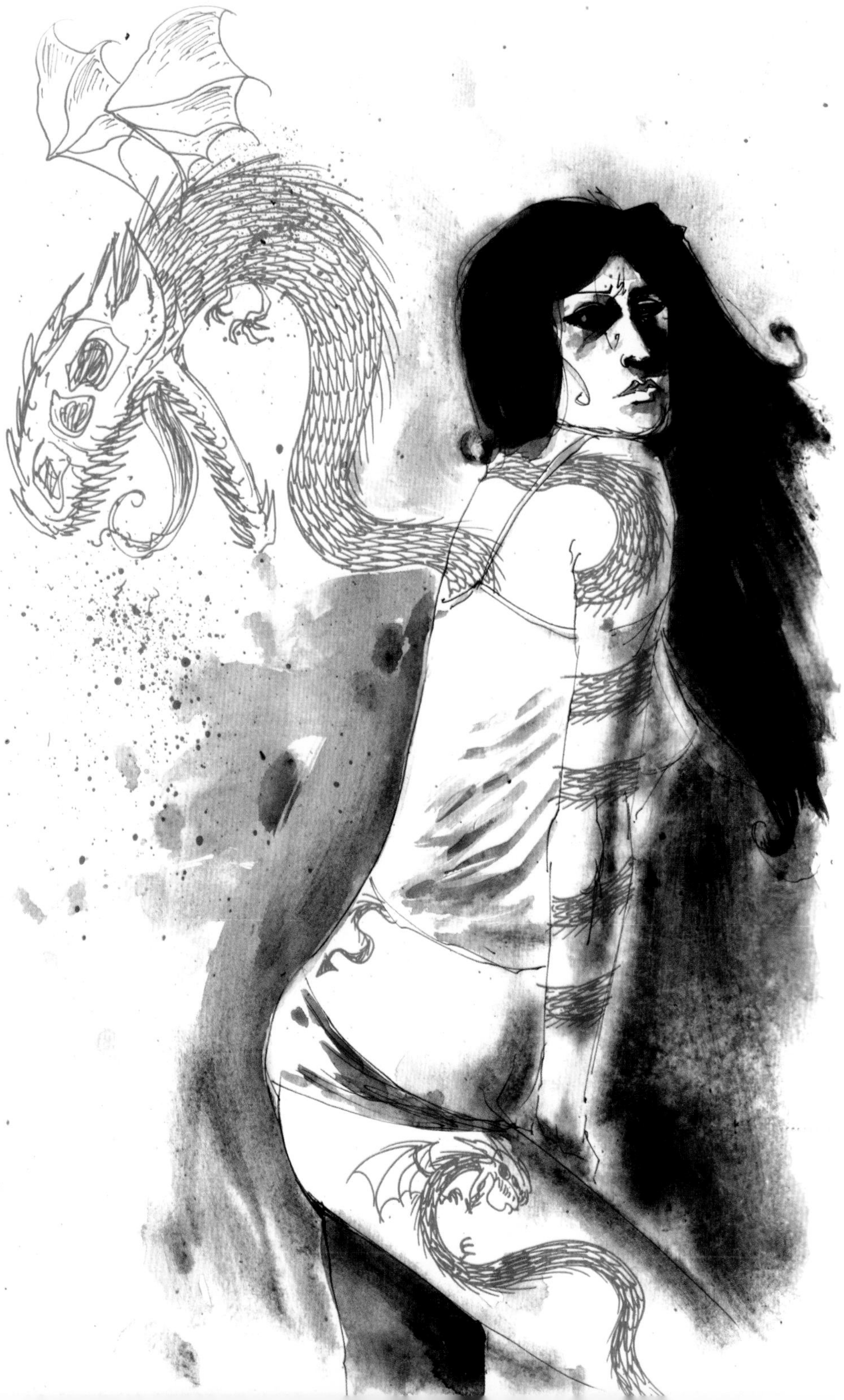

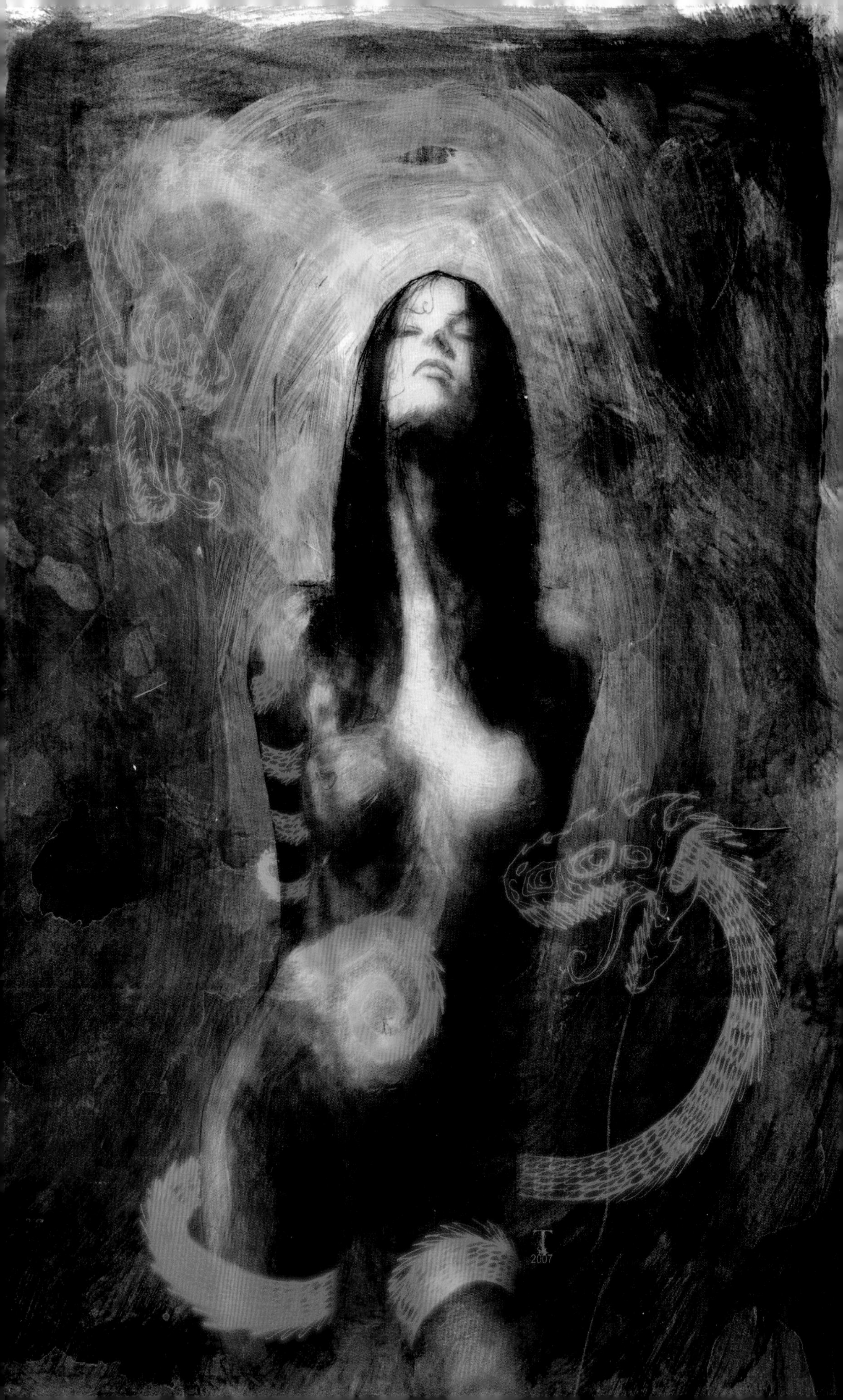
T
2007

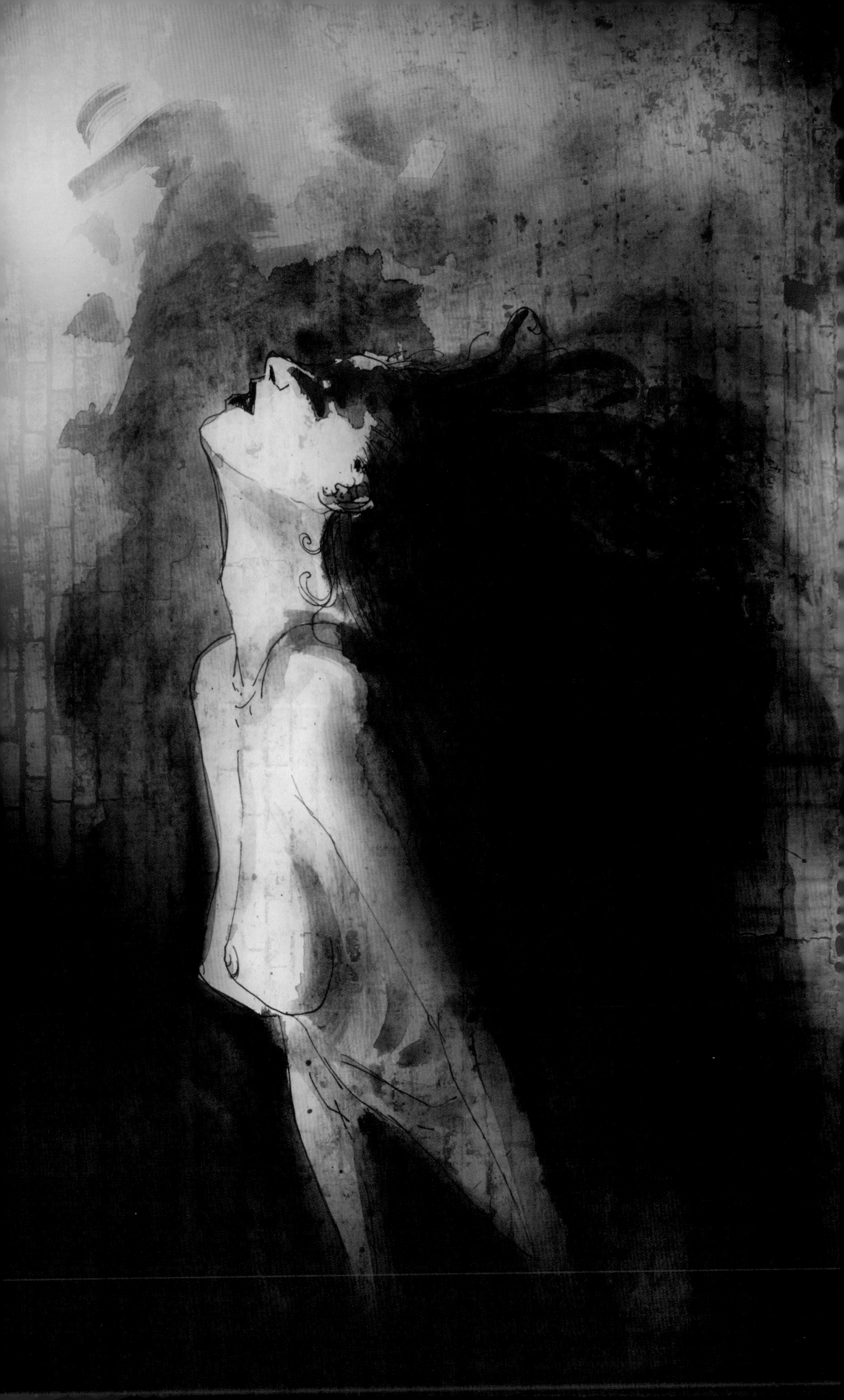

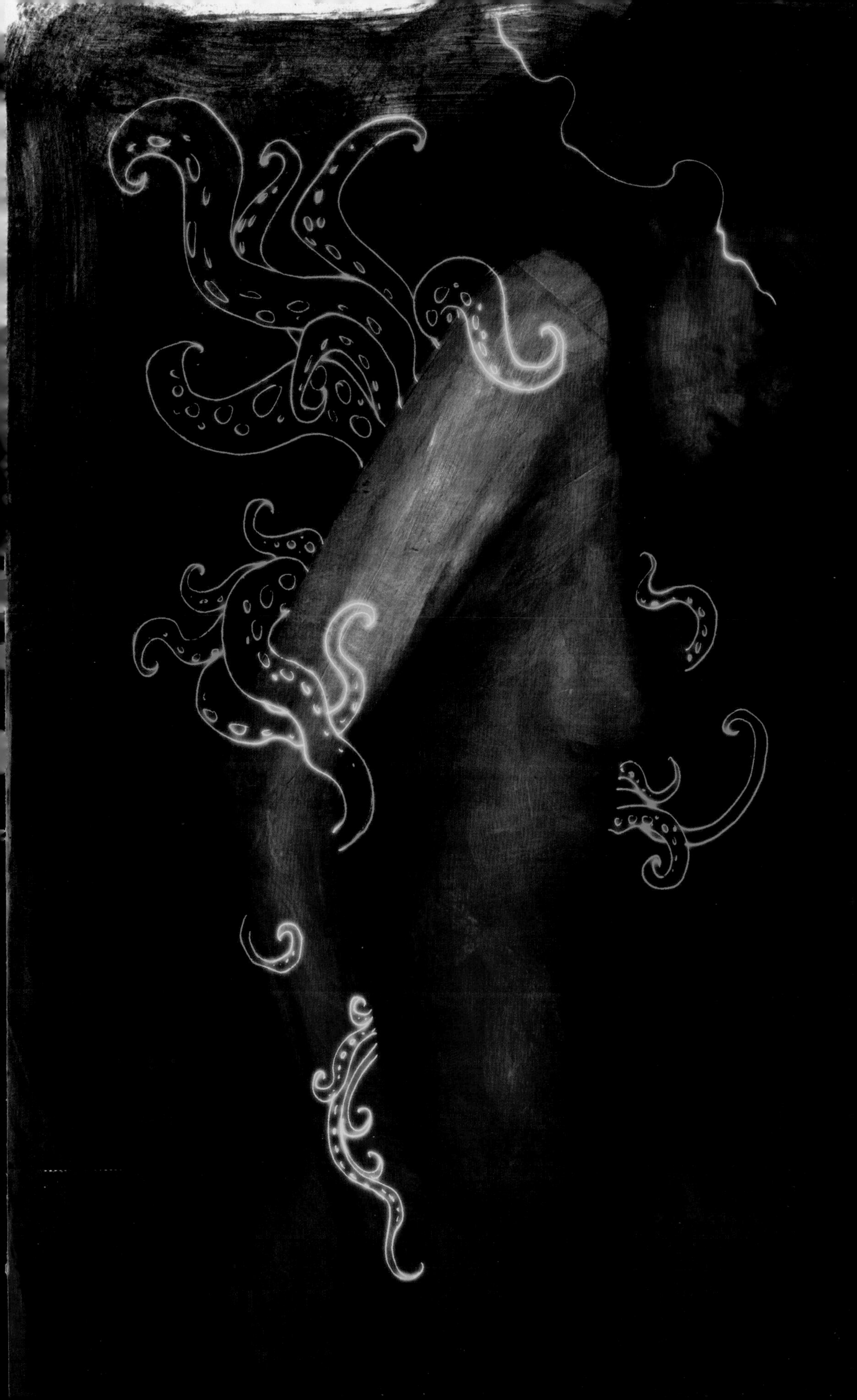

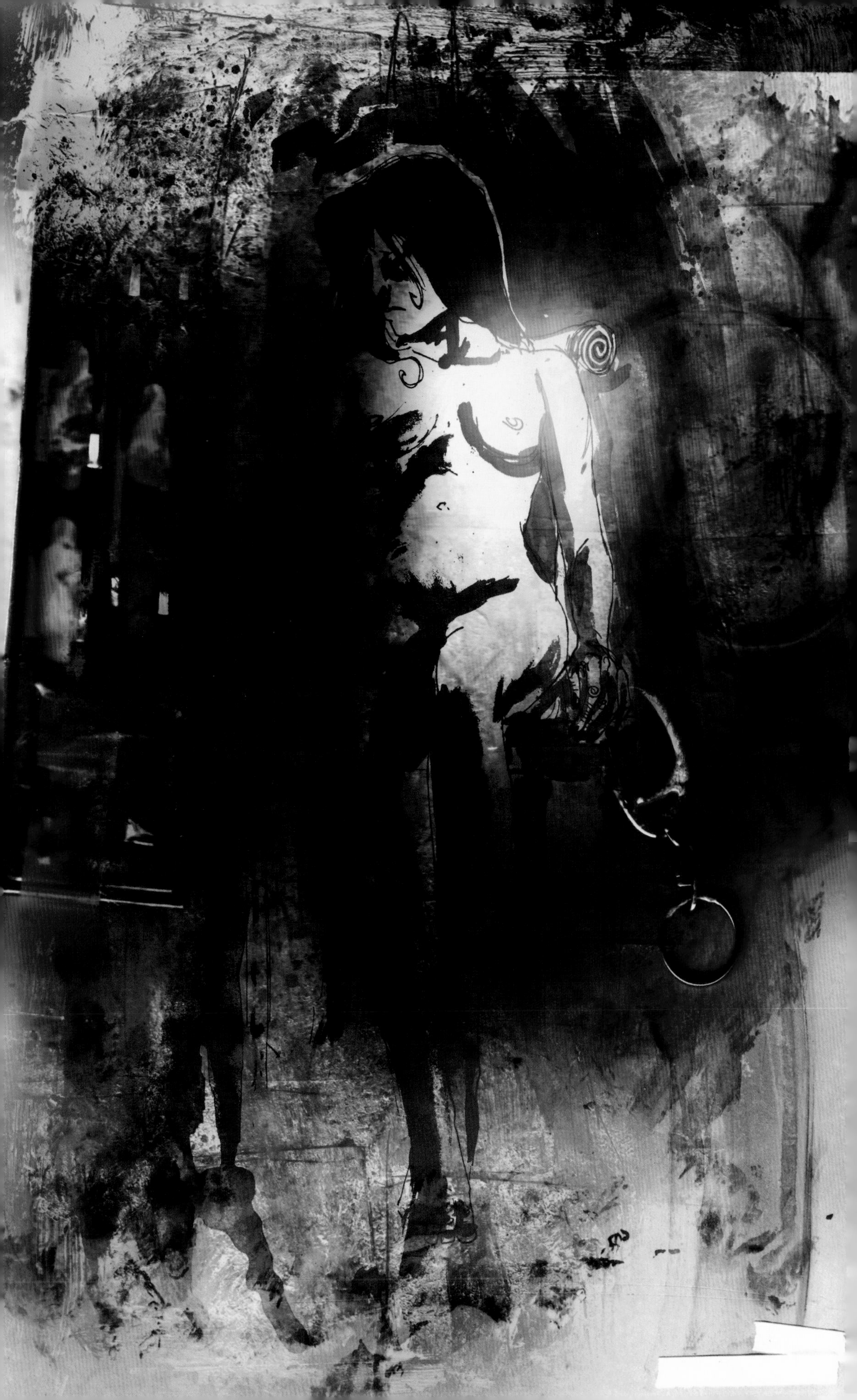

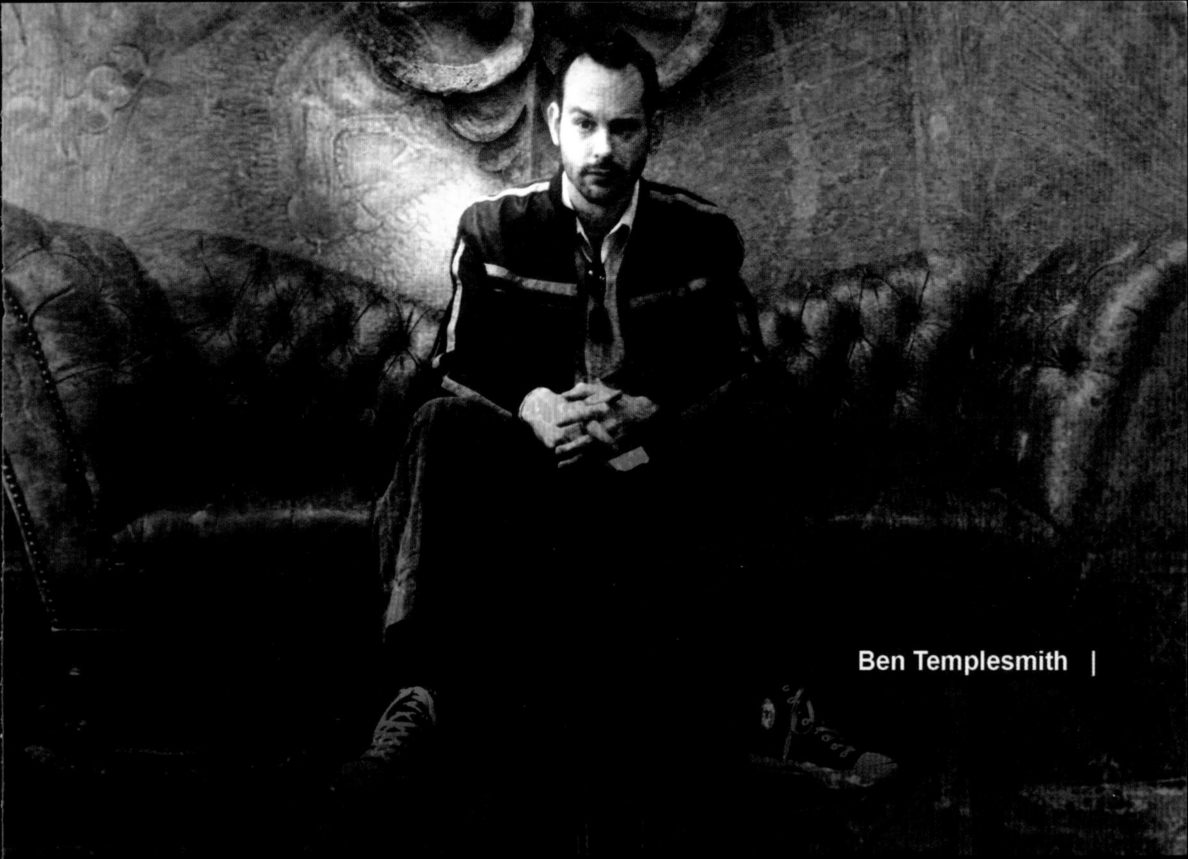

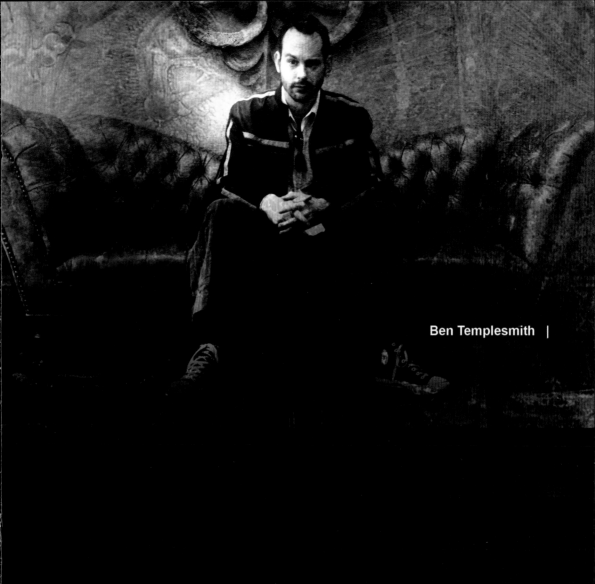

Ben Templesmith |

Ben Templesmith is an artist and writer most widely known for his work in the American comic book industry where he has received multiple nominations for the industry's top prize, the Eisner Award.
As a comic artist his most notable works have been *30 Days of Night*, *Fell* & *Wormwood: Gentleman Corpse*.
He's also worked on such things as *Singularity7*, *Hatter M*, *Conluvio*, *Star Wars*, *Army of Darkness*, *Silent Hill* and *Buffy: The Vampire Slayer* properties and produces art and design for music bands, dvds, toys, and film concept work.
Ben was raised in Western Australia and earned a degree in Design from Curtin University.
He currently lives and works in San Diego, USA.

More books from the imagination of
Ben Templesmith

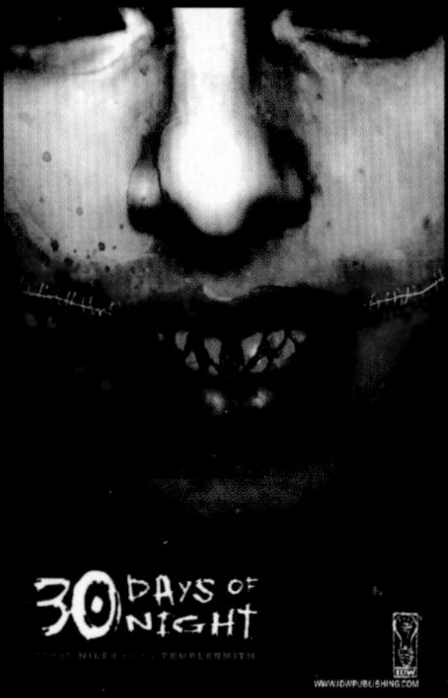
30 DAYS OF NIGHT

30 Days of Night
ISBN: 978-0-9719775-5-6
$17.99

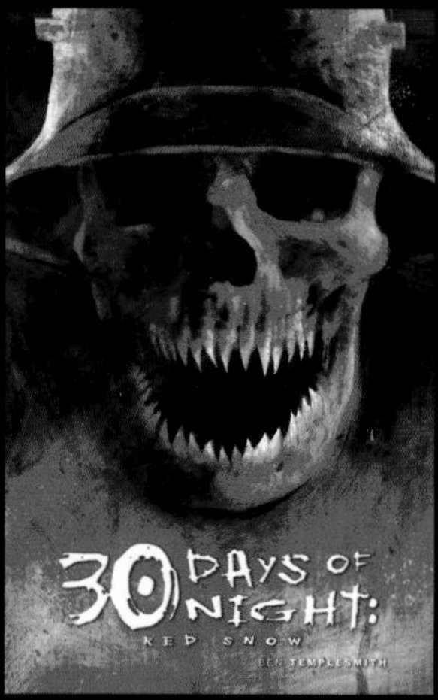
30 DAYS OF NIGHT:
RED SNOW
BEN TEMPLESMITH

30 Days of Night: Red Snow
ISBN: 978-1-60010-149-6
$17.99

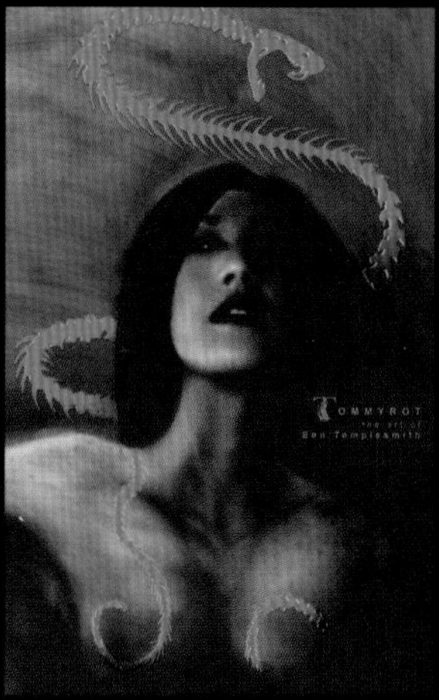

**Tommyrot:
The Art of Ben Templesmith**
ISBN: 978-1-60010-005-5
$19.99

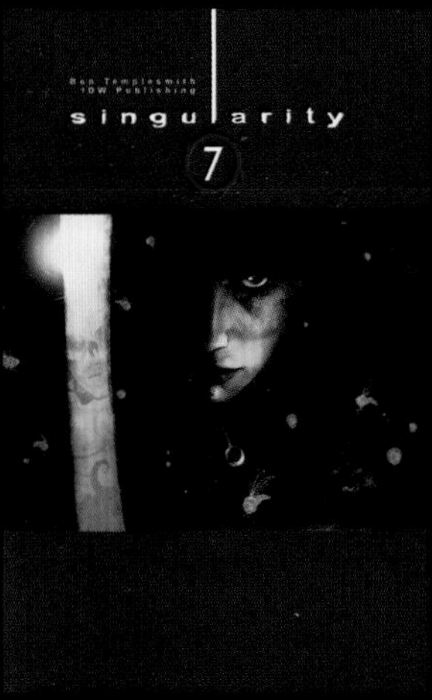
singularity
7

Singularity 7
ISBN: 978-1-932382-53-2
$19.99

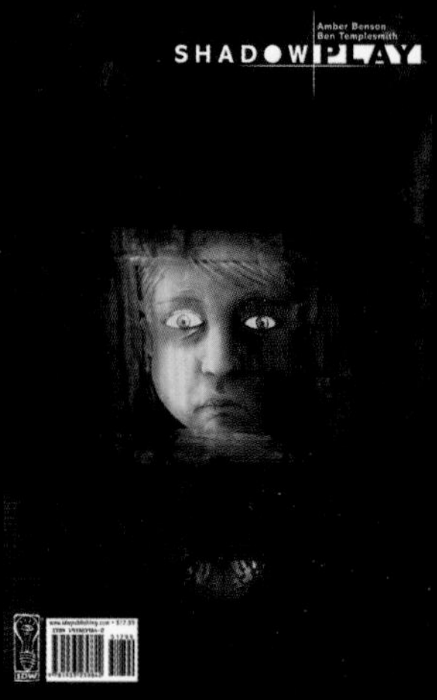
Amber Benson
Ben Templesmith
SHADOWPLAY

Shadowplay
ISBN: 978-1-933239-84-2
$17.99

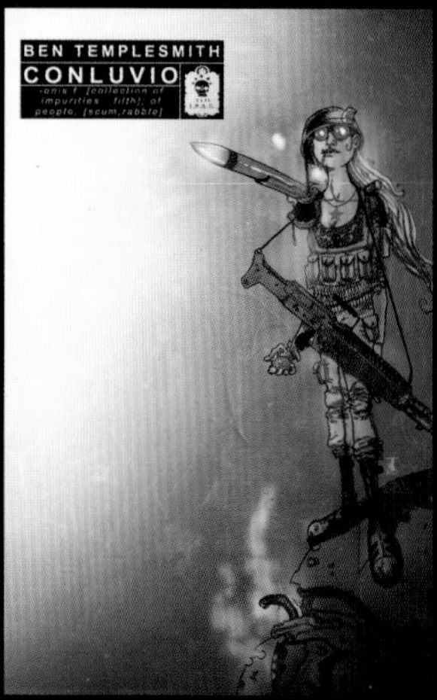
BEN TEMPLESMITH
CONLUVIO

**Conluvio: The Art of
Ben Templesmith, Vol. 1**
ISBN: 978-1-60010-053-6
$19.99